THE COURTSHIP OF
ROBERT BROWNING
AND
ELIZABETH BARRETT

Dr Karlin is a Lecturer in
the Department of English
Language and Literature,
University College,
London.

The Courtship of Robert Browning *and* Elizabeth Barrett

DANIEL KARLIN

Oxford   New York

OXFORD UNIVERSITY PRESS

1987

Oxford University Press, Walton Street, Oxford OX2 6DP
Oxford New York Toronto
Delhi Bombay Calcutta Madras Karachi
Petaling Jaya Singapore Hong Kong Tokyo
Nairobi Dar es Salaam Cape Town
Melbourne Auckland
and associated companies in
Beirut Berlin Ibadan Nicosia

Oxford is a trade mark of Oxford University Press

First published 1985 by Oxford University Press
First published as a paperback 1987

British Library Cataloguing in Publication Data
Karlin, Daniel
The courtship of Robert Browning and
Elizabeth Barrett.
1. Browning, Robert, 1812–1889
2. Browning, Elizabeth Barrett
I. Title   II. Series
821'.8'09   PR4231
ISBN 0–19–282039–7

Printed in Great Britain by
Richard Clay Ltd.
Bungay, Suffolk

For Pat

'Always with you in the spirit, always yearning to be
with you in the body,—always, when with you, praying,
as for the happiest of fortunes, that I may remain with
you for ever.'

Acknowledgements

The text of the letters between Browning and Elizabeth Barrett is reprinted with minor changes (see Note on the Text) by kind permission of the publishers from *The Letters of Robert Browning and Elizabeth Barrett Barrett, 1845–1846*, edited by Elvan Kintner, Cambridge, Mass.: The Belknap Press of Harvard University Press, Copyright © 1969 by the President and Fellows of Harvard College. Besides being an invaluable work of reference, Kintner's edition has a lucid and sensible discussion of the courtship in the Introduction, to which I am indebted.

The originals of the letters are held in the English Poetry Collection, Wellesley College Library, Wellesley College, Massachusetts, who have kindly given me permission to quote from them, together with extracts from Elizabeth Barrett's critical notes on Browning's poems, and to reproduce photographs of various letters and envelopes. I should like to extend special thanks to Ms Anne Anninger, Special Collections Librarian.

The portrait of Browning by D. G. Rossetti is reproduced by kind permission of the Fitzwilliam Museum, Cambridge. The portrait of Elizabeth Barrett by Field Talfourd is reproduced by kind permission of the Trustees of the National Portrait Gallery. The copy of R. H. Horne's *A New Spirit of the Age*, from which the portrait of Browning engraved by J. C. Armytage was taken, was kindly lent by the Cambridge University Library. The photograph of the Barrett house at 50 Wimpole Street is reproduced by kind permission of Westminster City Libraries: Archives and Local History Department, Marylebone Library. The entry of the Brownings' marriage in the register of St Marylebone Parish Church is reproduced by kind permission of the Rector.

I should like to thank Kim Scott Walwyn, at Oxford University Press, for her unfailing attention and encouragement.

To Mr John Woolford, and to Professor Christopher Ricks, I express my warm gratitude and affection.

Contents

Note on the Text

All quotations from the correspondence between Browning and Elizabeth Barrett are from *The Letters of Robert Browning and Elizabeth Barrett Barrett 1845–1846*, edited by Elvan Kintner (2 vols., Cambridge, Mass., 1969). Passages are identified first by their date (as assigned by Kintner), and then by reference to the page number of his edition; the volume number is not given, since the page numbers run consecutively. The date of the letters will in most cases (but not all) help readers with access to the first edition (1899) to find the passages quoted. Where Kintner's editorial material has been quoted, it is given the short title Kintner, followed by the page reference. Details of other short titles may be found by referring to the Bibliography.

Kintner's text is quoted without the indications he gives of deletions and additions to the manuscript, or of the placing of words or passages, except in cases where a manuscript deletion, indicated by angle brackets, is the subject of comment. Kintner's punctuation is that of the original; readers should note that both Browning and Elizabeth Barrett often use two dots (. .) where modern punctuation would use a dash or three dots; the appearance of this punctuation mark is therefore not a mistake, nor an indication of an elision in the quotation. All elisions are indicated by '[. . .]'. Idiosyncracies and archaisms of spelling and usage (for example 'sate' for 'sat') have not been noted by '[*sic*]' unless they affect the sense.

For the sake of simplicity the contracted forms 'cd', 'shd', 'wd' etc. in the letters are not printed with the d in superscript as in the original manuscripts.

List of Illustrations

Introduction

In 1899, ten years after his father's death, and thirty-eight years after that of his mother, Robert Wiedemann Barrett Browning published *The Letters of Robert Browning and Elizabeth Barrett Barrett, 1845–1846*; or, as they soon became known, the 'Browning love letters', since they told the story of the nineteen months which led from the first exchange of letters between Robert Browning and Elizabeth Barrett in January 1845, to their elopement in September 1846. Rightly anticipating a storm of protest from the surviving partisans of Elizabeth Barrett's father (who none the less was not to escape his dubious apotheosis in *The Barretts of Wimpole Street*), Robert Browning Jr. placed a brief note at the head of the first volume, in explanation of his filial piety and exculpation of his familial treason:

In considering the question of publishing these letters, which are all that ever passed between my father and mother, for after their marriage they were never separated, it seemed to me that my only alternatives were to allow them to be published or to destroy them. I might, indeed, have left the matter to the decision of others after my death, but that would be evading a responsibility which I feel that I ought to accept.

Ever since my mother's death these letters were kept by my father in a certain inlaid box, into which they exactly fitted, and where they have always rested, letter beside letter, each in its consecutive order and numbered on the envelope by his own hand.

My father destroyed all the rest of his correspondence, and not long before his death he said, referring to these letters: 'There they are, do with them as you please when I am dead and gone!'

The children of great artists are rarely as gifted as their parents, and the son of Robert Browning and Elizabeth Barrett was no exception—despite acquiring the nickname 'Pen'. Nevertheless, in the act for which the above brief statements stand as the only and enigmatic justification, 'Pen' Browning did indeed 'write' his parents; his publication of their massive correspondence gave a decisive imprimatur to the legend of heroic love which had been gathering in gossip and anecdote for fifty years: it composed the two poets into their eternal attitudes of chivalry and romance.

It is probably true to say that there are many people who, like those who know nothing more of Van Gogh than that he cut off his ear, or of Beethoven than that he might as well, know nothing more of Robert Browning and Elizabeth Barrett than that they eloped to Italy to escape Elizabeth's tyrannical and perverted father. One aspect of the two poets' lives and personalities has split off from all the others, and inhabits an area of popular culture where poets rarely establish themselves; the story of patriarchy defied, of miraculous rejuvenation and romantic flight has secured a place for Browning and Elizabeth Barrett which only Anon. achieves by work.

So powerful and enduring a story deserves attention. And because of Pen Browning we have, in two massive volumes, 573 letters between the two principals in the story. The existence in a body of these letters not only invites us to enjoy the story in all its sweep of action and fullness of detail; it makes a vital difference to our reading.

It made just such a difference to the writers themselves. Already, as the correspondence progressed, both parties to it became aware of the modifying presence of previous letters. 'A hundred letters I have, by this last', wrote Elizabeth Barrett, 'to set against Napoleon's Hundred Days—did you know *that*?' (18 Jan. 1846, p. 403.) She was still haunted by the fear that her unlooked for 'return' from the exile of sickness and seclusion might lead to some calamitous Waterloo, the final loss of Browning's affection. Browning responded with his own characteristic boldness and subtlety: 'of letters, this makes my 104th and, like Donne's Bride, "I take my jewels from their boxes; call / My Diamonds, Pearls, and Emeralds, and make / Myself a constellation of them all!" ' (19 Jan. 1846, p. 405.)[1] As she had taken a male persona, so he took a female one; reminding her, moreover, that some portents are ominous in a happy sense, and that her letters

---

[1] Misquoting ll. 33–6 of Donne's 'Epithalamion, or Marriage Song on the Lady Elizabeth and Count Palatine being Married on St. Valentine's Day': 'Up, up, fair Bride, and call, / Thy stars, from out their several boxes, take / Thy rubies, pearls, and diamonds forth, and make / Thyself a constellation, of them all'. The lines quoted below are ll. 36–7 and ll. 47–8. The text is from *The Complete English Poems*, ed. A. J. Smith (Harmondsworth, 1973).

'by their blazing, signify / That a great Princess falls, but doth not die'. Donne's 'Epithalamion . . . on St. Valentine's Day' is, indeed, a textbook for Browning's idea of love as 'inseparable union . . . Since separation / Falls not on such things as are infinite, / Nor things which are but one, can disunite'. Can we go further, and say that his allusion to a poem which celebrates the union of 'two phoenixes' implicitly acknowledges, before it was even fully formed, the mythical nature of their relationship? That the existence of under half the letters already presupposed the story told in the remainder? What becomes, then, of the notion of process, of human contingency? The correspondence, and the courtship itself, unfold before us not as a historical sequence, a pattern of choices and chances, but as a self-determined and authoritative structure, or, in other words, a fiction.

Rudolf Besier's *The Barretts of Wimpole Street*, especially in its film version, and non-fiction studies such as Dormer Creston's *Andromeda in Wimpole Street*, have made the outline of this fiction sufficiently familiar. Francis Thompson puts it concisely: 'Browning stooped and picked up a fair-coined soul that lay rusting in a pool of tears'. But it is worth remembering that, though Pen's publication of the letters set the seal of authority on the story, it did not by any means initiate it; on the contrary, the publication as a commercial venture depended on a history of gossip and innuendo which had been going strong ever since the marriage itself took place. We have a letter written by one of Browning's close friends, Joseph Arnould (future Judge of the Supreme Court at Bombay) to another, Alfred Domett (future Prime Minister of New Zealand), two months after the elopement. It gives a vivid picture of the pro-Browning case at a critical stage of formation, and sets the tone for many later accounts:

I think the last piece of news I told you of was Browning's marriage to Miss Barrett—which I had then just heard of. She is, you know [. . .] our present greatest living English 'poetess.' She had been for some years an invalid, leading a very secluded life in a sick room in the household of one of those tyrannical, arbitrary, puritanical rascals who go sleekly about the world, canting Calvinism abroad, and acting despotism at home. Under the iron rigour of this man's domestic rule she, feeble and invalided, had grown up to eight and thirty years of age in the most absolute and enforced seclusion from society: cultivating her mind to a wonderful amount of accomplishment, instructing herself in all languages, reading Chrysostom in the original Greek, and publishing the best metrical translation that has yet appeared of the 'Prometheus Bound'—having also found time to write three volumes of poetry, the last of which raised her name to a place second only to that of Browning and Tennyson, amongst all those who are not repelled by eccentricities of external form from penetrating into the soul and quintessential spirit of poetry [. . .] Well, this lady so gifted, so secluded, so tyrannised over, fell in love with Browning in the spirit, before ever she saw him in the flesh—in plain English loved the writer before she knew the man. Imagine, you who know him, the effect which his graceful bearing, high demeanour, and noble speech must have had on such a mind when she first saw the man of her visions in the twilight of her darkened room. She was at once in love as a poet-soul only can be: and Browning, as by contagion or electricity, was no less from the first interview wholly in love with her. This was now some two years back; from that time his visits to her have been constant. He of course wished to ask her of her father openly. 'If you do,' was her terrified answer, 'he would immediately throw me out of [the] window, or lock me up for life in a darkened room.' There was one thing only to be done, and that Browning did: married her without the father's knowledge, and immediately left England with her for Italy, where they are now living at Pisa in as supreme a state of happiness as you can fancy two such people in such a place. The old rascal father of course tore his beard, foamed at the mouth, and performed all other feats of impotent rage: luckily his wrath is absolutely idle, for she has a small independence of some £350 per ann., on which they will of course live prosperously. I heard from him a week back [. . .] he is a glorious fellow, by God! Oh, I forgot to say that the *soi-disante* invalid [. . .] once emancipated from the paternal despotism, has had a wondrous revival, or rather, a complete metamorphosis; walks, rides, eats and drinks like a young and healthy woman—in fact is a healthy woman of, I believe, some five and thirty—a little old—too old for Browning—but then one word covers all: they are in Love, who lends his own youth to everything.

(RB & AD, 133–6)

It would be interesting to know exactly who supplied Arnould with which of his 'facts'. As a rising lawyer, he may be faulted on at least one piece of hearsay evidence, since no one who had actually read Elizabeth Barrett's 1833 version of *Prometheus* could possibly speak of it as 'the best metrical translation that has yet appeared'— except, of course, Browning himself. But would Browning describe his new father-in-law—with whom he was making strenuous efforts to be reconciled—as a 'tyrannical, arbitrary, puritanical rascal'? Would he even have given Arnould an impression on which to found such a judgement? Then there is the matter of money. How like a member of the liberal professional class to sound such a practical note in the midst of his fairy-tale! But who informed him (accurately enough) of the size of Elizabeth Barrett's 'small independence'? With poignant naiveté, Arnould readjusts Elizabeth's age from thirty-eight at the beginning of the passage to thirty-five at the end, proof of her 'metamorphosis', though she is still 'too old for Browning'. (She was, in fact, forty, and he was thirty-four.) Arnould finishes with a schoolboy howler of ironic import. He calls Elizabeth 'the *soi-disante* invalid', unhappily implying that she was a self-created *malade imaginaire*.

The 'Browning version' of the courtship is riddled with inconsistencies. (The Barrett version, that Browning was a jumped-up fortune-hunter, is equally absurd; but it has no literary consequences, and we accordingly ignore it.) These inconsistencies focus, in Arnould's account, on the character and motivation of Elizabeth Barrett and her father. On the one hand, we are required to believe that Elizabeth was the passive victim of Mr Barrett's malevolent despotism (Arnould speaks of '*enforced* seclusion'); on the other hand, that she had the strength of mind to become 'our present greatest living English "poetess" '. She is 'terrified' of her father, and yet capable of receiving Browning's (clandestine? Arnould does not say) visits for two years. She is the heroine of a silly romance ('the man of her visions in the twilight of her darkened room'; incidentally, Arnould does not say how Browning gained admittance), and a resolute woman whose *choice* it must have been, though you would not guess it from Arnould's phrasing, to undergo her 'metamorphosis'. Last but not least, she has an income on which two people are expected to 'live prosperously'; why, then, had the lady 'so tyrannised over' not simply walked out long before?

As for Mr Edward Moulton Barrett, Arnould's portrait of him as, at best, a travestied King Lear, with his 'feats of impotent rage', and at worst a man capable of actual violence—but let us look more closely at the words which Arnould reports. 'He would immediately throw me out of [the] window, or lock me up for life in a darkened room.' Here we do come close to the actual phrasing of the letters, which suggests that Arnould must have had some information from Browning, at first or second hand. For example, Elizabeth Barrett told Browning that 'from the moment of a suspicion entering *one mind*, we should be able to meet never again in this room, nor to have intercourse by letter through the ordinary

channel [. . .] letters of yours, addressed to me here, would infallibly be stopped & destroyed—if not opened. [. . .] And then, I
might be thrown out of the window or its equivalent' (15 Jan. 1846,
pp. 393–4). Notice, however, the qualification attached to that last
phrase. All that is said here is that Mr Barrett would use the legal
power he had to control access to his own house. (It would be
unlawful of him to stop Elizabeth Barrett's mail, but then she was
not obliged to live in Wimpole Street.) A similar note is sounded in
a letter written a month earlier: 'I might be prevented from receiving you here, & *should*, if all were known: but', she immediately
continues, 'with that act, the adverse power would end' (12 Dec.
1845, p. 318). Elizabeth Barrett was perfectly aware that, as she put
it to Browning, 'If two persons have one will on a matter of that
sort, they need not be thwarted here in London' (5 May 1846, p.
681). As for being thrown out of the window, that is a nervous joke
about Mr Barrett's known intransigence on the subject of his
children's marrying. When Browning suggested a marriage in form
'so as to enable me, if difficulties should thicken, to be by your bed-
side at least' (9 June 1846, p. 770), Elizabeth Barrett replied that his
proposal 'could not work *at all*, unless circumstances were
known—and if they were known, at the very moment of their being
known you would be saved, dearest, all the trouble of coming up
stairs to me, by my being thrown out of the window to you' (9 June
1846, p. 771). Arnould's implication—that Elizabeth Barrett
believed that her father would actually assault her—is simply false.
What is significant is the *imagery* with which Elizabeth Barrett, in
Arnould's travesty, contrasts two forms of death, being flung into
the open and incarcerated in darkness, imagery which gives a direct
insight into Elizabeth Barrett's state of mind at the time of the
courtship. Images of windows and dark places, the sky and the
grave, recur in her letters, each ambiguously poised between fear
and desire. Take the image of the window, for example. 'Oh—this
life, this life!' she exclaimed in only her fifth letter to Browning.
'There is comfort in it, they say, & I almost believe—but the brightest place in the house, is the leaning out of the window!' (27 Feb.
1845, p. 31.) 'But where, pray, did I say . . & when . . that "everything would end well"?' she objected to him in a later letter, pointing out that

'well' is how you understand it. If you jump out of the window you succeed in getting to the ground, somehow, dead or alive . . but whether *that* means 'ending well,' depends on your way of considering matters.

(16 Mar. 1846, p. 541.)

The image of her father throwing her out of the window may tell us something, therefore, about Mr Barrett's temper, but it tells us much more about Elizabeth Barrett's own divided feelings at the prospect of 'ending well'. Now, what reason could Browning have for giving this image to Arnould, or to Arnould's source, as it seems likely he did? The effect of it is to cover up for Elizabeth Barrett—to disarm her anxiety by making Mr Barrett threaten to do to her literally what she wanted to do, figuratively, to herself. A surprising motive begins to emerge for the odium which Mr Barrett attracts in the story. He was bad enough, in all conscience, but not in the particular way which Arnould's account suggests: his identity as pantomime demon was imposed on him by the fiction in which he, along with the others, had got caught up.

By the end of the courtship, both Browning and Elizabeth Barrett had strong motives for shaping it into a form which would act, for them, as a ground of hope for their coming life together. Indeed without such an act of interpretation they could not have brought themselves to marry at all. On the very day of their marriage, when he had returned alone to New Cross, Browning wrote to his bride: 'I look back, and in every one point, every word and gesture, every letter, every *silence*—you have been entirely perfect to me—I would not change one word, one look—' (12 Sept. 1846, p. 1062). And in reply to his wish to have been better to *her*, Elizabeth Barrett wrote: 'What could be better than lifting me from the ground and carrying me into life & sunshine? I was yours rather by right than by gift, (yet by gift also, my beloved!—) for what you have saved & renewed is surely yours' (13 Sept. 1846, p. 1064).

In absolute terms, the act of elopement could only be justified by results, and both Browning and Elizabeth Barrett were fully conscious of the gamble they were taking. But to define what had gone before in terms of its *rightness*—that is, not only its moral validity, but its fitness to their respective natures—to see each other's behaviour in terms of perfection and salvation—this is to charm the future with the spell of a retrospective judgement. That future, remember, is blank for the two lovers, like the blankness at the end of a novel; they cannot foresee what we know to have occurred, the fourteen

years of love and marriage in Italy. They look back with distorting
authority over their journey to this cut-off point, a journey which
offers them—and us after them—all the satisfactions of a structure.
Arnould's story is merely the most basic form of the design which a
'mythical' reading of the letters might modify in emphasis and
enrich in detail, but would not fundamentally alter.

There is, however, a *history* of the courtship to be written; and
this history cannot afford to pre-empt its own conclusions by
adopting a framework of meaning devised, for their own purposes,
by the participants in the very events with which the history is to
concern itself. If we wish to *reconstruct* the courtship, as opposed to
accepting and expounding its self-construction, we must cease to
collaborate and begin to read.

In February 1846, Elizabeth Barrett sent to Browning a letter
which she had recently received from the writer and journalist
Harriet Martineau. In his comments on her letter, Browning
referred with heavy-handed sarcasm to Harriet Martineau's admittedly rather pretentious request to her friends to burn her letters to
them, and continued:

burn anybody's *real* letters, well & good—they move & live [. . .] in a
self-imposed circle limiting the experience of two persons only—*there* is
the standard, and to *that* the appeal—how should a third person know? His
presence breaks the line, so to speak, and lets in a whole tract of country on
the originally inclosed spot [. . .] the significance is lost at once, and the
whole value of such letters—

(15 Feb. 1846, p. 463.)

'*Real* letters', in this scheme, constitute a private and privileged discourse, an 'originally inclosed spot' reminiscent of Eden before a
'third person' intruded. And yet, in handing the letters to Pen at the
end of his life (perhaps because, though he had no scruples about
destroying his own letters, he could not bear to destroy hers),
Browning was implicitly permitting the intrusion of a multitude of
'third persons' into the garden of his correspondence with Elizabeth
Barrett.

At least one great critic thought there were grounds for objection
to the publication of some of the letters—apparently for the reason
Browning gave. In his book on Browning (still, to the shame of its
successors, the best general study of him to appear), G. K. Chesterton declared:

when a work contains expressions which have one value and significance when read by the people to whom they were addressed, and an entirely different value and significance when read by anyone else, then the element of the violation of sanctity does arise. It is not because there is anything in this world too sacred to tell. It is rather because there are a great many things in this world too sacred to parody. [. . .] As far as any third person is concerned, Browning might as well have been expressing the most noble and universal sentiment in the dialect of the Cherokees [. . .] If Browning or Mrs. Browning had not desired any people to know that they were fond of each other, they would not have written and published 'One Word More' or 'The Sonnets from the Portuguese.' Nay, they would not have been married in a public church [. . .] But the words of a poem or the words of the English Marriage Service, which are as fine as many poems, is a language dignified and deliberately intended to be understood by all. If the bride and bridegroom in church, instead of uttering those words, were to utter a poem compounded of private allusions to the foibles of Aunt Matilda, or of childish secrets which they would tell each other in a lane, it would be a parallel case to the publication of some of the Browning Letters. [. . .] Our wisdom, whether expressed in private or public, belongs to the world, but our folly belongs to those we love.

(Chesterton, pp. 64–5.)

Chesterton then quotes with relish a couple of passages in support of his claim that the correspondence is 'not of the sort which can be pursued very much by the outside public', and that it is written in 'an almost exasperatingly impressionist language, a language chiefly consisting of dots and dashes and asterisks and italics, and brackets and notes of interrogation':

It would be amusing to watch any one who felt an idle curiosity as to the language and secrets of lovers opening the Browning Letters. He would probably come upon some such simple and lucid passage as the following: 'I ought to wait, say a week at least, having killed all your mules for you, before I shot down your dogs. . . . but not being Phoibos Apollon, you are to know further that when I *did* think I might go modestly on . . . ὤμοι, let me get out of this slough of a simile, never mind with what dislocated ankles!'

What our imaginary sentimentalist would make of this tender passage it is difficult indeed to imagine. The only plain conclusion which appears to emerge from the words is the somewhat curious one—that Browning was in the habit of taking a gun down to Wimpole Street and of demolishing the live stock on those somewhat unpromising premises. Nor will he be any better enlightened if he turn to the reply of Miss Barrett [. . .] 'But if it could be possible that you should mean to say you would show me. . . .

Can it be? or am I reading this "Attic contraction" quite the wrong way. You see I am afraid of the difference between flattering myself and being flattered,—the fatal difference. And now will you understand that I should be too overjoyed to have revelations from the Portfolio . . . however incarnated with blots and pen scratches . . . to be able to ask impudently of them now? Is that plain?' Most probably she thought it was.

(Chesterton, pp. 66–7.)

If she did, she was perfectly justified; it is Chesterton who is responsible for the obscurity here, not least in calling Elizabeth Barrett's remarks a reply to Browning's, which they are not, and for cutting off the first part of Browning's sentence which makes the source of his image (Apollo's infliction of plague on the Greek camp in the *Iliad*, bk.I), and its application (to letter-writing), reasonably clear; it is coy of Chesterton, in any case, to disguise his own evident recognition of the image with bluff facetiousness. Neither passage, incidentally, is about love (this being May 1845, when the 'tender' passion was not yet openly at issue); Browning, as I have said, is worrying about the frequency of his letters, and Elizabeth Barrett is responding, with a suitable mixture of eagerness and restraint, to a separate point—Browning's hint that he might show her some of his unpublished work. All the phrases in the two passages are either self-explanatory or refer to other letters, and can be easily followed by an attentive reader.

The language of the letters is all accessible in this way (like that of Browning's poetry, in fact), and here Chesterton's point diverges sharply from Browning's; Browning argues that 'real' letters imply a private world of *meaning*, Chesterton that they imply a private world of *reference*. Of the meaning Chesterton has no doubt: after all, it springs from his account of the relationship itself, in which love, 'the most noble and universal sentiment', is the dominant term; that there might be a complexity in the sentiment itself would not appeal to Chesterton, whose view of Browning rests mainly on the paradox of essential simplicity expressing itself in complex forms. If we follow Browning's line, however, we must look beyond the superficial difficulties which we may encounter in understanding the letters; we must attempt to comprehend them, to get our minds round the minds whose operations they figure. And here the letters tell us, as no other source could in such detail and over so long a period, how Browning and Elizabeth Barrett thought. Because the main interest, historically, has been in whether, or to what degree, the letters matched the legend, their manner has gone almost un-analysed, except (as in the case of Chesterton) in terms of their 'exasperatingly impressionist language'. Yet this very manner is the most invaluable evidence we have for the conceptual bases of the work of these two complex and self-aware poets, each of whom wrote to the other, for all their respective denials, as a reader as well as a lover.

In Browning's case, such revelations are especially welcome because of the relative scarcity of comparable material. Elizabeth Barrett wrote many more letters than Browning, and the proportion of those that have survived is also greater than his, since she never asked for any to be returned or destroyed; for Browning, the harvest of 'real' letters, to use his term, is meagre indeed, and the letters to Elizabeth Barrett occupy a unique place in it; they are the only letters of his which can be said to resemble his poems in the depth of mind they display. In one especial sense, indeed, they provide the reader of Browning's poems with an invaluable correlate of the mental processes which govern his writing. Browning's *idea of creativity*, the dualism of finite and infinite, divine and human, desire and fulfilment, perception and language, extends into the expression of his feeling for Elizabeth Barrett with all-pervasive force and influence. It is not too much to say that he composes his love for her in the same terms as he composes the action of his poems. These terms appear at every level of his discourse to Elizabett Barrett, from the profoundest movements of the heart to the most trivial lover's gossip. They suggest that Browning was committed to the relationship with his whole identity and that this identity itself was peculiarly strong and self-possessed. After all, we are used to thinking of Elizabeth Barrett's experience of the courtship and subsequent marriage as a transforming one. She begins, in the myth, as a bedridden spinster, and ends as a triumphantly rejuvenated bride. With Browning there is no such alteration of personality. Courtship and marriage did not change him, they conformed to him. He had already anticipated his affair with Elizabeth Barrett in numerous aspects of his poems, from *Pauline* onward, not out of prescience, but because his nature followed its bent in whatever sphere it operated, and because it was a nature unalterable by external circumstances. Browning lived by and for the imagination, and he imagined Elizabeth Barrett. The letters show him doing it; and if the process illuminates the poems, it is no less true that the poems illuminate the courtship: they provide us with a working model of his

disposition as a lover, and his letters confirm and extend our understanding of his creativity and his aesthetics. The correspondence
would be invaluable on that score alone, without the wealth of what
else it has to give us.

The courtship of Robert Browning and Elizabeth Barrett, and the
correspondence which records it, have never, in my opinion, been
convincingly related and interpreted, because their true interest and
significance have been usurped by a legend which the two poets
themselves did much to foster; this book sets out, accordingly, to
remedy that deficiency. (Inevitably, I have had to leave out a great
deal of material which did not bear immediately on my chosen
topics; this book cannot hope to substitute for a reading of the letters themselves.) I shall begin by painting the portraits of the principals, and I shall then tell at some length the story of the events of the
courtship in a way which will dispel some of the myths that sur-
round it, but which will not, I believe, detract from its interest as a
human document. In Part Two I shall examine five aspects of the
courtship and the correspondence which I think of key importance
in any account of them. The first is the question of Browning's
creativity about which I have just been speaking. The second concerns the way in which Browning and Elizabeth Barrett thought
about letters, both the writing and the receiving of them, and the
interplay during their courtship between letters and meetings. The
third concerns the presentation of other people in the letters, and
the fourth concentrates specifically on the image of Mr Barrett. The
fifth and final chapter is concerned with the question of Elizabeth
Barrett's 'metamorphosis' during the courtship.

PART ONE

1

Backgrounds

1 The man with the wand

London, September 12 1846; a Saturday. At a quarter past eleven in the morning, a small group of people emerges from St. Marylebone Parish Church, which stands in Marylebone Road opposite the York Gate entrance to Regent's Park. It is the wedding party of Robert Browning (Condition: Bachelor; Rank or Profession: Gentleman, says the register) and Elizabeth Barrett Moulton Barrett (Condition: Spinster; Rank or Profession:—). The party consists of the Gentleman and — themselves; their witnesses, James Silverthorne (Browning's cousin) and Elizabeth Wilson (Elizabeth Barrett's maid); and the church usher. The latter has accompanied them out with a 'philosophic sentiment' (expressed between 'two bursts of gratitude' for the lavish tip he has just received) about 'marriage being a very serious event in one's mortal life'. At which point the bride and bridegroom part 'on the best terms possible', get into separate carriages, and drive off in opposite directions. 'The man with the wand' stands in the doorway, 'his speech scarcely ended on his lips' and his 'mouth wide open in surprise! "Never had he seen anything more remarkable than *that*, in the whole course of his practice!" ' (Elizabeth Barrett to her sister Henrietta, cited in Miller p. 126.)

Had the usher's wand been a magic one, he might have divined some of the other circumstances which surrounded this 'remarkable' wedding; but whether knowledge of them would have diminished his astonishment, or increased it, is hard to say. The forty-year-old bride had left her father's house in Wimpole Street, not a quarter of a mile away, under the pretence of paying a visit to an old friend; she had nearly fainted on the short walk to the hackney carriage stand in Marylebone Street, and had had to call at a chemist's for sal volatile; and after the wedding she drove to the house of the old friend whom she was supposed to have been visiting, was collected from there in another carriage by her two sisters, and taken for a drive to Hampstead Heath, pretending all the while that nothing unusual had happened. As for the bridegroom, he too, at the age of thirty-four, lived with his parents, in suburban New Cross; he drove there straight after the wedding, and wrote his wife the two-hundred-and-eightieth letter which he had written to her since they had first begun to correspond, twenty months earlier. During all this time, Elizabeth Barrett's father was unaware that she and Browning were anything other than literary acquaintances. For a week after the marriage, the couple remained apart; at the end of that week, they left England as stealthily as they had married.

The conventional idea of a clandestine liaison against parental opposition is enshrined in *Romeo and Juliet*, or, to take an example nearer home, in Browning's play *A Blot in the 'Scutcheon* (1843), with its young lovers and dominating guardian; most children in the modern period are dependent on their parents past the age of sexual maturity, and secret marriage is a way of defying or evading this economic constraint. In the case of Browning and Elizabeth Barrett, however, no such constraint existed. They were both (to quote the register again) 'of full age', and, thanks to Elizabeth Barrett, they were financially secure; moreover, whereas Mr Barrett would have been implacably opposed to the match (had he known about it), Browning's parents were sympathetic and supportive: Browning borrowed £100 from his father to pay the immediate expenses of the trip, since Elizabeth Barrett could not lay her hands on that amount of cash without exciting suspicion. It was Mr Barrett who managed her money.

There were, therefore, no legal or economic obstacles to the match; nor was there any question of physical force being exercised by Mr Barrett against his daughter. He might—would—have made things exceedingly difficult and unpleasant for her; he would almost certainly have ended, if not begun, by throwing her out of his house; but the notion that he had the desire, let alone the power, to lock her up, is absurd.

Nor were Browning and Elizabeth Barrett, in their flight from

England, escaping the outrage of society, as Shelley and Mary God-win had in 1818. To put it mildly, Mr Barrett was not the arbiter of public opinion as to the moral right of middle-aged, middle-class adults of independent means to marry whom they chose. With regard to his treatment of his family in general, he had not a single supporter in his immediate circle; Elizabeth Barrett was being urged on all sides, during most of the courtship period, to defy his dis-approval and go to Italy for the sake of her health; and this by people who had no inkling of her relationship with Browning. As for the match itself, close friends such as John Kenyon, who had every opportunity to feel slighted by not having been told before-hand, were practically unanimous in their approval; in the outside world, the storm which broke was a storm of gossip. Eliza Ogilvy, who was later to know the Brownings well in Italy, heard of their elopement from a friend in these terms: 'Have you heard that Miss Barrett who was said to be in a decline has jumped up out of bed and run off with Robert Browning?' The comic relish of this view is present even in Wordsworth's malicious remark that he hoped the two poets would understand each other, as nobody else would. (But then, perhaps someone had drawn his attention to the fact that he was the model for Browning's 'The Lost Leader', published the year before, the scathing portrait of a poet who played Judas to the radical cause: 'Just for a handful of silver he left us, / Just for a riband to stick in his coat'). There is no trace, even in Wordsworth's unkind cut, of moral or even social censure.

It is plain that, had Browning and Elizabeth Barrett chosen to conduct their relationship in the light of day, there would have been an uproar in Wimpole Street, but nowhere else; they might have married and settled in London (or abroad, if they chose, for the sake of Elizabeth Barrett's health) openly and with perfect freedom. There was nothing abnormal, except the continued breach with Mr Barrett, about their subsequent dealings with England, their visits, the publication of their books, their relations with family and friends. No one refused to receive them, or read their poems, on Mr Barrett's account—except Mr Barrett. Most of Elizabeth Barrett's brothers, who had reacted badly to the elopement, came round in time; and their hostility (including the ludicrous accusation that Browning was after Elizabeth Barrett's money) seems to have arisen more from their embarrassment at the clandestine form of the mar-riage than from solidarity with their father's opposition to it taking

place at all. The blare of gossip cannot have been pleasant, especially
when it accompanied an aria of paternal fury; Browning and Elizabeth Barrett, insulated by distance and intimacy at Pisa, had left
them to face the music.

What reason did Browning and Elizabeth Barrett have for what
she called, in the letter she wrote to her brother George on the eve
of her elopement, Browning's 'omission of the usual application to
my father & friends'? It was not Browning's responsibility, she
emphasized: 'he was about to do it—anxious to do it—& I stopped
him' (*Letters to George Barrett*, 151). Indeed she did. 'The danger
does not come from the side to which a reason may go', she told
him. 'Only one person holds the thunder—& I shall be thundered
at; I shall not be reasoned with—it is impossible.' And she quoted
to him what she had said once 'in a jest' about Mr Barrett's welcome
to prospective sons-in-law:

'If a prince of Eldorado should come, with a pedigree of lineal descent
from some signory in the moon in one hand, & a ticket of good-behaviour
from the nearest Independent chapel, in the other'—?—

'Why even *then*,' said my sister Arabel, 'it would not *do*.' And she was
right, & we all agreed that she was right. It is an obliquity of the will—&
one laughs at it till the turn comes for crying.

                                        (12 Dec. 1845, pp. 318–19.)

But if Mr Barrett had no power to enforce his 'obliquity of the
will', why did Browning and Elizabeth Barrett not defy it openly?
Elizabeth Barrett explained to George: 'I could not *physically bear*
to encounter agitating opposition from those I tenderly loved—&
to act openly in defiance of Papa's will, would have been more
impossible for me than to use the right which *I believe to be mine*,
of taking a step so strictly personal, on my own responsibility.'
'More impossible' is odd; she did not, in the end, find it 'impossible'
to use her 'right . . . of taking a step so strictly personal.' On the
other hand, she stressed, in letter after letter, the real impossibility
to her of facing her father's anger. On one occasion, Browning lost
his temper at the thought of Mr Barrett's attitude: 'the absurdity
and tyranny suddenly flashed upon me . . it must not be borne—
indeed its only safety in this instance is in its impotency' (12 June
1846, p. 776). Browning acknowledges that Mr Barrett had no real
power to prevent Elizabeth Barrett from doing what she liked; but
her father's mere presumption of authority, however unfounded,

was enough to intimidate her, as she sorrowfully explained in her reply:

And do you think that because this may be done, or not done . . & because *that* ought *not* to be borne ⸱⸱. we can make any change . . act any more openly . . face to face, perhaps—voice to voice? Alas, no!—You said once that women were as strong as men, . . unless in the concurrence of physical force. Which is a mistake. I would rather be kicked with a foot, . . (I, for one woman! . .) than be overcome by a loud voice speaking cruel words. I would not yield before such words,—I would not give you up if they were said . . but, being a woman & a very weak one (in more senses than the bodily), they would act on me as a dagger would, . . I could not help *dropping*, dying before them—I say it that you may understand.

(12 June 1846, p. 779.)

As a matter of fact, she had made Browning understand very well in an earlier exchange, when she described the 'dreadful scenes' which had taken place when her sister Henrietta ('who never offended as I have offended [. . .] only because she had seemed to feel a little') was browbeaten into submission: 'she was carried out of the room in strong hysterics, & I, who rose up to follow her, though I was quite well at that time & suffered only by sympathy, fell flat down upon my face in a fainting-fit. (15 Jan. 1846, p. 394). Browning entered fully into her feelings, and reinforced them on his own account: the 'repetition of those "scenes" ', he told her, was 'the one trial I *know* I should not be able to bear [. . .] intolerable—not to be written of, even—my mind *refuses* to form a clear conception of them' (19 Jan. 1846, pp. 403–4). Eleven days before the wedding, Elizabeth Barrett was still expressing her anxiety about 'breaking down [. . .] in nervous excitement & exhaustion. I belong to that pitiful order of weak women who cannot command their bodies with their souls at every moment, & who sink down in hysterical disorder when they ought to act & resist' (1 Sept. 1846, p. 1032). After the marriage, writing a long account of the court-ship to her friend Julia Martin, she recapitulated the whole question: and the energy of her self-justification is proof, if proof were needed, of the sting both of her self-knowledge and of her resentment against her father for, as she saw it, coercing her into deceiving him:

An application to my father was certainly the obvious course, if it had not been for his peculiar nature and my peculiar position. But there is no speculation in the case; it is a matter of *knowledge* that if Robert had applied to him in the first instance he would have been forbidden the house without a moment's scruple; and if in the last (as my sisters thought best as a respectable *form*), I should have been incapacitated from any after-exertion by the horrible scenes to which, as a thing of course, I should have been exposed. Papa will not bear some subjects, it is a thing *known*; his peculiarity takes that ground to the largest. [. . .] Now if for the sake of the mere form I had applied to my father, and if, as he would have done directly, he had set up his 'curse' against the step I proposed to take, would it have been doing otherwise than placing a knife in his hand? [. . .] In my actual state of nerves and physical weakness, it would have been the sacrifice of my whole life [. . .] and, above all, of what the person dearest to me persisted in calling *his* life, and the good of it—if I had observed that 'form'. [. . .] That I was *constrained* to act clandestinely, and did not *choose* to do so, God is witness, and will set it down as my heavy misfortune and not my fault.

(*Letters of EBB*, i. 292–4.)

It was weakness, then, which, according to her, drove Elizabeth Barrett (and Browning with her) to secrecy and deception. She is not entirely clear, however, about the reason for this weakness. To Browning she speaks of a general (or generic) timidity, of belonging to 'that pitiful order of weak women who cannot command their bodies with their souls at every moment'; to Mrs Martin, of a specific condition, 'my actual state of nerves and physical weakness'. Both explanations may be true; but behind both there is a history which Elizabeth Barrett does not relate—the history of how and why she joined 'that pitiful order of weak women', since she was certainly not born into it; the history of how her 'actual state of nerves and physical weakness' came about. Without this history, the triangular relation between herself, her father and her lover will remain fixed in the fairy-tale terms of ogre, victim, and rescuer; and our own attitude to it will be no more enlightened than that of the hapless usher, left standing in the doorway of St. Marylebone Church.

2   From Hope End to Wimpole Street

Elizabeth Barrett's father, Edward Barrett Moulton, was born in Jamaica in 1785. He came to England with his mother and his younger brother Samuel in 1794–5; their father had left them some years earlier. They eventually settled at Coxhoe Hall, near Durham, a mansion leased for them by Mrs Moulton's father, Edward Barrett. He was a very wealthy man; the family's fortune (as Elizabeth Barrett later told Browning with shame and revulsion) was founded on the slave-labour of the sugar-plantations. In 1798, Edward and Samuel Moulton became their grandfather's heirs, and adopted his surname. Edward Barrett Moulton Barrett started school at Harrow, 'but received there so savage a punishment for a supposed offence ("burning the toast") by the youth whose "fag" he had become, that he was withdrawn from the school by his mother, and the delinquent was expelled' (this tradition is preserved by Browning, curiously enough, in the 'Prefatory Note' to a collected edition of Elizabeth Barrett's poems, 1887). In 1801, he was entered as a commoner at Trinity College, Cambridge; but did not matriculate or graduate. In 1805, he married Mary Graham-Clarke, the daughter of a friend and business partner of his grandfather's. He and his wife lived for a while with his mother, at Coxhoe Hall; it was here, on 6 March 1806, that their eldest child, Elizabeth Barrett Moulton Barrett, was born. There were to be twelve children in all; nine were living when Browning and Elizabeth Barrett began to correspond in 1845.

In 1809, Mr Barrett and his wife moved to Hope End, an estate near Ledbury in Herefordshire. (The name, as biographers nervous about the connotations assure us, means 'a closed valley'.) Mr Barrett enlarged and ornamented the house: in 1831 it was described (admittedly by an auctioneer) as 'a chef d'œuvre, unrivalled in this kingdom'. The feature which caught everyone's attention was its 'eastern style of architecture'; 'a Turkish house', as Elizabeth Barrett later described it to Browning, 'crowded with minarets & domes, & crowned with metal spires & crescents' (11 July 1845, p. 119). There were over four hundred acres of land: 'excellent grass and meadow, arable, and wood land, hop garden, and plantation . . . a most eligible property for residence and investment'.

It was certainly an idyllic setting for childhood. Elizabeth Barrett grew up, the lively, high-spirited, strong-willed child of indulgent parents, in an atmosphere of material and emotional security. The Barretts were fond of nicknames; Elizabeth became 'Ba' (the 'a' pronounced as in 'car'). She was a bookish child, an avid reader and scribbler, who demanded a share of her eldest brother Edward's lessons in Greek and Latin (and far outstripped him); but she was also physically energetic, riding, walking, climbing, playing; and she had an impetuous and imperious temper. In an autobiographical sketch written when she was fourteen,[1] she recalled herself at the age of three 'reigning in the Nursery and being renowned amongst the servants for self-love and excessive passion'. 'Headlong I was at first,' she wrote in her second letter to Browning, 'and headlong I continue—precipitously rushing forward through all manner of nettles & briars instead of keeping the path,—guessing at the meaning of unknown words instead of looking into the dictionary . . tearing open letters, and never untying a string,—and expecting everything to be done in a minute, & the thunder to be as quick as the lightning' (15 Jan. 1845, p. 8). Often, as a child, she had 'upset all the chairs & tables & thrown the books about the room in a fury'; such 'good open passion which lies on the floor & kicks' was 'the born weakness of my own nature' (18 Dec. 1845, p. 326). This 'weakness' seems not to fit with the other, more conventionally feminine 'weakness' with which Elizabeth Barrett later excused herself from facing her father's anger; but, as we shall see, one was a development of the other.

There is no doubt that Mr Barrett was the ruling spirit of Hope End, as he was later to be of Wimpole Street; but, as Elizabeth Barrett's more recent biographers have emphasized, it would be wrong to picture him as a harsh, unfriendly figure in the early lives of his children. On the contrary: it took years of altered behaviour to uproot the affection and loyalty planted in them during this period; some of them, indeed, took his part to the bitter end. Elizabeth Barrett herself, on almost every occasion when she criticized her father to Browning, tried to make him understand that there was another side to the man, a side not only of uprightness and fortitude and other such Roman virtues, but of tenderness, tact and love. She left Wimpole Street in the belief that her father no longer loved her; or even that he had never loved her, as she understood the feeling. Whether that was true or not in a sense makes no difference: what is significant is that Elizabeth Barrett needed to believe it.

For the rest, Mr Barrett had a set of attitudes and prejudices by no means untypical of his class and generation. He was a Liberal, active in local politics (elected Sheriff of his county in 1812 and 1814), but neither a radical nor a free thinker. He was a devout Protestant, who attended both Church of England and Dissenting services, and

---

[1] *Glimpses into My Own Life and Literary Character*, in *The Brownings' Correspondence*, ed. P. Kelley and R. Hudson, vol. i. p. 349.

inclined his daughter to prefer the plainness and simplicity of the latter. There were family prayers daily, and strict Sunday observance. Discipline in these matters was less than fanatical, however. Elizabeth Barrett described to Browning how, as a little girl enchanted with Greek and Roman mythology, she 'went out one day with my pinafore full of little sticks (& a match from the housemaids' cupboard) to sacrifice to the blue eyed Minerva who was my favorite goddess on the whole because she cared for Athens' (15 Jan. 1846, p. 392). In the same letter, she spoke of the 'strength & opportunity for breaking the bonds all round into liberty & license' which her father had given her, despite his own religious and moral conservatism. Mr Barrett may not have been especially fond of literature and learning himself, but he had a country gentleman's large, miscellaneous library. He forbade Elizabeth Barrett to read Gibbon's *Decline and Fall of the Roman Empire* ('it's not a proper book'), and Fielding's *Tom Jones*; '& none of the books on *this* side, mind'. 'So I was very obedient', she demurely commented, 'and never touched the books on *that* side, & only read instead Tom Paine's Age of Reason, & Voltaire's Philosophical Dictionary, & Hume's Essays, & Werther [Goethe, *The Sorrows of Young Werther*], & Rousseau, & Mary Wollstonecraft [*Vindication of the Rights of Woman*] . . books, which I was never suspected of looking towards, & which were not 'on *that* side' certainly, but which did as well.' Mr Barrett admired his daughter's intellectual proficiency, and he probably winked at her reading of 'unsuitable books'. The combination of formal prohibition and informal latitude lasted throughout Elizabeth Barrett's time under her father's roof. As late as 1844, she wrote to Mary Russell Mitford that she dared not reveal to her father that she had read (and admired) the novels of George Sand: 'he would think I was mad and required his paternal restraint in all manner of ways. He has very strict ideas about women and about what they should read'. 'At the same time,' she went on, 'I fancy that he has a high opinion of my curiosity about books, and is content that I should be supposed to have read them, right and left, through a filter, without having done myself much harm' (*EBB to MRM*, 226–7). And she felt able to publish two sonnets to Sand in her 1844 *Poems*, which were dedicated to her father.

Mr Barrett fostered, too, his daughter's precocious talent for verse. 'I used to write of virtue with a large "V," & "Oh Muse" with a harp—, & things of that sort', she told Browning. 'At nine years old I wrote what I called 'an epic'—& at ten, various tragedies, French & English, which we used to act in the nursery' (15 Jan. 1846, p. 391). In her early autobiographical sketch, she recalled receiving a reward from Papa for one of these poems on 'virtue with a large "V" ', written at the age of six: 'a ten shilling note enclosed in a letter which was addrest to *the Poet Laureat of Hope End* [. . .] I received much more pleasure from the word *Poet* than from the ten shilling note'. At the age of fourteen, her father gave her the even greater pleasure of seeing her minor epic, *The Battle of Marathon*, appear in print. Soon after that, she began contributing poems to magazines and annuals on her own account, and her public reputation was launched with the publication, in 1826, of *An Essay on Mind, with Other Poems*. With the exception of her first translation of Aeschylus's *Prometheus Bound* (1833), which was hastily written and severely criticized, her reputation from then on followed a steady upward curve, in which controversy over her boldness and disregard of convention (in metre, morality, and politics alike) served only to boost her sales. It was not until some considerable time after her death that her fame began to decline. Unlike Browning, she never experienced a long period of unjust neglect, unless she is experiencing it now.

At the same time as Elizabeth Barrett's intellect was expanding, her health was declining. She became seriously ill in 1821, to the extent that she spent a year away from home, at Gloucester, in order to be nearer treatment. What was wrong with her? The question is vexed by the medical ignorance of the period and the speculation of later observers. She had recently fallen from her pony, and the idea grew up that she had an aggravated injury to her spine; when Browning first knew her, he believed from the gossip he had heard that she was incurably paralysed. But Elizabeth Barrett's accident had probably nothing to do with her illness. A detailed diagnosis by Dr William Coker, in a letter sent to another physician, discusses the possibility of disease, not injury, to the spine, though Coker admits that there was no evidence for this, either. The suspicion arose in Elizabeth Barrett's own family that she was malingering, and Betty Miller (Miller, pp.90–1) unhesitatingly ascribes her illness to repressed jealousy of her eldest brother, Edward. He, as a male, was to be given the privilege of formal education denied to her; she, at puberty, faced the prospect of relegation to the indignities of marriage and domestic duty. She countered by becoming a *sufferer*, a position from which she could exert power through incapacity, and which enabled her to evade the 'normal' responsibilities of her sex and class. But, though there is no doubt that Elizabeth Barrett exploited her situation along the lines that Miller suggests, there is equally no doubt that she was really ill; that she contracted a form of tuberculosis at this period, from which she was never free, and that she died of it forty years later. Tuberculosis is an impressionable disease. Elizabeth Barrett's health fluctuated according to variations in climate and state of mind; she had periods of remission followed by crises, and the crises generally corresponded with times when she was under nervous strain. In these circumstances, there is little point in drawing distinctions between 'physical' and 'psychological' illness.

Elizabeth Barrett's parents cared for her devotedly in the first stage of her illness; but Mr Barrett alone was to witness the full extent of his daughter's transformation from active girl to neurotic, invalid woman. His wife, Mary, died in 1828, four years after the birth of her twelfth child. 'A sweet, gentle nature, which the thunder a little turned from its sweetness—as when it turns milk—One of those women who never can resist,—but, in submitting & bowing on themselves, make a mark, a plait, within, . . a sign of suffering' (27 Aug. 1846, p. 1012). So Elizabeth Barrett described her mother to Browning, in the only reference to her in the entire correspondence. The 'thunder', of course, is Mr Barrett: Elizabeth Barrett was terrified of storms, and several times in her letters to Browning she uses storm imagery to mark her alienation from her father. This, and the date of the passage so late in the courtship, make the eloquence of Elizabeth Barrett's sympathy a little suspect here; she, after all, was doing the reverse of 'submitting & bowing', and she had an interest in identifying her mother as the victim of a tyranny which she was about to defy.

Whether or not Mr Barrett had 'thundered' at his wife, he was shocked and distressed by her death. He was now solely responsible for bringing up eleven children (one daughter, Mary, had died young); and he was already harassed by financial difficulties. The tide of the Moulton Barrett fortunes had turned. Mr Barrett and his brother Samuel were absentee landlords of the property which they had inherited from their grandfather; not only was this property badly managed on their behalf, but it was the subject of litigation by another branch of the family, the Goodin-Barretts. The case—one of those, long, tangled inheritance disputes—was decided in 1824, and the decision went against the Moulton Barretts. It is difficult to feel any sympathy for the losers in a case involving the ownership of 'parcels' of slaves, but the fact remains that this reverse was the first of a series which ended by greatly diminishing Mr Barrett's resources. He and his brother were forced to take a more active interest in their own affairs; Samuel (after a bitter argument with his brother as to which of them should go) went to Jamaica in 1827, and Mr Barrett began to spend time in London, dealing in the City as a merchant as well as trying to preserve the remains of his rentier income. At the same time, he began to make economies in his way of life (withdrawing his two eldest sons from Charterhouse, for example; none of the others went to public school), while striving to preserve the Hope End estate itself. He did not succeed. His creditors foreclosed in 1831, and the estate (valued at £50,000) was put up for auction. The Barretts left in August 1832, for a rented house in Sidmouth. It was a shattering blow to the whole family, especially the older children, who felt the loss of social status as well as the loss of a home which had seemed invulnerably secure; but the full force of the humiliation fell on Mr Barrett, who had failed alike in his ambitions and his responsibilities. Elizabeth Barrett admired the iron self-control with which he struggled with his difficulties, though she, in common with the others, was driven to despair by his refusal to share his troubles; for many months, the Barrett children heard of the progress of their father's unavailing attempts to stave off the sale of Hope End only from the gossip of their friends. Mr Barrett's policy of hiding his anguish behind 'a thick mask of high spirits' set his daughter a potent example of the excitements and perils of self-repression.

In prosperity, Mr Barrett had been cheerful and outgoing; in adversity, he became gloomy and withdrawn. He had never confided much in his wife; now he confided in no one, except in the God who had afflicted him. His religion became a resource of fortitude, but also of sternness and absolutism. God, in Mr Barrett's belief, had the right to do what he liked with his 'children'; and Mr Barrett assumed the same right towards his own. If he was not answerable to them, then the loss of his fortune could not be seen as a failure on his part. At the same time, the family which he had so prolifically engendered must not be allowed to deviate from its loyalty. The one thing which Jehovah could not stand was the Children of Israel whoring after strange gods; and, *mutatis mutandis*, that seems to have been the reasoning behind Mr Barrett's refusal to allow any of his children an independent sexual life. As the children grew up, they became aware, first of their father's determination that none of them should marry without his consent, and then that this consent would never be forthcoming. Mr Barrett did not openly state his objection to marriage in principle; that would have been absurd, given his own history. He merely affirmed that he had the right to decide on the suitability and timing of any match, and it became clear that, on one pretext or another, he would always decide against. This particular assumption of authority was only one of what Elizabeth Barrett called his 'patriarchal ideas of governing grownup children "in the way they *must* go!" ' (20 Aug. 1845, p. 169); but it was the one which had the most dramatic consequences.

Why did the children themselves endure it? Elizabeth Barrett told Browning that they were 'constrained *bodily* into submission . . apparent submission at least . . by that worst & most dishonoring of necessities, the necessity of *living*' (ibid.). But the explanation is surely more complicated than that. The Barretts were a close-knit family, and the children may have sensed in their father's attitude a feeling to which they could respond, a desire to keep the family intact after the shock of its personal, social and financial misfortunes. Mr Barrett's perverse and unjust behaviour (again the analogy with the God of Israel irresistibly suggests itself) could be seen as the obverse of his love; he laid upon them the bondage of his affection. Moreover, the fact that they suffered their father did not mean that they agreed with the overt principle of his conduct. This principle of 'passive filial obedience', as Elizabeth Barrett explained to Browning, was 'held . . drawn (& quartered) from Scripture. He *sees* the law & the gospel on his side' (21 Jan. 1846, p. 408). But she went on to describe a scene which gives us a graphic insight into the limitations of Mr Barrett's hold over his children, and of their clear-sighted understanding of the rationality of his declared position:

Only the other day, there was a setting forth of the whole doctrine, I hear, down stairs—'passive obedience, & particularly in respect to marriage.' One after the other, my brothers all walked out of the room, & there was left for sole auditor, Captain Surtees Cook, who had especial reasons for sitting it out against his will,—so he sate and asked 'if children were to be considered slaves' as meekly as if he were asking for information. I could not help smiling when I heard of it.

Captain Surtees Cook was a cousin of the Barretts, who was clandestinely courting Henrietta, the eldest of Elizabeth Barrett's sisters (they married in 1850, and Henrietta was duly cast off). Surtees Cook, unlike Browning, was allowed by his cousinship to visit Wimpole Street as often as he liked, and naturally did not want to jeopardize his privilege; yet even he, in his comically feeble way, dissented from what others did not hesitate to call Mr Barrett's 'monomania'.

By the time the family moved to Sidmouth in 1832, Mr Barrett's ideas would have become clear to the older members of the family, though they were not yet fully reconciled to bearing with them; there was trouble in store for both Edward and Henrietta (the oldest children after Elizabeth). As for Elizabeth Barrett herself, her father's objection to suitors met with her own distaste for what she perceived as the deceitful and materialistic transactions between men and women in her social circle. 'I have not a high appreciation of what passes in the world [. . .] under the name of love', she told Browning; 'that word which rhymes to glove & comes as easily off and on' (21 Dec. 1845, pp. 340, 341). The conventional processes of courtship and marriage are treated with complete lack of respect in her letters to Browning: sometimes with outright bitterness—'To see the marriages which are made every day!—worse than solitudes & more desolate!' (ibid., p. 340.)—sometimes with an eye to black comedy. 'Yesterday I heard some delightful matrimonial details of an "establishment" in Regent's Park, quite like an old pastoral in the quickness of the repartee. "I hate you"—"I abhor you"—"I never liked you"—"I always detested you." A cup and saucer thrown bodily, here, by the lady!—On which the gentleman upsets her, . . chair & all, . . flat on the floor. The witness, who is a friend of mine, gets frightened & begins to cry. She was invited to be godmother to their child, & now she is pressed to stay longer to witness the articles of separation' (20 May 1846, p. 717). 'As for *men*,' she told Browning, 'you are not to take me to be quite ignorant of what they are worth in the gross. The most blindfolded women may see a little under the folds . . & I have seen quite enough to be glad to shut my eyes' (26 Mar. 1846, p. 565). She was scathing about their vanity, their bullying, their meanness. 'Oh—to see how these things are set about by *men*! to see how a man carefully holding up on each side the skirts of an embroidered vanity to keep it quite safe from the wet, will contrive to tell you in so many words that he . . might love you if the sun shone!' (21 Dec. 1846, p. 341.) And again: 'I understand perfectly, how as soon as ever a common man is sure of a woman's affections, he takes up the tone of right & might . . & he *will* have it so . . & he *won't* have it so [. . .] Of such are "Lovers' quarrels" for the most part. The growth of power on one side . . & the struggle against it, by means legal & illegal, on the other' (4 July 1846, p. 844). 'When I was a child', she remarks in another letter, 'I heard two married women talking. One said to the other . . "The most painful part of marriage is the first year, when the lover changes into the husband by slow degrees." The other woman agreed, as a matter of fact is agreed to. I listened with my eyes & ears, & never forgot it . . as you observe. It seemed to me, child as I was, a dreadful thing to have a husband by such a process' (6 July 1846, p. 853). She was equally observant, and equally sharp, about the pettiness of domestic life. 'Did you ever observe a lord of creation knit his brows together because the cutlets were underdone, shooting enough fire from his eyes to overdo them to cinders [. . .] Did you ever hear of the litany which some women say through the first course . . low to themselves . . Perhaps not!—it does not enter into your imagination to conceive of things, which nevertheless *are*' (7 Apr. 1846, pp. 599–600). The light note of reproach here is sounded more fully and authoritatively, in *Aurora Leigh*, against the whole male sex for its unthinking behaviour towards women, and its ignorance of the fact that women feel it. Not, of course, that such pettiness was entirely confined to men. 'I *saw* a woman, once, burst into tears, because her husband cut the bread and butter too thick. [. . .] "You ALWAYS do it"! she said' (18 Dec. 1845, p. 326).

Given such a satirical eye, it is perhaps not surprising that Elizabeth Barrett, before her relationship with Browning, should have found it easier than others in the family to conform to her father's will. Poor Mr Barrett certainly believed himself to be safe from that quarter. 'Once I heard of his saying of me that I was "the purest woman he ever knew,"—which made me smile at the moment, or laugh I believe, outright, because I understood perfectly what he meant by *that*—viz—that I had not troubled him with the iniquity of love-affairs, or any impropriety of seeming to think about being married' (14 Sept. 1846, p. 1072). She too, however, disavowed obedience in principle to her father's claim to authority over her sexual and emotional choices. 'I have been a submissive daughter,' she told Browning, '& this from no effort, but for love's sake [. . .] yet I have reserved for myself ALWAYS that right over my own affections which is the most strictly personal of all things, and which involves principles & consequences of infinite importance & scope' (24 Oct. 1845, p. 248).

As an alternative to the 'iniquity of love-affairs' which did not tempt her anyway, she engaged in close friendships, with both men and women, which avoided her father's ban. Of her friendships with men, three stand out, from different periods of her life: at Hope End, with the classical scholar Hugh Stuart Boyd, who was many years older than she, married, and blind; at Sidmouth, with the Reverend George Barrett Hunter, minister of an Independent chapel, also older, and a widower; and in London, with a 'cousin' (so-called) of her father's, John Kenyon. The relationship with Boyd was intense, and aroused the jealousy of his wife and gossip in the Barrett household; but whatever sexual edge it had was inevitably qualified by cicumstance, and part of its attraction for Elizabeth Barrett seems to have been its safety. If she was looking for the same kind of equivocal relationship with Hunter, she was disappointed; he ended by falling in love with her, openly and in earnest, and pestered her with his unwanted attentions until her marriage. With Kenyon, however, she formed the happiest and most stable friendship of her life. Like Mr Barrett, he had been born in Jamaica and brought up in England; but he had kept his wealth, and used it to patronize the arts, and especially literature. He was the friend of Wordsworth, Coleridge, Southey, and Lamb, among many others; when he got to know Elizabeth Barrett, he more or less adopted her literary career, introducing her to Wordsworth, to Walter Savage Landor, to Mary Russell Mitford; he became her critic, her confidant, and the equivalent of her literary agent. He had also, as it happened, been a schoolfellow of Robert Browning's father, and the young poet was another of his protégés. In 1843, he made an abortive attempt to introduce him to Elizabeth Barrett; and in 1845, the correspondence between them began at his encouragement.

More significant than any of these friendships, however, was Elizabeth Barrett's relationship with her eldest brother, Edward, who was nicknamed 'Bro'. Intense rivalry and intense sympathy made Bro the most important figure in Elizabeth Barrett's emotional life before she knew Browning: her 'first and chiefest affection', 'what I loved best in the world beyond comparison & rivalship', she told Browning, 'far better' even than her father (20 Aug. 1845, p. 169). Betty Miller persuasively suggests that Elizabeth Barrett underwent a kind of trauma when she realized that the opportunities which were available to Bro, as a man, were denied to her; but Miller disguises the fact that the result was the reverse of that which Elizabeth Barrett might have feared. Her intellect was much stronger than Bro's; he was a mediocre pupil at Charterhouse while she was a prodigy of self-education; and the upshot was that the balance of power between them, when they became adults, lay decisively with her. It was Bro, not Elizabeth Barrett, who ended up by not having a career; he never went to university, took up no profession, and seems to have spent much of his life in attendance on his sister. He idolized and idealized her no less than she him, but with somewhat different results. Elizabeth Barrett may have felt her own intellectual growth unfairly thwarted in relation to her brother's, but grow she did; he did not. In Elizabeth Barrett's later accounts of him, she stresses the complete sympathy of tastes and views between them, the fact that he alone of her family was attuned to her sensibility. You might put it another and less kind way, and say that her identity completely overshadowed his.

The consequence of Bro's devotion to Elizabeth Barrett was momentous. In 1835 the Barrett family left Sidmouth and settled in London, first in a house in Gloucester Place, and then, in 1837, at 50 Wimpole Street. In the late summer of 1838, not long after the publication of her volume *The Seraphim, and Other Poems*, which confirmed her growing reputation, Elizabeth Barrett suffered a relapse in health: it is from this time that she dated her invalidism, in the sense of a completely disabling condition. She was advised to leave London for the warmer climate of Torquay, on the Devonshire coast. Her father had at first opposed her going. She later wrote to Miss Mitford that she had gone 'not indeed against his desire, but against the bias of his desire. I was persuaded—he was entreated. On his side, it was at last a mere yielding to a majority' (*EBB to MRM*, 73). In the course of one of the longest and most painful letters she ever wrote to Browning, she described what followed this overruling of her father's will:

They sent me down you know to Torquay—Dr. Chambers saying that I

could not live a winter in London—The worst . . —what people call the
worst—was apprehended for me at that time. So I was sent down with my
sister [Henrietta] to my aunt there [her maternal aunt, Arabella Graham-
Clarke]—and he, my brother whom I loved so, was sent too, to take us
there & return. And when the time came for him to leave me, *I*, to whom he
was the dearest of friends & brothers in one . . the only one of my family
who . . well, but I cannot write of these things; & it is enough to tell you
that he was above us all, better than us all & kindest & noblest and dearest
to *me*, beyond comparison, any comparison, as I said—& when the time
came for him to leave me *I*, weakened by illness, could not master my spirits or drive back my tears—& my aunt kissed them away instead of reprov-
ing me as she should have done; & said that *she* would take care that I
should not be grieved . . *she*! . . and so she sate down & wrote a letter to
Papa to tell him that he would 'break my heart' if he persisted in calling
away my brother—As if hearts were broken *so*! I have thought bitterly
since that my heart did not break for a good deal more than *that*! And
Papa's answer was—burnt into me, as with fire, it is—that 'under such circumstances he did not refuse to suspend his purpose, but that he considered
it to be *very wrong in me to exact such a thing*.' So there was no separation
then: & month after month passed—& sometimes I was better & sometimes worse—& the medical men continued to say that they wd not answer
for my life . . they! if I were agitated—& so there was no more talk of a separation. And once *he* held my hand, . . how I remember! & said that he
'loved me better than them all & that he *would not* leave me . . till I was
well,' he said! how I remember *that*! And ten days from that day the boat
had left the shore which never returned; never—& he *had* left me! gone!
For three days we waited—& I hoped while I could—oh—that awful agony
of three days! And the sun shone as it shines to-day, & there was no more
wind than now; and the sea under the windows was like this paper for
smoothness—& my sisters drew the curtains back that I might see for
myself how smooth the sea was, & how it could hurt nobody—& other
boats came back one by one.

(20 Aug. 1845, p. 170.)

Bro, along with three companions, was drowned in a sudden squall
while sailing in Babbacombe Bay, on 11 July 1840. Three of the
four bodies, including that of Bro, were eventually washed ashore;
he was buried in Torquay on 6 August. Elizabeth Barrett's grief was
aggravated by an incident she did not mention in this account to
Browning—on that particular day, she and Bro had parted after a
quarrel; but the main, overpowering burden was that of guilt. It was
at her insistence that Bro had stayed in Torquay; she had imposed
her will on him and on her father: this was the retribution. It is

possible, too, that, as Betty Miller suggests, she recoiled from an unconscious intention arising out of her long-suppressed rivalry with her closest sibling. At any rate, her reaction was extreme. She suffered a complete breakdown: for months she lay prostrate, unable to shed a tear, barely able to sleep, and suffering from terrifying hallucinations; she was close to madness, she thought later. She wanted to die; at first, she believed she would. 'And although what I cannot help feeling as an unnatural tenacity to life prevented my following my beloved, quietly quietly as I thought I should', she wrote to Miss Mitford, '—and although I have learnt even to be calm and to talk lightly sometimes, yet the heavy sense of loss weighs at my heart day and night, and *will*, till my last night or day' (*EBB to MRM*, 73).

Gradually, as she says, Elizabeth Barrett recuperated her strength and spirits; nine months after Bro's death, she wrote to Mrs Martin, 'I don't give up much to the pernicious languor—the tendency to lie down to sleep among the snows of a weary journey' (*Letters of EEB*, i. 87). By the time she wrote to Browning, she had recognized the irrationality of her first 'acrid thoughts': 'I *know* that I would have died ten times over for *him*, & that therefore though it was wrong of me to be weak, & I have suffered for it [. . .] *remorse* is not precisely the word for me—not at least in its full sense' (20 Aug. 1845, p. 171). But this recovery of mental balance was partial and inadequate. 'Still you will comprehend from what I have told you', she went on to Browning, 'how the spring of life must have seemed to break within me *then*;—& how natural it has been for me to loath the living on—& to lose faith (even without the loathing) to lose faith in myself . . which I have done on some points utterly.'

It was not simply that Elizabeth Barrett could never bear to speak Bro's name (not even to Browning after their marriage), or to hear it spoken, or that she had ever afterwards a morbid fear of the sea and a dislike of its sound—'you must never go away in *boats*', she warned Browning shortly before their marriage (26 Aug. 1846, p. 1007); it was, as she described it, a reversal of her whole former attitude to life. 'My castle-building is at an end!' she wrote to Miss Mitford. 'A great change has passed both upon my inward and outward life [. . .] I scarcely recognize myself sometimes. One stroke ended my youth' (cited in Taplin, 82). Whether this sentiment is true or not is irrelevant: it determined Elizabeth Barrett's self-construction for the next five years, the crucial years of her return to Wimpole Street, her isolation and her achievement of fame with her 1844 *Poems*.

More than anything, it determined her attitude towards her father. 'He was generous & forbearing in that hour of bitter trial,' she told Browning, 'and never reproached me as he might have done & as my own soul has not spared [. . .] It would have been *cruel*, you think, to reproach me. Perhaps so!—yet the kindness & patience of the desisting from reproach, are positive things all the same' (20 Aug. 1845, pp. 169, 171). Since it was by the opposition of her will to his that 'the crown of his house' had fallen, she set herself to submit to that will as completely as she could. 'Under the circumstances and in the state of feeling natural to me at this time,' she wrote to Miss Mitford nearly a year after the tragedy, 'my only full contentment can be in his doing his own full pleasure [. . .] you will understand from all, that my poor most beloved Papa's *biases* are sacred to me, and that I would not stir them with a breath' (*EBB to MRM*, 73–4). Nevertheless she carried one more point: she successfully negotiated a return to Wimpole Street from Torquay, where she had feared that her father might leave her; or else, he might settle her in some other place, where, as she insisted to her brother George, she would allow none of her family to be with her; she would not divide them again. 'All that remains to me of earthly happiness seems to me dependent on my return to Wimpole Street. [. . .] I want to be with you *all*—none away, but those whom God has taken' (*Letters to George Barrett*, 54). Her father eventually agreed; she wrote to Mr Boyd, 'I go as "the doves to their windows," to the only earthly daylight I see here. I go to rescue myself from the associations of this dreadful place. I go to restore to my poor papa the companionship of his family' (*Letters of EBB*, i. 88). She was later to use exactly the same apocalyptic quotation about the doves (from Isaiah 60: 8) to describe her feeling for Browning (4 Jan. 1846, p. 362); but then it was rescue *from* Wimpole Street which was at issue, and 'poor papa's' susceptibilities counted for nothing. Unconscious of this coming reversal, Elizabeth Barrett travelled from Torquay to Wimpole Street (in a carriage specially fitted with a bed), starting on 1 September 1841, and arriving ten days later 'with a sense of being thoroughly *beaten*, as she told Miss Mitford; but also in profound relief at being 'with Papa—in the midst of all left! No more partings—nor meetings which were worse—almost *much* worse, sometimes' (*EBB to*

MRM, 84). She settled into her room, up two flights of stairs at the back of the house, carefully shielded from the draughts which were said by the doctors to be her greatest danger. With her books, her correspondence, and her poetry for occupation; with Flush, the spaniel given to her by Miss Mitford, as her companion and recreation; cared for by a personal servant; with the constant tribute of her family's affection and attention; convinced that her physical condition was practically irremediable, and content that it should be so; both excited and enervated by opium (in 1845 she was 'in the habit of taking forty drops of laudanum a day, and *cannot do with less*'—*Letters of EBB*, i. 269): Elizabeth Barrett built up an identity which enabled her to cope with other people, and to face herself, with a degree of equanimity. As for her father, he prayed with her each evening before she went to sleep, 'one of my hands held in his and nobody besides him and me in the room' (*EBB to MRM*, 138); 'God knows that I had as much joy as I imagined myself capable of again,' she wrote to Browning, 'in the sound of his footstep on the stairs, & of his voice when he prayed in this room,—my best hope, as I have told him since, being, to die beneath his eyes' (26 Jan. 1846, p. 422). It was this 'peace & rest', this *'safety of heart'* (*Letters to George Barrett*, 70), which she was to put deliberately at risk, five years and one day after her arrival in Wimpole Street, on the morning of her marriage.

3 Youth and art

The man Elizabeth Barrett married had had (relatively speaking) a very different life from hers. Not for Robert Browning the enjoyment of rentier wealth and the social position of a country gentleman (followed by their decline); not for him the experience of a dominant father, a rival sibling, and numerous other brothers and sisters; not for him the anguish of bereavement or ill health, nor the comforts of seclusion and morphine. He was born in 1812 into the professional middle class: his family, settled in what were then the rural suburbs of Camberwell and New Cross, had connections with the law, with banking and merchant shipping. His father, a clerk in the Bank of England, was a gentle man, with a talent for drawing and a passion for rare books, whose library, containing several thousand volumes, was the young poet's inexhaustible resource, the guide to his passion for history, for biography, for metaphysics, and for the occult. His mother, Sarah Anna Wiedemann, of German and Scottish descent, ten years older than her husband, and the stronger personality of the two, was a devout Nonconformist, who passed on to her son, along with the foundations of her religion, her love of music, of plants and animals, and especially of the small wild creatures—songbirds, lizards, snails, spiders, and beetles—which populated her garden and colonized Browning's poetry. Browning's only sister, Sarianna, was two years younger than him; devotion to her family subsumed her considerable qualities of intellect and character—devotion to her mother while she lived, especially in the last invalid years of her life; to Browning while he lived at home, where she assiduously fair-copied his poems; to her father after her mother's death; to Browning again, as housekeeper and companion, after her father's. Though Browning did not enjoy quite the perfect health in his youth which he later claimed (to Elizabeth Barrett, for example), he was essentially strong, active, and energetic, a lover, as she had been, of walking and riding. Twice in letters to her he speaks of dancing all night and hearing the birds singing in the dawn as he came home. (His attitude to Elizabeth Barrett's ill health, always tender and supportive, has an element of personal incredulity. He could not imagine himself taking morphine.) When he first broke into the London literary world, he sought the acquaintance of writers, journalists, critics, and above all people of the theatre. The disillusion with 'society' which he expressed so forcefully to Elizabeth Barrett came, as she remarked, from 'satiety' (20 Mar. 1845, p. 42). When he disparaged the advantages of foreign travel, she reminded him again that he did so from 'the point of attainment' (17 Apr. 1845, p. 48): he had been to Russia, to France, to the Low Countries and northern Germany, and twice to Italy. Above all, he had, as Elizabeth Barrett soon realized, been 'spared, up to this time, the great natural afflictions, against which we are nearly all called, sooner or later, to struggle and wrestle' (5 Mar. 1845, p. 35). There had been no death in the family.

The most striking contrast of all is between the two fathers, because it springs from a connection between them. Like the Barretts, the Brownings had links with the West Indies. Robert Browning, the poet's grandfather, 'an able, energetic, and worldly man' (Orr, *Life*, 4), who achieved a senior position in the Bank of England by his own uncompromising efforts, had married Margaret Tittle, who came from a family with large plantation holdings on the island of St. Kitts. Robert Browning, the poet's father, was sent out to St. Kitts at the age of twenty to make his career on his mother's family's estates; and there, according to Browning (the first words are his mother's, which he is relaying to Elizabeth Barrett), he ' "conceived such a hatred to the slave-system in the West Indies," [. . .] that he relinquished every prospect,—supported himself, while there, in some other capacity, and came back, while yet a boy, to his father's profound astonishment and rage' (26 Aug. 1846, pp. 1005–6). There had been, Browning speculated 'some abominable early experience', but his father had an 'invincible repugnance to allude to the matter [. . .] if you question him about it, he shuts his eyes involuntarily and shows exactly the same marks of loathing that may be noticed while a piece of cruelty is mentioned . . and the *word* "blood," even, makes him change colour' (27 Aug. 1846, p. 1011). On his return from St. Kitts, he 'had the intention of devoting himself to art, for which he had many qualifications and abundant love—but the quarrel with his father [. . .] induced him to go at once and consume his life after a fashion he always detested' (26 Aug. 1846, p. 1006). John Maynard (Maynard pp. 25–7) points out the note of melodramatic exaggeration in that last statement: Browning's father's appointment to a clerkship in the Bank of England, the same institution where his father worked, was hardly the martyrdom that Browning makes it out to be; rather, 'the foundation stone of an agreeable and comfortable way of life'. (Anyway, is not there something suspect, readers of 'Pictor Ignotus', 'Andrea del Sarto', and 'Youth and Art' might ask, about the notion of the artist *manqué*, thwarted by circumstance and not by defect of will?) Nevertheless, the basic fact remains that while Mr Barrett struggled to retain his position in the 'slave-system', Mr Browning renounced his. The strength of mind which the son showed on this occasion translated itself, in later life, into an extreme tender-heartedness as a husband and father, and a general reluctance to impose his will in any situation: qualities which he passed on, in turn, to his own son, who once broke with a friend because he saw him bullying his wife, and denounced to Elizabeth Barrett 'the execrable policy of the world's husbands, fathers, brothers, and domineerers in general' (4 Sept. 1846, p. 1044). When Elizabeth Barrett referred to her father treating his children as 'chattels' and called it 'a mistake of the intellect rather than of the heart' (3 Mar. 1846, p. 514), Browning refused to have any truck with what he recognized as a half-apology: 'all faults are such inasmuch as they are "mistakes of the intellect" ', he replied; 'but if I ever see it right, exercising my intellect, to treat any human beings like my "chattels"—I shall pay for that mistake one day or another, I am convinced—and I very much fear that you would soon discover what one fault of mine is, if you were to hear anyone assert such a right in my presence' (4 Mar. 1846, p. 516).

In one respect, Browning and Elizabeth Barrett were alike: they were both precocious versifiers, and their talent was admired and encouraged, without being fully comprehended, by their indulgent parents. Whereas Elizabeth Barrett eventually made her own way into print, however, Browning relied on his father until his marriage for the expenses of publishing his poetry. This support was given, too, long after Mr Browning had lost his appetite for his son's complex and apparently inharmonious verses. He gave up on *Sordello* (1840), unable, in common with almost everyone else then or since, to make head nor tail of it. *Sordello* is written in couplets which, to the lover of Pope, must have seemed a barbaric travesty. Indeed, a character in *Pippa Passes* (1841), Browning's next work, expresses, in thinly-disguised form, Browning's barbed recognition that his father and those like him could not be expected to approve of his style. Speaking of an unnamed poet whose 'immortal poem' is expected to fail miserably, the character remarks: 'His own fault, the simpleton! Instead of cramp couplets, each like a knife in your entrails, he should write [. . .] classically and intelligibly' (i. 297–300).

But Browning's parents had other, and more serious misgivings, about fostering his writing, at any rate in the early stages. For Browning made a deliberate decision to have no career, and he did so, as John Maynard acutely notes, some years before his vocation as a poet can have been completely clear to him—after his youthful effusions, that is, but before the writing of his first major work, *Pauline* (1833). His decision took concrete form at the moment when he decided to withdraw from the new London University (later University College London), where he had studied Classics and German for most of the acadamic year 1828–9. He would not study law; he would not go into business; over the next few years, he flirted with the idea of a diplomatic career, but he never seriously took it up. Essentially, he committed himself to a process of self-education (by study, travel, and social life) which led him, in the

1830's, to the determination to be a poet—irrespective of whether that entailed making a living. By 1842 (three years before they met) Elizabeth Barrett knew enough about Browning's choice of life to compare him (as well as Tennyson) with Wordsworth, as one who knew what 'a true poet's crown is worth', and who dedicated himself to 'a silent, blameless, heroic life of poetic duty'; but, as she herself recognized, she was crying in the wilderness of worldly wisdom: ' "Art," it was said long ago, "requires the whole man," and "Nobody," it was said later, "can be a poet who is anything else;" but the present idea of Art requires the segment of a man, and everybody who is anything at all is a poet in a parenthesis'.[2] Browning determined that the parenthesis would not embrace him: he argued the point with his parents, and won it. He established his right to an 'absolute independence', which he had, as he told Elizabeth Barrett, 'fought so many good battles to preserve' (16 Sept. 1845, p. 200). Echoes of these 'battles' reach us in gossip which came to Elizabeth Barrett's ears about Browning's lack of serious occupation and his family's dissatisfaction with his idleness and dependence (see chapter five, below). Elizabeth Barrett dismissed such gossip as illfounded, and in the case of Browning's immediate family she was probably right; by 1845, he had won his parents over completely, unless his accounts of their sympathy and support in his letters to Elizabeth Barrett are diabolically perjured.

It took considerable force of character for Browning both to abjure the conventional careers and compromises of his class, and to persuade his parents to support him in doing so. The struggle told on him as much as on them. He had always been a restless, nervously energetic child (he is recorded as gnawing the top of his pew in exasperation at a long sermon); the evidence from the outset of his literary career is that of a mind operating under extreme pressure, working at an abnormal pace and with irregular effect. There is a combination of brashness and humility, of aggressive self-reliance and something not far from fawning, in some of his letters of the 1830's and early 1840's—particularly those to men who were in a position to advance his literary prospects, such as the editor of the *Monthly Repository*, W. J. Fox, or the actor-manager William Macready—which testifies to insecure ambition, and the desperate need to show himself worthy of the privileges he had arrogated to

---

[2] 'The Book of the Poets', in *Works of EBB*, pp. 650–1.

himself. There is something ominous, as well as comic, in Macready's entry in his diary for 27 August 1840: 'Browning came before I had finished my bath, and really *wearied* me with his obstinate faith in his poem of *Sordello*, and of his eventual celebrity, and also with his self-opinionated persuasions upon his *Return of the Druses* [a play which Macready refused to produce]. I fear he is for ever gone' (cited in DeVane, *Handbook*, 133). The same unease appears in some of the impressions we have of Browning's social presence at this period—pushy, self-conscious, dominating and yielding by turns. Mary Russell Mitford thought him effeminate; Jane Welsh Carlyle thought him insincere and affected. It is difficult, perhaps, to like someone who has something to prove, even (perhaps especially) when they are in the process of proving it.

This process itself began with the anonymously-published *Pauline* (1833), which sank without trace and which remained unacknowledged by the poet for over thirty years, until the threat of pirated publication forced him ('with extreme repugnance') to include it in his collected works. Then came the *succès d'estime* of *Paracelsus* (1835) and, in a lesser degree, of *Strafford* (1837), Browning's first stage play, which launched his ill-fated attempt to achieve fame in the theatre. At this point, Browning stood on the brink of a moderate commercial success; then he published *Sordello* (1840). The failure of this great poem, which had taken him seven years to write, was incomparably more serious, more wounding (to Browning personally, and to his reputation) than that of *Pauline*. It blighted criticism and sales for a quarter of a century. The stereotype of Browning as the hearty, blustering Victorian optimist was a relatively late arrival; for much of his career, he was denounced as wilfully and pretentiously obscure, the worst kind of avant-garde élitist. This stereotype survived *Pippa Passes* (1841), *Dramatic Lyrics* (1842), *Dramatic Romances and Lyrics* (1845), even *Men and Women* (1855). It began to wane with *Dramatis Personae* (1864), and was routed by *The Ring and the Book* (1868). But the experience of neglect and ridicule cannot have made Browning's position, as a self-appointed poet, easier to bear. He talked of doing his duty, of being answerable only to the God who had given him his task, of not caring for the world's opinion; but he knew perfectly well, and resented bitterly, the fact that he was not receiving the critical and public esteem which was his due. Elvan Kintner (Kintner, p. xlii) draws the parallel with Keats, and there is confirmation of this from

Browning himself. Just as the tide of his own popularity was turning, in 1865, he wrote to Julia Wedgwood strongly asserting his
belief that Keats '*did* have death accelerated, if not induced' by the
ridicule he had suffered: 'don't believe a man of average sensibility
is ever insulted by a blackguard without suffering enough: despise
it? yes,—but you feel the slap in the face, too [. . .] Don't suppose
that joking about such a person's pestle and mortar and so on, did
not drop hell fire on the sore-place' (*RB & JW*, 128). In the laughter
at Keats for not sticking to his 'pestle and mortar', for having cock-
ney pretensions to higher things, Browning senses the nightmarish
might-have-been of his own career. His social class was not that far
removed from Keats's; behind the harsh reviews of his early poems,
he may have felt the lurking implication that he, too, would be
better off plying some honest trade; a thin partition of luck (the luck
of his parents' continuing support) separated him from Keats's fate.

It is not surprising, therefore, to find that in Browning's early
work the problems of creative ambition, of achievement and failure
both in the outer world and in the world of the imagination, are of
central importance. The very structure of *Paracelsus*—five books,
entitled 'Paracelsus Aspires', 'Paracelsus Attains', 'Paracelsus', 'Paracelsus Aspires', and 'Paracelsus Attains'—points to Browning's
preoccupation with the falling and rising rhythm of the mind's drive
towards supremacy. But for our purpose there is one crucial feature
of Browning's treatment of these topics—a feature which will help
us to understand why he was drawn so irresistibly to the poetry and
personality of Elizabeth Barrett. It concerns the doubleness of
human creativity. The imagination *desires* to be free, untrammelled,
autonomous; it *needs* to be dependent, bound by obligation to
acknowledge the authority which gave it life. Milton's Satan claims
to be 'self-begot'; his Adam is 'inspired' by God with the breath of
life. One rebels, making an impossible claim; the other worships,
owing an unpayable debt. These dual impulses, in Browning's view,
can never be reconciled within human nature in general, and within
the mind of the artist in particular; it is this very fact, the unresolv-
able struggle of consciousness, which makes life worth living and
poetry worth writing.

The relation of this idea to Browning's own career is straightforward enough. In choosing to 'become' a poet, he was making the
equivalent of a Satanic or Promethean gesture of self-assertion,
which invoked a backlash of guilt and anxiety. In 'meaning, on the

whole, to be a Poet, if not *the* Poet . . for I am vain and ambitious some nights' (24 May 1845, p. 75), he was setting his will against the will of the world, and against another 'will', the long legacy of ambition and triumph represented by the poetry of the past. Yet he could only pursue his chosen vocation in terms which enforced his sense of humility and obligation—whether to Divine Providence which had endowed him with his talent, or to the public he must address, or to his predecessors, who offered him the two-edged gift of their language.

Accordingly, Browning gives the characters in his early work identities and relationships which are governed by the see-saw of defiance and deference. He rings the changes on the way in which the balance of power shifts as between egotism and self-abnegation, both within the individual's mind, and in relations between individuals, and in the relations of individuals to their society or their God. This tension is especially significant for us in the way it affects relationships between people—for example, the speaker of *Pauline* and Pauline herself; Paracelsus and Aprile in *Paracelsus*; Sordello and Palma in *Sordello*; Jules and Phene in *Pippa Passes*. Male and female roles may change, or the relation may be between two people of the same sex, but the essential structure remains. Love is governed by conflicting impulses of action and passivity, possessiveness and self-surrender. Desire is both selfish and selfless; lovers seek to possess the beloved, but also to give away their identity; to triumph in the act of surrender, and surrender in the act of triumph. The problem becomes acute for the figures in Browning's early poetry who represent, however partially, his sense of his own identity. These 'heroes' (of *Pauline*, of *Paracelsus*, of *Sordello*) are all driven to acknowledge that their need to love is as great as their desire to be loved. In Christian terms, 'whosoever will save his life shall lose it' (Mark 8:35): only in deference, in devotion, in self-sacrifice, can the ego assert its power to create and act.

In this light, Browning's relationships with women before Elizabeth Barrett show a clear pattern. 'There is no love but from beneath, far beneath', he told her (10 Aug. 1846, p. 950); he needed, therefore, 'a woman to whose intellect, as well as goodness' he could 'look up' (13 Aug. 1846, p. 960). This need was dictated by a sense not of weakness, but of excessive strength. Like the hero of *Pauline*, Browning felt himself 'made up of an intensest life, / Of a most clear idea of consciousness / Of self', which was 'linked

[. . .] to self-supremacy [. . .] And to a principle of restlessness /
Which would be all, have, see, know, taste, feel, all—'(ll. 268–78).
The incoherent rush of verbs in that last line represents the power
which must be checked; and the speaker therefore proposes (in
terms equally extreme) to devote himself to Pauline: 'We will go
hand in hand, / I with thee, even as a child—love's slave, / Looking
no farther than his liege commands'(ll. 947–9).

But, as Browning assured Elizabeth Barrett again and again, he
had failed in his prior search for someone to whom he could act the
part of 'love's slave'. 'I seem to have foretold, *foreknown* you in
other likings of mine', he told Elizabeth Barrett, adding that the
very fact that these 'likings' had been transient emphasized their
inadequacy. (4 Feb. 1846, p. 435.) All these women—Eliza and
Sarah Flower in his adolescence, and Fanny Haworth in his early
manhood, are the most notable—were, like Elizabeth Barrett, older
than Browning: speaking of his 'male prudery with respect to
"young ladies" ', he told Elizabeth Barrett that he had never seen
'any attractiveness in the class', and had been 'very little inclined to
get involved in troubles & troubles for nothing at all' (22 May
1846, p. 723). Age guaranteed at least one kind of *priority* in the
beloved; there must also be a superiority of mind and character. But
though all the women to whom Browning was attached had varied
artistic and intellectual gifts, none of them had the concentration of
identity which he required in answer to his own. 'Before I knew
you,' he wrote to Elizabeth Barrett, 'women seemed not so much
better than myself,—therefore, no love for them!' (10 Aug. 1846,
p. 950.) By the time he came to know Elizabeth Barrett, he claimed
to have despaired of finding this essential 'disproportionateness in a
beloved object'. He had calculated his 'whole scheme of life' on a
basis which 'supposed *you*, the finding such a one as you, utterly
impossible—because in calculating one goes upon *chances*, not on
providence—how could I expect you?' (13 Sept. 1845, p. 193.) He
was 'no longer in the first freshness of life', and had 'for many years
now made up my mind to the impossibility of loving any woman';
he had 'wondered at this in the beginning, and fought not a little
against it [. . .] acquiesced in it at last, and accounted for it all to
myself, and become, if anything, rather proud of it than sorry'(16
Sept. 1845, p. 198). He took all the more credit, therefore, that
'when real love [. . .] *did* reveal itself to me at last, I *did* open my
heart to it with a cry'.

2

First Letters

1 Exchanges of courtesy

Browning and Elizabeth Barrett were not strangers to one another before they began to correspond, in the sense that they read and admired each other's work, and heard news of each other from their common friend John Kenyon. Most of the evidence for their feelings about each other before their relationship began is on Elizabeth Barrett's side, partly because more of her letters survive, and partly because of Browning's reticence: he had an aversion, he told her later, to 'the foolish crowd of rushers-in upon genius . . who come and eat their bread and cheese on the high-altar—and talk of reverence without one of its surest instincts—never quiet till they cut their initials on the cheek of the Medicean Venus to prove they worship her' (16 Nov. 1845, p. 271). Nevertheless, as this imagery implies, Browning claimed to have recognized Elizabeth Barrett's 'genius' long before he had any personal motive for doing so, and there is no reason to doubt his word. Elizabeth Barrett records her delight at seeing a letter of his to Kenyon in 1843, praising a poem of hers which Kenyon had shown him in manuscript (*Letters of EBB*, i. 143). In her own opinion of Browning's poetry, from *Paracelsus* to the plays and poems of the *Bells and Pomegranates* series, Elizabeth Barrett showed a judgement and discrimination well in advance of most contemporary criticism. She, like everyone else, had her laugh at Browning's obscurity: ' "Pippa passes" . . comprehension, I was going to say!' she wrote to Miss Mitford after her first reading (*EBB to MRM*, 78); but, unlike most others, she persevered, and *Pippa Passes* became her favourite among Browning's works, the one which, as she told him, she most wished she had written herself. Her tolerance even extended to *Sordello*. 'Study is necessary to it,' she admitted, 'as, indeed, though in a less degree, to all the works of this poet' (*Letters of EBB*, i. 254); but the point she stuck to, from first to last, was that Browning was a 'true poet', that his essential creative strength outweighed his accidental faults of obscurity and lack of harmony: 'the power of objecting dies away before the palpable presence of poetic genius everywhere' (*EBB to MRM*, 134).

It was not only Browning's poetry that Elizabeth Barrett felt called upon to defend. Miss Mitford, for example, consistently denigrated Browning's character, saying that with his 'extreme irritability of nerve' he should turn 'to occupations of less excitement' than poetry (*EBB to MRM*, 115), that he was effeminate (ibid., pp. 140, 241), or that he was ambitious in worldly terms (ibid., p. 241). Elizabeth Barrett was able to counter such accusations by reference to Mr Kenyon's repeated praise of Browning as noble, generous and manly. There is no doubt that Kenyon's opinion predisposed Elizabeth Barrett to like Browning, and above all to trust him; without such a predisposition, she might never have consented to meet him.

It was not enough, nevertheless, to secure a meeting when, in March 1842, 'Mr. Kenyon proposed [. . .] to introduce to my sofa-side—Mr. Browning the poet—who was so honor-giving as to wish something of the sort. I was pleased at the thought of his wishing it—for the rest, *no!*' (*Letters to George Barrett*, 81.) Kenyon had assured her that Browning was 'one of the lions of London who roared the gentlest and was best worth my knowing; but I refused then, in my blind dislike to seeing strangers' (*Letters of EBB*, i. 288). As we shall see, Browning kept this failed opportunity in mind when he wrote his first letter to Elizabeth Barrett. Meanwhile, the complimentary exchanges continued at a distance; and finally, in 'Lady Geraldine's Courtship', a work added at the last minute to her 1844 *Poems*, Elizabeth Barrett made the gesture which precipitated the first direct contact. The poem, subtitled 'A Romance of the Age', and written in the swinging metre of Tennyson's 'Locksley Hall', turned out to be one of the most popular of Elizabeth Barrett's shorter pieces. It tells the story of how the beautiful and talented Lady Geraldine chooses, instead of marriage with someone of equal rank, the love of Bertram, a famous (but low-born) poet. The poem had much to attract Browning in any case (Bertram

occupies exactly the kind of ambivalent position, as a lover, to which
Browning could respond, a position compounded of supremacy and
humility), but the lines to which his attention must have been drawn
were those in which his own name was directly invoked. Bertram is
reading aloud to Lady Geraldine, from 'the pastoral parts of
Spenser', and 'Petrarch's sonnets':

Or at times a modern volume, Wordsworth's solemn-thoughted idyl,
Howitt's ballad-verse, or Tennyson's enchanted reverie,—
Or from Browning some "Pomegranate," which, if cut deep down the
     middle,
Shows a heart within blood-tinctured, of a veined humanity.

                                                         (ll. 163–4.)

Browning was in Italy when the two-volume *Poems* appeared, in
August 1844. By the time he returned, in December, their resound-
ing critical and popular success had enhanced the value of the compliment to himself. He read it in his sister Sarianna's copy, a present
from Mr Kenyon; and, meeting Kenyon 'a day or two after', he
asked if it would be in order for him to write to Miss Barrett. 'He
assured me with his perfect kindness, you would be even "pleased"
to hear from me [. . .] he wrote me a note soon after to re-assure
me on that point' (16 Nov. 1845, p. 271). 'THEN I *did* write,'
Browning continued, 'on *account of my purely personal obligation*'.
In fact, Browning did not mention the allusion to himself in his letter to Elizabeth Barrett: he wrote as if in straightforward praise of
her work, and not in gratitude for her compliment; the point he is
making to her is that this gratitude caused him to write the letter,
where previously his 'admiration [. . .] went its natural way in
silence'. Moreover, Browning remarked, 'I did write, on the whole,
UNWILLINGLY . . with consciousness of having to *speak* on a subject which I *felt* thoroughly concerning, and could not be satisfied
with an imperfect expression of'. Browning made this last point,
about the inadequacy of expression to feeling, the basis of the letter
itself.

2   Browning's first letter

Three months before their marriage, and seventeen months after his
first letter, Browning wrote to Elizabeth Barrett:

Do you remember that the first word I ever wrote to you was 'I love you,

dear Miss Barrett?' It was so,—could not but be so—and I always loved
you, as I shall always—

(16 June 1846, p. 787.)

That is what the myth-makers want to hear! But here is what
Browning wrote:

New Cross, Hatcham, Surrey.

I love your verses with all my heart, dear Miss Barrett,—and this is no
off-hand complimentary letter that I shall write,—whatever else, no prompt
matter-of-course recognition of your genius, and there a graceful and natural end of the thing: since the day last week when I first read your poems, I
quite laugh to remember how I have been turning and turning again in my
mind what I should be able to tell you of their effect upon me—for in the
first flush of delight I thought I would this once get out of my habit of
purely passive enjoyment, when I do really enjoy, and thoroughly justify
my admiration—perhaps even, as a loyal fellow-craftsman should, try and
find fault and do you some little good to be proud of hereafter!—but
nothing comes of it all—so into me has it gone, and part of me has it
become, this great living poetry of yours, not a flower of which but took
root and grew—oh how different that is from lying to be dried and pressed
flat, and prized highly and put in a book with a proper account at top and
bottom, and shut up and put away . . and the book called a 'Flora,' besides!
After all I need not give up the thought of doing that, too, in time; because
even now, talking with whoever is worthy, I can give a reason for my faith
in one and another excellence, the fresh strange music, the affluent
language, the exquisite pathos and true new brave thought—but in this
addressing myself to you—your own self, and for the first time, my feeling
rises altogether. I do, as I say, love these books with all my heart—and I
love you too: do you know I was once not very far from seeing—really seeing you? Mr. Kenyon said to me one morning 'Would you like to see Miss
Barrett?'—then he went to announce me,—then he returned . . you were
too unwell—and now it is years ago—and I feel as at some untoward passage in my travels—as if I had been close, so close, to some world's-wonder
in chapel or crypt, only a screen to push and I might have entered, but there
was some slight . . so it now seems . . slight and just-sufficient bar to
admission; and the half-opened door shut, and I went home my thousands
of miles, and the sight was never to be!

Well, these Poems were to be—and this true thankful joy and pride with
which I feel myself.

Yours ever faithfully,
Robert Browning

(10 Jan. 1845, pp. 3–4.)

On the cover of Dormer Creston's book, *Andromeda in Wimpole Street*, it states that she 'has selected the most interesting and revealing passages' of the letters. The condensed version of Letter One, not surprisingly, quotes the first sentence only as far as 'a graceful and natural end of the thing', and then jumps forward to 'do you know I was once not very far from seeing—really seeing you?' The intervening passage is arguably 'the most interesting and revealing' of the letter; but I can sympathize with the urge, in a book claiming to tell 'one of the world's immortal love stories' with 'both understanding and sensitive reticence', to omit it. What on earth was Browning up to?

That concluding lament—'the sight was never to be!'—rules out the notion that Browning had, at this initial stage, any idea of gaining admittance to Wimpole Street. From everything Browning knew about Elizabeth Barrett, she was an incurable invalid who saw nobody; he himself had been refused three years earlier, since when it was not to be assumed that her health had improved; and the whole simile of the 'world's-wonder in chapel or crypt' plays on the popular image of Elizabeth Barrett as a secluded genius. (In fact, the morbid associations of the 'crypt' did not in the least appeal to Elizabeth Barrett, as we shall see.) This is certainly not a 'love letter' in the usual sense. But it *is* a love letter, none the less; one which is addressed to a peculiar object. The nature of this object is both personal (in that it is embodied in a human being) and intellectual (in that it consists of an idea). Understanding it is the key to Browning's behaviour throughout the entire courtship.

The opening statement, 'I love your verses with all my heart', is set off by being placed before the conventional beginning, 'dear Miss Barrett'; the reversal expresses Browning's determination not to write an 'off-hand complimentary letter'. So far, so good. The personal declaration is not, however, left to stand on its own. (Would that it had been, the reader may think!) The remainder of the sentence manages, at first glance, to be both sprawling and contorted. It reads like a prose parody of the poems which Browning's critics accused him of writing, garbled effusions, ostentatiously and intolerably obscure. But, as with those poems themselves, if we want to make sense of this letter, we must begin by presuming, unlikely though it may seem, that Browning knew what he was doing.

The general purport of the opening sentence is that Browning cannot tell Elizabeth Barrett what it is about her poetry that he loves so much, because he loves it so much; and that this inability is a good thing. In fact the whole meaning is contained in the first clause, except that Elizabeth Barrett could not be expected to know that its plain language concealed such a complicated idea. The bulky contortions of the second part of the sentence are a comment on the naked simplicity of the opening declaration. It is like an annotated text—a text from the Bible, say, with a theological gloss. Loving Elizabeth Barrett's poetry with all his heart, says Browning, means that he will *not* be able to give reasons for his admiration—'no prompt matter-of-course recognition of your genius'—since the very strength and depth of his feeling preclude his adequate expression of it. And in fact, as the concluding image of the dried flowers suggests, this inability to 'justify my admiration' is a proof of that admiration's genuine nature: Elizabeth Barrett's 'great living poetry' has become part of Browning, not something external to himself which he can criticize in academic terms.

Why should the gloss be so much longer and more complicated than the text? There are two reasons. First (again, as in the Bible) the apparent plainness of the surface conceals a ramification of significance which it is the business of the commentator to uncover. In this case, the phrase 'love . . . with all my heart' is the crucial one—Browning emphatically repeats it further on, once he has explored and exposed its meaning. Second, and more important, the rhetoric of the sentence—the plain short energetic opening, followed by the long reflexive commentary, doubling back on itself and using elaborate figures of speech—articulates the very core of Browning's state of mind in relation to Elizabeth Barrett.

To understand this state of mind, we need to take into account the way in which Browning thought about creativity and language. I have dealt with this topic in detail in Part Two (pp. 173–90); here, it is only necessary to mention three main principles on which Browning worked. First, there is a fundamental and unbridgeable gap between the conception of something, and its execution or expression. Poems, for example, are conceived in 'moments' of timeless perfection, but are written in the 'real time' of language. Second, and following from this, language is the human and fallible instrument of a divine and perfect inspiration. 'God is the perfect poet,' says a character in Browning's early poem *Paracelsus*, 'Who in his person acts his own creations'. Human beings, in a version of

Original Sin, are cursed with the necessity of using an external medium to convey their 'own creations'. Their inspirations may be divine, but their productions are human, and therefore flawed, damaged, corrupt. Third, and most important for our purpose, the two preceding principles can be applied to any form of creative process, whether in art or life. Hence Browning's intense interest in painters and musicians; hence, too, his interest in bishops and politicians, grammarians and doctors, spiritualists and alchemists. For they, too, are trying to create or express or accomplish something—a work of art, a political system, a vision. And, of course, lovers—in a sense the ultimate artists in Browning's work—who attempt to 'realize', in the medium of the flesh, the ideal communion of their souls. The speaker of 'Two in the Campagna' (1855) utters their characteristic lament:

> I would I could adopt your will,
>   See with your eyes, and set my heart
> Beating by yours, and drink my fill
>   At your soul's springs,—your part my part
> In life, for good and ill.
>
> No. I yearn upward, touch you close,
>   Then stand away, I kiss your cheek,
> Catch your soul's warmth,—I pluck the rose
>   And love it more than tongue can speak—
> Then the good minute goes.

This 'good minute' is equivalent to the 'first flush of delight' with which Browning responded to Elizabeth Barrett's poems, and it is of the essence of this 'minute' that it should be 'more than tongue can speak', that it should be impossible to 'thoroughly justify' it in any medium of human communication. This is 'the old trick', humanity's curse: what the speaker of the poem, in the famous final lines, calls 'Infinite passion, and the pain / Of finite hearts that yearn'. 'I *know* that I don't make out my conception by my language,' Browning wrote to Ruskin, 'all poetry being a putting of the infinite within the finite.'

That is what Browning is doing in his first letter: putting the infinite within the finite. Or rather, he is making a studied display of not doing so—he declines, in an elaborate rhetorical charade, to express *directly* his admiration for Elizabeth Barrett's poems; to say *to her* what he thinks their real qualities are. No, he tells her, he can list their merits when he is 'talking with whoever is worthy', that is, discussing her poems with other admirers (Browning probably has Mr Kenyon in mind here), 'but in this addressing myself to you—your own self [. . .] my feeling rises altogether'. And so he returns to the initial declaration: 'I do, as I say, love these books with all my heart'. This return is the result of his failed attempt to express his feeling—'nothing comes of it all'—but that failure leads to a compensating triumph of the feeling itself—'into me has it gone, and part of me has it become, this great living poetry of yours'.

Can we dismiss Browning's claim (not to have done justice to his admiration for Elizabeth Barrett) as an exasperating piece of flummery? After all, do not the actual phrases ('fresh strange music', 'affluent language' etc.) shine through their ornate semantic and syntactical costume? But that is really the point of the whole exercise. Browning deliberately presents himself in this light; he has 'composed' his approach to Elizabeth Barrett, and offers her the spectacle of his stammering sincerity, produced, directed, written by, and starring himself. Browning the writer *of* the letter stands behind Browning the character *in* the letter—and this is the ultimate, the decisive proof of what the drama is about in the first place.

Browning's script has a role for Elizabeth Barrett, too, though it is not made explicit until his second letter. He told her then,

your poetry must be, cannot but be, infinitely more to me than mine to you—for you *do* what I always wanted, hoped to do [. . .] You speak out, *you*,—I only make men & women speak—give you truth broken into prismatic hues, and fear the pure white light, even if it is in me [. . .]

(13 Jan. 1845, p. 7.)

The 'pure white light' of Browning's admiration for Elizabeth Barrett's poetry was 'broken into prismatic hues', the complicated language of his letter. But the point is comparative: Elizabeth Barrett does not suffer from the same defect as Browning, her poetry *is* 'pure white light', the very essence of her personality: 'you speak out, *you*'. That is why Browning laid such emphasis in the first letter on 'this addressing myself to you—your own self', and that is why he was able to add, after repeating that he loved her books with all his heart, 'I love you too'. Poet and poetry were one. No wonder Browning feels compensated for having missed seeing Elizabeth Barrett: 'the sight was never to be', but 'these Poems were to be'—it comes, ideally, to the same thing. 'I believed in your glorious genius

and knew it for a true star from the moment I saw it,' he wrote later,
'—long before I had the blessing of knowing it was MY star, with
my fortune and futurity in it' (9 Nov. 1845, p. 261). The image
makes their respective positions unequivocally plain: she and her
work together are the high, divine, pure, unchanging radiance; he is
the passionately humble and inadequate worshipper. Browning's
first letter concerns the work, not the woman, because that was the
aspect his devotion could reach. In her reply, Elizabeth Barrett
showed him that the way to the woman was also open.

3   Elizabeth Barrett's reply

Browning was treading on dangerous ground when he implied an
identity between Elizabeth Barrett and her poetry, for her own
opinion was exactly the reverse. 'If my poetry is worth anything to
any eye,' she wrote to him later, '—it is the flower of me [. . .] the
rest of me is nothing but a root, fit for the ground & the dark' (15
May 1845, p. 65). She later looked back on the state of mind in
which she made this comment, when Browning first knew her,
when she was

> so weary of my own being that to take interest in my very poems I had to
> lift them up by an effort & separate them from myself [. . .] making
> indeed a sort of pleasure & interest about the factitious personality associ-
> ated with them . . but knowing it to be all far on the outside of *me* . .
> *myself* . . not seeming to touch it with the end of my finger . . & receiving it
> as a mockery & a bitterness when people persisted in confounding one with
> another.
>
> (31 Oct. 1845, p. 255.)

This picture may not be entirely accurate, since Elizabeth Barrett
had a motive for contrasting her former state of existence with the
one she enjoyed after Browning's advent; I have discussed this 'self-
construction' in Part Two (pp. 252–72). But assuming there is
some truth in it, was not Browning one of these same people who
'persisted in confounding' Elizabeth Barrett with her work? And
she went on to make a scathing remark on the kind of fan mail such
people sent her, and which she had become sick of receiving—'these
heaps of letters which go into the fire one after the other, & which,
because I am a woman & have written verses, it seems so amusing to
the letter-writers of your sex to write'—a description which, in a

nightmare, Browning might have felt applicable to him. A comment in the letter she wrote to Mary Russell Mitford, on the eve of her elopement, shows that, in the early stages, Elizabeth Barrett did indeed think Browning's admiration 'a mere poet's fancy . . an illusion of a confusion between the woman and the poetry'. She repeated, too, the point that her experience had not prepared her for anything different: 'I have seen a little of the way of men in such respects, and I could not see beyond that with my weary, weeping eyes, for long' (*EBB to MRM*, 273).

It is in this context that we should consider Elizabeth Barrett's reply to Browning's first letter. It would not be surprising if, as far as she was concerned, he was only a more respectable specimen of the men who wrote to her 'because I am a woman & have written verses'—more respectable because of her own long-standing admiration of his work, because of Mr Kenyon's recommendation, and because of the courtesy of the letter itself—different in degree, therefore, but not in kind. Evidence of her self-possession may be seen in her allusions to this first letter of Browning's and to the ones which immediately followed. For if Browning felt from the start under an implicit obligation not to gossip about being in correspondence with her, Elizabeth Barrett had no such scruples—at first. 'I had a letter from Browning the poet last night, which threw me into ecstasies,' she wrote to Mrs Martin about this first letter; 'Browning the author of *Paracelsus*, and king of the mystics' (Griffin and Minchin, 148). The tinge of exaggeration here means that it's not to be taken seriously— that Elizabeth Barrett felt tickled, but not touched. She later wrote to Mrs Martin that she was 'getting deeper and deeper into correspondence with Robert Browning, poet and mystic, and we are growing to be the truest of friends' (*Letters of EBB*, i. 238). Her remark immediately following shows how little she differentiated between Browning and other celebrities, and how he fitted into her paradoxical sense of herself as someone whose social opportunities came to her because of her seclusion: 'If I live a little longer shut up in this room, I shall certainly know everybody in the world.' She even joked, in a letter to Miss Mitford, that Browning 'writes letters to me [. . .] saying he "*loves*" *me*. Who can resist *that*?' Of course, she added, after asking Miss Mitford not to gossip on the subject, 'it is all in the uttermost innocence' (*EBB to MRM*, 239). She was later bitterly to regret this levity; but, as she explained to Browning, it came of her own 'uttermost innocence' about the consequences of his overture to her. When he offered her the mythical version of his opening letter which I quoted above ('Do you remember that the first word I ever wrote to you was "I love you, dear Miss Barrett?" '), she replied:

Do I remember? Yes indeed, I remember. How I recalled and wondered afterward, though at the moment it seemed very simple & what was to be met with in our philosophy every day. [. . .] Then I remember all the more [. . .] through an imprudence of my own [. . .] of which I will tell you. I was writing to Miss Mitford [. . .] & I just then writing of you, added in my headlong unreflecting way that I had had a real letter from you which said that you loved me—'Oh—but,' I wrote on, 'you are not to mistake this, not to repeat it—for of course it is simply the purest of philanthropies' . . . some words to that effect—and if yours was the purest of philanthropies, mine was the purest of innocences, as you may well believe, . . for if I had had the shadow of a foresight, I should not have fallen into the snare. So vexed I was afterwards!—Not that she thought anything at the time, or has referred to it since, or remembers a word now. Only I was vexed in my innermost heart . . & *am* . . do you know? . . that I should have spoken lightly of such an expression of yours—though you meant it lightly too. Dearest!—It was a disguised angel & I should have known it by its wings though they did not fly.

(16 June 1846, pp. 789–90.)

Elizabeth Barrett's acceptance of Browning's version of the letter only throws into relief her integrity in refusing to rewrite her own response, and her gentle insistence, enforced by the image of the angel with folded wings, that Browning himself 'meant it lightly'. 'I foresaw nothing, . . looked to you for nothing,' she went on; love had seemed a 'quaint word' to her then.

Are we, then, to dismiss altogether the notion that Elizabeth Barrett was stirred in any way by Browning's letter? Not quite; we come back to her consistent and creditable belief in Browning's stature as a writer (creditable in the light of the differences between them, and the general critical denigration of his work), and the supportive judgements of friends like Kenyon and Richard Horne; a structure of feeling remains even after the props of the myth have been removed. Nor should we disregard the impact of Browning's letter in itself, at once energetic and oblique, intensely and enjoyably *odd*. It was a letter well suited to the 'king of the mystics'. Here is her reply:

50 Wimpole Street
Jan. 11, 1845.

I thank you, dear Mr. Browning, from the bottom of my heart. You meant to give me pleasure by your letter—and even if the object had not been answered, I ought still to thank you. But it is thoroughly answered. Such a letter from such a hand! Sympathy is dear—very dear to me: but the sympathy of a poet, & of such a poet, is the quintessence of sympathy to me! Will you take back my gratitude for it?—agreeing, too, that of all the commerce done in the world, from Tyre to Carthage, the exchange of sympathy for gratitude is the most princely thing?

For the rest you draw me on with your kindness. It is difficult to get rid of people when you once have given them too much pleasure—*that* is a fact, & we will not stop for the moral of it. What I was going to say . . after a little natural hesitation . . is, that if ever you emerge without inconvenient effort from your 'passive state,' & will *tell* me of such faults as rise to the surface and strike you as important in my poems, (for of course, I do not think of troubling you with criticism in detail) you will confer a lasting obligation on me, and one which I shall value so much, that I covet it at a distance. I do not pretend to any extraordinary meekness under criticism, & it is possible enough that I might not be altogether obedient to yours. But with my high respect for your power in your Art & for your experience as an artist, it wd be quite impossible for me to hear a general observation of yours on what appear to you my master-faults, without being the better for it hereafter in some way. I ask only for a sentence or two of general observation—and I do not ask even for *that*, so as to teaze you—but in the humble, low voice, which is so excellent a thing in women—particularly when they go a-begging! The most frequent general criticism I receive is, I think, upon the style, 'if I *would* but change my style' ! But *that* is an objection (isn't it?) to the writer bodily? Buffon says, and every sincere writer must feel, that '*Le style c'est l'homme*;' a fact, however, scarcely calculated to lessen the objection with certain critics.

It is indeed true that I was so near to the pleasure and honour of making your acquaintance?—& can it be true that you look back upon the lost opportunity with any regret? BUT . . you know . . if you had entered the 'crypt,' you might have caught cold, or been tired to death, & *wished* yourself 'a thousand miles off'—which would have been worse than travelling them. It is not my interest however to put such thoughts in your head about its being 'all for the best'—and I would rather hope (as I do) that what I lost by one chance I may recover by some future one. Winters shut me up as they do dormouse's eyes: in the spring, *we shall see*: & I am so much better that I seem turning round to the outward world again. And in the meantime I have learnt to know your voice, not merely from the poetry but from the kindness in it. Mr. Kenyon often speaks of you—dear Mr.

Kenyon!—who most unspeakably, or only speakably with tears in my eyes, . . has been my friend & helper, & my book's friend and helper! critic & sympathiser, true friend of all hours! You know him well enough, I think, to understand that I must be grateful to him.

   I am writing too much—& notwithstanding that I am writing too much, I will write of one thing more. I will say that I am your debtor, not only for this cordial letter & for all the pleasure which came with it, but in other ways, & those the highest: & I will say that while I live to follow this divine art of poetry . . in proportion to my love for it and my devotion to it, I must be a devout admirer & student of your works. This is in my heart to say to you— & I say it.

And, for the rest, I am proud to remain

> Your obliged and faithful
> Elizabeth B. Barrett

> (11 Jan. 1845, pp. 4–6.)

As with Browning's letter, there is a rhetorical movement here to which we must pay attention. This movement is carried by the change in Elizabeth Barrett's tone, which modulates from the mannered and gracious opening, through the skittishness of the second paragraph about 'my master-faults', to the much more (and surprisingly) personal notes of the third and fourth paragraphs. It is as though Elizabeth Barrett had set out to write Browning one kind of letter, and ended up writing a quite different kind, in which conventional cordiality turns out, unexpectedly, really to come 'from the bottom of my heart'.

   That last phrase is part of Elizabeth Barrett's conscious echo of Browning's opening; she also follows him (a little more timidly) in ignoring the conventional form of opening address. Still, her first sentence, by stopping short where Browning's had paused before its spiralling leap, gives a much more balanced impression. The sequence of ideas in the first paragraph is clearly articulated. The exclamations ('Such a letter from such a hand!' 'the quintessence of sympathy to me!') are controlled by the easy flow of the writing; they are polished, almost polite: compare them to the emotional exclamations about Kenyon at the end of the third paragraph. The whole performance is keyed to the image of herself (and of Browning) which Elizabeth Barrett offers in the concluding image. The rentier's daughter, guiltily conscious that the family fortune was founded on the slave-labour of the Jamaican sugar-plantations, has a genteel and literary scorn for 'all the commerce done in the world';

writing to the bank clerk's son, she manages, with a classical allusion and a metaphorical twist, to transmute the base metal of commerce into a 'princely thing', 'the exchange of sympathy for gratitude'. (Browning's commercial imagery tends to be less fanciful: in his fourth letter, for example, he compared his poems to cabbages, for which he was not receiving 'a fair proportion of the Reviewers' gold-currency', unlike 'the other traders [who] pouch their winnings'—11 Feb. 1845, p. 18.) This, however, is the limit of Elizabeth Barrett's highbrow courtesy.

The second paragraph does three things. It invites Browning to continue the correspondence—that is the clear signal of the second sentence, for all its protestations ('if ever you emerge without inconvenient effort' etc.). In conjunction with this, it invites Browning to take the dominant (male) role in this correspondence—the '*exchange* of sympathy for gratitude', which implies parity, becomes the gift of Browning's critical judgement, the conferment of 'a lasting *obligation*' which Elizabeth Barrett 'value[s] so much, that I covet it at a distance', and for which she goes 'a-begging'. And that leads on to the third point, the tone of the paragraph. Elizabeth Barrett's disclaimer of 'any extraordinary meekness under criticism' looks rather odd in the light of that winsome reference to 'the humble, low voice, which is so excellent a thing in women'. But perhaps the allusion is less coy than it seems.

> Cordelia, Cordelia! stay a little. Ha!
> What is't thou sayst? Her voice was ever soft,
> Gentle and low, an excellent thing in woman.
> (*King Lear*, V. iii. 273–5.)

A trick of memory revises 'gentle' to 'humble', something unwarranted by the play: Cordelia's soft voice is never heard 'a-begging'. On the contrary, this daughter of a vile-tempered old patriarch (we should do both Lear and Mr Barrett the justice of saying that the parallel does not really work) has a mind and spirit of her own. A satirical and subversive implication lurks in the shade of Elizabeth Barrett's deference; but that does not prevent the deference from being, with respect to Browning, perfectly sincere. Elizabeth Barrett was quite capable of holding that women writers in general were unfairly judged by male critics, and at the same time that she, as a writer, was inferior to Browning; she was also, of course, profoundly ambivalent about the operation of male power.

If the second paragraph invites Browning to continue writing, the third does something more. In it, Elizabeth Barrett all but invites Browning to come and see her. In letters to her friends, Elizabeth Barrett gave the impression that Browning had charmed her against her will: 'he writes me letters praying to be let in, quite heart-moving and irresistible,' she wrote to Mary Russell Mitford (*EBB to MRM*, 239). This, besides being false in itself (Browning wrote no such letters), disingenuously suppresses the fact that it was she who had taken the initiative. Why had she done so? Perhaps because she rebelled against Browning's image of her as 'some world's wonder in chapel or crypt'. It is one thing to use images of darkness and captivity and entombment about oneself, but it is disconcerting to find them complacently echoed. Elizabeth Barrett had the same objection to Horne's portrait of her as a 'fair shade' in *A New Spirit of the Age*. So she takes Browning up on it—'if you had entered the "crypt," you might have caught cold, or been tired to death' (which makes the tired old idiom look a little more lively). The image of the 'dormouse's eyes' makes her seclusion seem natural and seasonal, and the phrase '*we shall see*' carries the image further: it means both that she will be better (the dormouse will see with its opened eyes) and that she will 'see about' receiving him when spring comes round. She adds that she is 'so much better that I seem turning round to the outward world again'; there goes another myth, that Elizabeth Barrett was rescued from a state of helpless and hopeless physical prostration by Browning's sole intervention.

When all is said and done, however, there still seems an element of the mysterious, of the unconsciously prophetic, about this permission which Elizabeth Barrett was so reluctant, usually, to grant even to women friends. Of course, our retrospective knowledge pulls us strongly, as it did the participants themselves, to make more of such passages than is warranted; but there is also no doubt that, had Elizabeth Barrett wished to keep Browning at epistolary arm's length, she could easily have done so. To say that it was a product of her 'headlong' impulsiveness is not to explain why she felt such an impulse in the first place. My own guess is that her recurrent sense of pain and frustration at being identified with her poems was sharply aroused by Browning's enthusiastic endorsement of this fallacy, and that, given who he was, it seemed to her momentarily possible and desirable to disabuse him; she acted, or half-acted, on that basis.

At any rate, after giving Browning this strong encouragement, Elizabeth Barrett rounds off with three significant comments. One is on the development of a personal relation between her and Browning: 'I have learnt to know your voice, not merely from the poetry but from the kindness in it.' The second follows naturally: the link between them of their friend John Kenyon, who, as we know, spoke warmly to Elizabeth Barrett of Browning's character. Browning had not mentioned in his own letter the part Kenyon had played in advising him to write, only the occasion in the past when he had failed to introduce him; Elizabeth Barrett responds by assuring him of Kenyon's active sponsorship ('Mr. Kenyon often speaks of you') and of her own affection for him. The third point picks up the earlier implication that Browning was her superior in poetry: it firmly and unequivocally places *him* on the divine side of 'this divine art of poetry'. In doing so, it reinforces Browning's opposite opinion by an unconscious irony: when Elizabeth Barrett writes, 'This is in my heart to say to you—& I say it', she puts forward a model of perfect and adequate self-expression which Browning felt himself utterly unable to achieve.

The first exchange of letters between Browning and Elizabeth Barrett announces the concern which was to become central to the courtship. The ways in which each praised the other's poetry—Browning because Elizabeth Barrett seemed to him an exemplar of 'pure' poetry, she because of Browning's 'power' and 'experience as an artist'—rapidly acquired a personal as well as an aesthetic edge. Browning and Elizabeth Barrett were to debate their relative status up to and beyond the altar, and it was in and through this debate that their feeling for each other defined and developed itself.

But the opening letters do more, for modern readers, than draw the lines along which the relationship between Browning and Elizabeth Barrett developed. They introduce us to the styles of the two writers, and in doing so they make it clear how distinctive these are, how different from each other and how expressive of wholly incompatible orders of experience and value. Browning's letter, for all its difficulty, is all of a piece, and stable in its own terms; Elizabeth Barrett, for all her experience in letter-writing, is far less sure of herself; her letter changes course in a way that Browning's does not. She is, after all, the one under pressure. There is a hardness in Browning's style, you might call it a worldliness, which contrasts strongly with Elizabeth Barrett's more impressionable manner. This is not to disparage her; far from it. In common with most readers of the correspondence, I come away with the feeling that she is a much better letter-writer than Browning, as good letter-writing is understood. She is, for the most part, easy, unaffected, and witty; she has a sense of humour and a sense of proportion, about her own concerns as well as others'; and her writing gives, as Browning's almost never does, that sense of a speaker which is one of the sleights of style we most prize in letters. But Browning's letters are different in kind; and their importance for our understanding of the courtship lies precisely in their being, as I said before, *compositions*. They are, in a sense, as impersonal, or to use his own term 'dramatic', as his poems, even though their motive and subject is exclusively personal. The self that Browning dramatizes in his letters is his own; but they are dramatic productions none the less. The fact that Browning's letters might not be *premeditated* does not mean that they are spontaneous. There is not a single casual allusion, there is not a single pointless digression; an all-embracing objective cannot tolerate unconnected images or associations. Elizabeth Barrett's best letters remind you of Byron; Browning's of St. Paul. And this difference, much more than the stereotyped difference of his being the 'aggressive' male, gave him an initiative in the courtship which, with one traumatic exception, he never lost.

3

First Meeting

1 Before

'You *influenced* me,' Elizabeth Barrett told Browning, 'in a way which no one else did [. . .] by two or three halfwords you made me see you, & other people had delivered orations on the same subject quite without effect. I surprised everybody in this house by consenting to see you' (23 Feb. 1846, p. 488). But Browning's path to Wimpole Street had its quirks and irregularities. We need to study them, because they affected whàt happened when he arrived.

Browning was not slow to see the opportunity which Elizabeth Barrett's reply to his first letter gave him. The 'half-opened door' had not shut in his face, as it had on the earlier occasion, but had been left deliberately ajar. In the following letters, he reminded Elizabeth Barrett, with unobtrusive but persistent touches, of her quasi-promise. 'I will joyfully wait for the delight of your friendship, and the spring, and my Chapel-sight after all!' he wrote in his second letter (13 Jan. 1845, p. 7); and in the next, 'After all, you know nothing, next to nothing of me [. . .] Spring is to come, however!' (27 Jan. 1845, p. 12); and in the next, 'mind that spring is coming, for all this snow' (11 Feb. 1845, p. 18). These remarks, placed at the ends of letters, are made in low-key or throwaway tones; and only, it seems, when Elizabeth Barrett failed to pick up on any of them, and seemed to be looking forward with equanimity to a merely epistolary friendship, did Browning make a more direct approach. His fifth letter opens:

Wednesday morning—Spring!
Real warm Spring, dear Miss Barrett, and the birds know it; and in Spring I
shall see you, surely see you . . for when did I once fail to get whatever I
had set my heart upon?—as I ask myself sometimes, with a strange fear.

(26 Feb. 1845, p. 25.)

This was too forthright for Elizabeth Barrett to ignore; she began
her next letter with a rebuttal:

Yes, but, dear Mr. Browning, I want the spring according to the new 'style'
(mine), & not the old one of you and the rest of the poets. To me unhappily, the snowdrop is much the same as the snow—it feels as cold under-
foot—and I have grown sceptical about 'the voice of the turtle,' the east
winds blow so loud. [. . .] A little later comes my spring,—and indeed
after such severe weather, from which I have just escaped with my life, I
may thank it for coming at all. How happy you are, to be able to listen to
the 'birds' without the commentary of the east wind—which, like other
commentaries, spoils the music.

(27 Feb. 1845, p. 29.)

In 1751, an Act of Parliament shifted the beginning of the year from
its customary date, 25 March (the Annunciation), to 1 January.
Elizabeth Barrett plays on the fact that the new year may have
begun, but spring has not yet been 'announced'. A traditional
feature of the iconography of the Annunciation is the representation
of the Holy Spirit in the form of a dove. But turtle-doves are also
symbols of erotic love, most famously in the verse from the Song of
Solomon which Elizabeth Barrett quotes:

My beloved spake, and said unto me, Rise up, my love, my fair one, and
come away. For lo, the winter is past, the rain is over and gone; the flowers
appear on the earth; the time of the singing of birds is come, and the voice
of the turtle is heard in our land; the fig tree putteth forth her green figs,
and the vines with the tender grape give a good smell. Arise, my love, my
fair one, and come away.

(2: 10–13.)

By linking the Annunciation with the Song of Solomon, Elizabeth
Barrett suggests the depth of her anxiety about the 'awakening'
which she had (perhaps inadvertently) started, and which Browning
was so tenaciously pursuing. Another passage from the same
chapter of the Song is echoed towards the end of her letter, when
she returns to Browning's provocative remark about his wishes
always fulfilling themselves:

Is it true that your wishes fulfil themselves?—And when they *do*, are they not bitter to your taste—do you not wish them *un*fulfilled? Oh—this life, this life! There is comfort in it, they say, & I almost believe—but the brightest place in the house, is the leaning out of the window!—at least, for me.

(p. 31.)

This is the first of a series of allusions to windows which, as I said in the Introduction, are a recurrent and ambivalent image for Elizabeth Barrett of the possibility of life and the opportunity of death. This ambivalence is sharpened when we recall the 'beloved' of the Song of Solomon: 'behold, he standeth behind our wall, he looketh forth at the windows, shewing himself through the lattice' (2: 9). The Song is a poem of desire, and it tells us that 'love is strong as death' (8: 6); leaning out of the window in the desire for death, Elizabeth Barrett evokes the desire for love and life with equal force.

   Taken together, these two passages from Elizabeth Barrett's letter, the one which mentions her fear of the east wind, and the one which mentions leaning out of the window of the house of life, mark an important point in the opening stage of her relationship with Browning. The letters which lead up to this point are crammed with information about both Browning's and Elizabeth Barrett's tastes and activities, but their tone is, on Elizabeth Barrett's side, determinedly chatty. Whereas Browning, from the first, makes every effort to give himself away (though he cannot help watching himself doing it), Elizabeth Barrett is bright, cheerful, good company—but not personal. She was quite willing for him to be so: when he wrote that 'what I have printed gives *no* knowledge of me' (11 Feb. 1845, p. 17), she replied, 'Well, then! teach me yourself . . you' (17 Feb. 1845, p. 22). On her own account, however, she was less forthcoming. Here, for example, are two passages from consecutive letters, in which each praises the other's writing. First, Elizabeth Barrett, in her second letter:

You have in your vision two worlds—or to use the language of the schools of the day, you are both subjective & objective in the habits of your mind. You can deal with both abstract thought & with human passion in the most passionate sense. Thus, you have an immense grasp in Art; and no one at all accustomed to consider the usual forms of it, could help regarding with reverence & gladness the gradual expansion of your powers.

(15 Jan. 1845, p. 9.)

Change this to the third person, and Browning would not have been surprised to find it in a contemporary periodical, except that his contemporary critics were rarely so intelligent—or so complimentary. But even the warmth here ('reverence & gladness') is appreciative in a public, almost an official sense; indeed, Elizabeth Barrett, with characteristic loftiness, takes it on herself to speak for the community of intelligent readers, 'those accustomed to consider the usual forms' of literature. Now compare the opening of Browning's third letter:

Your books lie on my table here, at arm's length from me, in this old room where I sit all day: and when my head aches or wanders or strikes work, as it now or then will, I take my chance for either green covered volume, as if it were so much fresh trefoil to feel in one's hands this winter-time [. . .]
(27 Jan. 1845, pp. 10–11.)

Note the concreteness with which Browning places himself at work, sitting at his table; such domestic details are scattered through his early letters—'Out comes the sun, in comes the "Times" and eleven strikes (it *does*) already, and I have to go to Town' (11 Feb. 1845, p. 19)—but there is a complete absence of them in Elizabeth Barrett's. The personal note is also dominant here in Browning's response to Elizabeth Barrett's poetry, which—woman's work!—is related not to a public, but to a private context, and is not shown in its intrinsic self, but in relation to something else; not in its nature, but its effects. These effects are not intellectual; at any rate they do not employ the intellectual terms ('the language of the schools of the day') which Elizabeth Barrett used about Browning's work. The two volumes of Elizabeth Barrett's 1844 *Poems* were bound in green cloth, and Browning compares them to trefoil, a plant with magical healing powers. It is an image with strong associations for him: 'mystic trifoly' had appeared in the same soothing and restorative role in *Sordello* (1840), iii. 2, as one of the cures for another disillusioned and weary poet. It is the physical sense of touch which is uppermost in Browning's image, the coolness and refreshment of touching the green books in the green-less winter, which is both the actual winter and the winter of his literary discontent.

Returning to Elizabeth Barrett's letter of 27 February, then, with its allusion to the 'new style' of Spring which she required, we can see that she was conceding something important to Browning by making such direct and personal references to the precarious state of her health and to her equivocal attitude to living. Browning began his next letter with a splurge of sentiment about the 'tragic chord' that Elizabeth Barrett had added to 'the octaves on octaves of quite new golden strings' with which she had 'enlarged the compass of my life's harp'. This 'tragic chord' refers to Elizabeth Barrett's remarking on the 'severe weather, from which I have just escaped with my life'; and Browning went on: 'But if my heart's truest wishes avail, as they have hitherto done, you shall laugh at East winds yet, as I do!' (1 Mar. 1845, p. 32.) He repeats the point to which she had objected previously, about his wishes fulfilling themselves, and he takes the opportunity she offered him of interesting himself personally in her well-being. He himself, he added, had been ' "spoiled" in this world' for happiness—'to such an extent, indeed, that I often *reason* out [. . .] that I might [. . .] take any step that would peril the whole of my future happiness—because the past is gained, secure, and on record'. The pressure of the implication here could only make itself felt because Elizabeth Barrett had abruptly lost the status of a 'Chapel-sight', and acquired that of flesh and blood. Now, indeed, she could be envisaged, she lived in a house, even if it was still the metaphorical House of Life: Browning concluded his letter by asking her 'not to "lean out of the window" when my own foot is only on the stair' (p. 33). Again, it must be emphasized that Elizabeth Barrett herself was responsible for this development.

In her reply (5 Mar. 1845, pp. 34–6), Elizabeth Barrett did nothing to weaken the personal note she had struck. She rejected the implication either that she was mortally ill ('As to "escaping with my life," it was just a phrase [. . .] I am *essentially better*, & have been for several winters'), or that she was 'desponding by nature'. But her way of denying that she was morbid left plenty of scope for the pathos which Browning had detected in her situation. 'Anguish has instructed me in joy—and solitude in society—it has been a wholesome & not unnatural reaction.' Brave words, but hardly those of a light-hearted optimist. And Elizabeth Barrett went on to make another of the significant contrasts of the correspondence, that between her own situation and Browning's. 'I do like to hear testimonies like yours, to *happiness*,' she wrote, underlining the word as though it were foreign to her. 'Still, it is obvious too that you have been spared, up to this time, the great natural afflictions, against which we are nearly all called, sooner or later, to struggle and wrestle—or your step would not be "on the stair" quite so lightly.' (This was a shrewd comment; Browning was devastated, four years later, by the first of the 'great natural afflictions' to strike him, the death of his mother.) It was from this perspective—that of the sufferer, speaking to the man of 'unscathed joy'—that Elizabeth Barrett commented on the relationship which she saw developing between them:

How kind you are!—how kindly & gently you speak to me!—Some things you say are very touching, & some, surprising—& although I am aware that you unconsciously exaggerate what I can be to you, yet it is delightful to be broad awake & think of you as my friend.

But, Browning replied, 'I never yet mistook my own feelings, one for another'; and, he added, 'Do you think I shall see you in two months, three months? I may travel, perhaps' (11 Mar. 1845, p. 39). It might seem tactless of Browning to remind Elizabeth Barrett that he was free to go where he liked, especially if she took the juxtaposition of the last two sentences as a kind of threat. Indeed she half took it so: 'If you mean "to travel," ' she wrote back, 'why, I shall have to miss you—do you really mean it?' (20 Mar. 1845, p. 43.) Browning laughed, he told her, at the idea that when he next left England he would 'leave off Miss Barrett along with port wine'; and he signed himself emphatically 'Yours every where, and at all times yours' (31 Mar. 1845, p. 45). But the intimation of physical absence remained; and, coupled with Browning's insistence that he 'never mistook his feelings', it gave Elizabeth Barrett a clear signal of impatience.

Her will wavered, 'April is coming', she conceded. 'There will be both a May and a June if we live to see such things, & perhaps, after all, we may' (20 Mar. 1845, p. 40). The rhyme of 'May' and 'may': May is the month of possibility; May (Browning's birth month) was the month in which the first meeting was to take place. But Elizabeth Barrett was not yet there:

There will be both a May and a June if we live to see such things, & perhaps, after all, we may. And as to seeing *you* besides, I observe that you distrust me, & that perhaps you penetrate my morbidity & guess how when the moment comes to see a living human face to which I am not accustomed, I shrink & grow pale in the spirit [. . .] I will indeed see you when the warm weather has revived me a little [. . .] But I shall be afraid of you at first— though I am not, in writing thus. You are Paracelsus, and I am a recluse, with nerves that have been all broken on the rack, & now hang loosely, . . quivering at a step and breath.

(ibid., pp. 40–1.)

'Paracelsus' here stands for the man of the world, the learned and experienced traveller, the male seeker and seer. The hero of what was still Browning's best-known and best-liked poem dies in 'a cell in the Hospital of Saint Sebastian', but his final seclusion is very different from Elizabeth Barrett's: it concludes a lifetime in which, like Tennyson's Ulysses (from the same period of the 1830s when the magical Romantic quests had come to their untimely ends) he has 'followed knowledge like a sinking star'; and death itself comes (as for so many of Browning's protagonists, Childe Roland foremost among them) in a flare of vision which lights up and consumes the embers of life. It was with this image of Browning's life that Elizabeth Barrett contrasted her own existence. Travel may broaden the mind; torture wrecks it. It is one thing to search out the secrets of Nature, quite another to be interrogated in bondage: the lurid process of the Inquisition ('nerves that have been all broken on the rack') replaces the search for knowledge. In the passage that followed, Elizabeth Barrett developed this contrast at length: she gave Browning a summary of her life, deepening and strengthening the personal notes which she had already sounded in previous letters.

You seem to have drunken of the cup of life full, with the sun shining on it. I have lived only inwardly,—or with *sorrow*, for a strong emotion. Before this seclusion of my illness, I was secluded still—& there are few of the youngest women in the world who have not seen more, heard more, known more, of society, than I, who am scarcely to be called young now. I grew up in the country . . had no social opportunities, . . had my heart in books & poetry, . . & my experience, in reveries. [. . .] It was a lonely life— growing green like the grass around it. Books and dreams were what I lived in—& domestic life only seemed to buzz gently around, like the bees about the grass. And so time passed, and passed—and afterwards, when my illness came & I seemed to stand at the edge of the world with all done, & no prospect (as appeared at one time) of ever passing the threshold of one room again,—why then, I turned to thinking with some bitterness [. . .] that I had stood blind in this temple I was about to leave . . that I had seen no Human nature, that my brothers & sisters of the earth were *names* to me, . . that I had beheld no great mountain or river—nothing in fact. I was as a man dying who had not read Shakespeare . . & it was too late!

(ibid., p. 41.)

How revealing that last analogy is of the very bookishness it laments! The perverse aptness of it is almost suspect; and we may look at Elizabeth Barrett's self-portrait with some scepticism in the light of her *Diary* (1830–1), in which 'social opportunities' are not so much absent as spurned when available. But whether Elizabeth Barrett's account of her childhood is true or false does not matter; it was the one she gave to Browning, the one she wanted him to believe. In this treacherous idyl, 'growing green like the grass' signifies both pastoral peace and innocence, but also immaturity ('greenness') and lack of feature. A landscape of grass has no contours: there is no relief (in both senses) of mountain or river, Romantic emblems of grandeur and the process of time. In later poems ('Love Among the Ruins', 'Two in the Campagna'), Browning was to articulate the sense of something timeless and foreboding in an expanse of grassland, 'The champaign with its endless fleece / Of feathery grasses everywhere'. One of the first things he and Elizabeth Barrett did after the immediate crisis of their elopement journey was to make an expedition to the fountain at Vaucluse, near Avignon, which (the words are hers) 'in its dark prison of rocks flashes and roars and testifies to the memory of Petrarch'; there Elizabeth Barrett seated herself, with Browning beside her, on a rock in the midst of the spray (Taplin, 185). From the prison of Wimpole Street to the 'prison of rocks'; from the seclusion of childhood to the intimacy of marriage; from the experience of 'books and poetry' to the physical sense of inspiration, of being in touch with one of the great sources of erotic language, expressed in the actual play of water. Here, at last, was transfiguration, the expression of the ideal by the real (and who better than Petrarch to occasion it?), the lack of which Elizabeth Barrett had so deplored, the hope of which she had given up. This was what Browning offered. But Elizabeth Barrett did not yet know it, and even if she had known it she was not yet ready to stretch out her hand.

Browning could only be alarmed by the contrast which he saw Elizabeth Barrett developing between himself and her. Having expressed his admiration of her as a 'world's-wonder in chapel or crypt', he now found his traveller's reputation rebounding on him: he was in danger of proving too worldly, too seasoned, to gain admittance to her seclusion. He hastened, therefore, to correct her misapprehension. 'All you gain by travel is the discovery that you have gained nothing,' he declared. 'After this, you go boldly on your own resources, and are justified to yourself, that's all.' And he illustrated his point:

Three scratches with a pen, even with this pen,—and you have the green little Syrenusae where I have sate and heard the quails sing. One of these days I shall describe a country I have seen in my soul only, fruits, flowers, birds and all.

(15 Apr. 1845, pp. 46–7.)[1]

Browning's sketch (plate 2) represents the three 'siren-isles' off the coast of Sorrento, which were to figure in his poem 'England in Italy' (later called 'The Englishman in Italy'), published in *Dramatic Romances and Lyrics* in November 1845. This poem directly reflects the discussion between Browning and Elizabeth Barrett in this period about the advantages of travel, a discussion which came to involve (by a process too complicated to follow here) the alleged inability of native Italian writers to do justice to the beauty of their own landscape, and the merits of a recently translated book by Hans Christian Andersen, *The Improvisatore*. At any rate, Browning's point is that 'even with this pen'—'even with my poor skill', he means, as well as 'even with this poor instrument'—he can adequately render his experience of foreign travel. The order of priority is reversed: Elizabeth Barrett, who wished to 'exchange some of this lumbering, ponderous, helpless knowledge of books, for some experience of life & man' (20 Mar. 1845, p. 41), is in fact better placed than he to 'describe a country I have seen in my soul only'.

'Ah—but you will never persuade me that I am the better, or as well, for the thing I have not', Elizabeth Barrett replied (17 Apr. 1845, p. 48). Browning had spoken of his achievements as all in prospect, and Elizabeth Barrett agreed that his best work lay in the future; but she was equally convinced that a man who had travelled through a good deal of Europe (his latest trip lasting five months), who knew Tennyson and Carlyle and Dickens personally and not simply by correspondence or repute, and who wrote that he had heard news of her between two dances at a London party (15 Apr. 1845, p. 45), had the advantage of her when it came to 'experience of life & man'—and that such experience *mattered*.

I have a profound conviction that where a poet has been shut from most of

---

[1] The plural 'Syrenusae' is emended from 'Syrenusa' in both Kintner and the first edition of the letters.

the outward aspects of life, he is at a lamentable disadvantage. Can you, speaking for yourself, separate the results in you from the external influences at work around you, that you say so boldly that you get nothing from the world? You do not *directly*, I know—but you do indirectly & by a rebound. Whatever acts upon you, becomes *you*—& whatever you love or hate, whatever charms you or is scorned by you, acts on you & becomes *you*.

(17 Apr. 1845, p. 48.)

This is one of many moments in the correspondence at which Elizabeth Barrett's bracing good sense cries out for a hearing. It did not get one from Browning, who understood the argument in different terms. For him, Elizabeth Barrett's 'lamentable disadvantage', her seclusion, was a necessary condition of the visionary utterance which had entranced him in her 1844 *Poems*; he prized it, therefore, above the process of interaction between the mind and 'external influences' out of which his own 'dramatic' poetry was made. Moreover, the contrast between himself and Elizabeth Barrett was based on an absolute division of qualities; to imagine her in some way *becoming* like himself, by going abroad, or frequenting London's literary salons, was absurd; she was 'other', and he knew, even if she did not, the value of her otherness. 'You do *not* know what I shall estimate that permission [to visit] at,' he wrote (13 May 1845, p. 63). At the same time, he was pressing on with his intimations of spring: 'Surely the wind that sets my chestnut-tree dancing, all its baby-cone-blossoms, green now, rocking like fairy castles on a hill in an earthquake,—that is South West, surely!' (3 May 1845, p. 56.) And eventually, Elizabeth Barrett consented: 'I will see you on any day unless there shd be an unforeseen obstacle, . . any day after two, or before six' (15 May 1845, p. 65).

Browning had still to fight against Elizabeth Barrett's sense of obligation to him for, as she saw it, condescending to want to see her. It was a feeling she never wholly got rid of; a year later he was still objecting to 'that notion of your being peculiarly isolated,—of any kindness to you, in your present state, seeming doubled and quadrupled' (25 Mar. 1846, p. 558). But this feeling was rooted in experiences of which Browning was as yet only hazily aware, and we can see the 'objective' paths of himself and Elizabeth Barrett converging to the point of the first meeting, while their 'subjective' paths were still widely divergent. Elizabeth Barrett not only 'grew pale in the spirit' at the thought of seeing an unfamiliar face; she felt an impulse of self-hatred, of revulsion at her own condition—which, she feared, drew people (men and women, she found it hard to decide which were the worse) because of its very debility. The idea of being a sofa-heroine, attractive in proportion to her pathos, was repugnant to her, perhaps because she did, in fact, exploit her disability in certain specific ways. (It gave her, for one thing, the freedom to see Browning alone in her room ninety-one times before her marriage.) She would not, she told him, 'make a company-show of an infirmity, & hold a beggar's hat for sympathy' (15 May 1845, p. 65). Elizabeth Barrett was as far as possible from being a coquette; it was not the thought that Browning might be disappointed in her *looks* that worried her, but the conviction that he would be disappointed in her *image*. She would not be (did not want to be) mysterious, glamorous, tragic; she would be anonymous, a let-down. In the same letter in which she invited him to call, she wrote:

There is nothing to see in me; nor to hear in me—I never learnt to talk as you do in London,—although I can admire that brightness of carved speech in Mr. Kenyon & others. If my poetry is worth anything to any eye,—it is the flower of me [. . .] the rest of me is nothing but a root, fit for the ground & the dark. And if I write all this egotism, . . it is for shame; and because I feel <afraid> ashamed of having made a fuss about what is not worth it,—and because you are extravagant in caring so for a permission, which will be nothing to you afterwards.

(15 May 1845, p. 65.)

The stress on *nothing* ('nothing to see in me . . . nothing but a root . . . nothing to you afterwards') makes painful reading; as does the sense of *shame*, which so preoccupied Elizabeth Barrett that she did not notice the redundance which her correction introduced into the syntax. She focuses on appearance: the eye becomes a metaphor for the mind which judges and values her poetry, and even speech has a surface 'brightness'. In all the letters which had passed between them, the word 'meet' had not been used: it was always 'see', and, moreover, from the 'Chapel-sight' onward, it was always the act of Browning seeing her. Elizabeth Barrett did not want to be *seen* in that way. She was distressed, too, at the thought that Browning might want it. 'When I wrote that letter to let you come the first time,' she told him later, 'do you know, the tears ran down my cheeks [. . .] I was vexed with you for wishing to come as other

people did, & vexed with myself for not being able to refuse you as I
did them' (31 Oct. 1845, p. 255).

Browning thought he understood her feelings: did he not have
the same reason for being nervous? Suppose *she* was disappointed in
him? And had *he* accused *her* of being

even as—'Mr. Simpson' who desireth the honour of the acquaintance of
Mr. B. whose admirable works have long been his, Simpson's, especial sol-
ace in private—and who accordingly is led to that personage by a mutual
friend—Simpson blushing as only adorable ingenuousness can, and twisting
the brim of his hat like a sailor giving evidence. Whereupon Mr. B. begin-
neth by remarking that the rooms are growing hot—or that he supposes
Mr. S. has not heard if there will be another adjournment of the House
to-night—whereupon Mr. S. looketh up all at once, brusheth the brim
smooth again with his sleeve, and takes to his assurance once more, in
something of a huff, and after staying his five minutes out for decency's
sake, noddeth familiarly an adieu, and spinning round on his heel ejacula-
teth mentally—'Well, I *did* expect to see something different from that little
yellow commonplace man . . and, now I come to think, there *was* some
precious trash in that book of his'—Have *I* said, 'so will Miss Barrett ejacu-
late?'

(16 May 1845, pp. 67–8.)

But Elizabeth Barrett was not deflected by this jocular analogy. Her
case was different from Browning's, and she knew they both knew
it. She rejected the charge of 'Simpsonism' out of hand: Browning
'should have been able to understand better, or misunderstand less,
in a matter like this' (17 May 1845, p. 69). This was, in fact, the last
letter before the first meeting; and the misunderstanding was not
cleared up, with consequences that nearly stopped the relationship
in its tracks.

There was one other aspect of his 'Paracelsus'-self which may
have given Browning some unease. Paracelsus was a healer, famous
in particular for discovering the medical use of opium-based drugs;
and, as Elizabeth Barrett herself told Browning, sleep 'will not
easily come near me except in a red hood of poppies' (5–6 May
1845, p. 57). Whether consciously or not, Browning found his way
here with unerring touch.

Suppose you found, unattributed, the following passage from one
of the letters, written two days after the wedding:

First, God is to be thanked for this great joy of hearing that you are better,
my ever dearest—it is a joy that floats over all the other emotions. Dearest,

I am so glad!—I had feared that excitement's telling on you quite in another way—When the whole is done, & we have left England & the talkers thereof behind our backs, you will be well, stedfastly & satisfactorily, I do trust.

(14 Sept. 1845, p. 1072.)

Encouragement from the vigorous and healthy Robert Browning to his invalid bride? Quite the reverse. The woman who nearly fainted on the way to church is here expressing her relief that the 'excitement' of the occasion has not incapacitated her husband with a crippling headache. Browning's ill health came into the open in May 1845—precisely when it would do him most good. He had hinted at it in his third letter ('when my head aches or wanders or strikes work'—27 Jan. 1845, p. 10), but the general impression he gave of himself was one of energetic well-being. Then, three months later, he wrote to Elizabeth Barrett: 'I have been surprised [. . .] with something not unlike illness of late—I have had a constant pain in the head for these two months, which only very rough exercise gets rid of [. . .] I thought I never could be unwell' (3 May 1845, p. 55). 'The legendary figure with unflagging courage, optimism, and moral energy sometimes mistaken for Browning is credited as well with robust and extraordinary health,' Elvan Kintner remarks, 'and the reader familiar with him may be somewhat surprised to find in these letters so many references to disabling headaches' (Kintner, p. xlii). In fact, Browning's health occupies as much attention, from this moment on, as Elizabeth Barrett's; and, while hers continued more or less on an upward curve, Browning's fluctuated from bad to worse; there is no unequivocal statement of well-being from him until a letter written the day after his marriage. 'Dearest, I woke this morning *quite well*—quite free from the sensation in the head—I have not woke *so*, for two years perhaps—what have you been doing to me?' (13 Sept. 1846, p. 1068; it was to this that Elizabeth Barrett was responding in the passage quoted above.) Browning's last question is double-edged; it might imply that Elizabeth Barrett had inflicted his headache as well as cured it. In a sense she had. At any rate the effect of Browning's constant ill health was to bring him within the scope of Elizabeth Barrett's solicitude. The relationship was no longer one-sided: Andromeda might be chained to the rock, but Perseus had migraine. She adjured him constantly to sleep more and write less, despite her own scorn for the 'absurd reasoning' of doctors who had prescribed abstinence from poetry to *her*

(11 Aug. 1845, pp. 151–2); she recommended, at various times, exercise and fresh air, tobacco and cold showers. How important this development was can be gauged from Elizabeth Barrett's eleventh letter. It is significantly short—barely more than a note—and it is the first one she wrote out of sequence, that is, without having received a reply from Browning to her preceding letter. It consists of three short paragraphs, all on the same subject. Browning had cancelled an engagement with Mr Kenyon (at which one of Elizabeth Barrett's sisters was also to be present):

> Sunday—in the last hour of it.
>
> May I ask how the head is? [. . .] Mr. Kenyon was here today & told me such bad news that I cannot sleep tonight (although I did think once of doing it) without asking such a question as this, dear Mr. Browning.
>
> Let me hear how you are—will you? [. . .] I had been thinking so of seeing you on Tuesday . . with my sister's eyes—for the first sight.
>
> [. . .] Just a word, to say how you are. I ask for no more than a word, lest the writing should be hurtful to you.
>
> May God bless you always.
> Your friend
>
> E.B.B.
> (11 May 1845, pp. 60–1.)

Everything about this letter—the heading with its unconventional notation of time, the postponing of 'dear Mr. Browning' to the end of the first paragraph, where it loses all its formality, the expression of personal concern ('I cannot sleep tonight'), the urgently repeated requests, the informal signature—everything speaks with the eloquence of intimacy—an eloquence which had been triggered in Elizabeth Barrett by Browning's sudden vulnerability. He himself seized on the signature: 'My own, dear friend', he opened his reply, explaining that he was 'quite well now, or next to it' (12 May 1845, p. 61). He had gained a crucial step; he had levelled, by at least a little, the ground of the meeting which was now about to take place.

2   After

Browning noted the date, time, and duration of the first meeting on the envelope of Elizabeth Barrett's letter of 17 May, the one immediately preceding the meeting; he made a similar note of every subsequent meeting, except one; his arithmetic went astray at number sixty-five, which he recorded twice. On this occasion he wrote:

Tuesday, May 20, 1845
3 – 4 $\frac{1}{2}$ p.m.

He always called at or just after three o'clock, when Mr Barrett was safely out. As for her brothers, and their 'public of noisy friends', she saw them 'only at certain hours'; besides, she assured Browning, 'as you have "a reputation" & are opined to talk in blank verse, it is not likely that there shd be much irreverent rushing into this room when you are known to be in it' (11 Aug. 1845, p. 152). On this first occasion, he was shown upstairs by one of Elizabeth Barrett's sisters (again, probably Arabel); later, he would be ushered by Elizabeth Barrett's personal maid, Elizabeth Wilson. Preparing for the meeting, Elizabeth Barrett, 'in a fit of shyness not quite unnatural', for which she had been 'cordially laughed at [. . .] by everybody in the house', had taken down from the wall the portrait of Browning reproduced from R. H. Horne's *New Spirit of the Age* (plate 3); and then, 'in a fit of justice', took down Tennyson's as well (4 Dec. 1845, p. 306.) (The portraits which remained were those of Wordsworth, Carlyle, and Harriet Martineau; Browning had hung below Wordsworth.) With this exception, the room was probably much as Elizabeth Barrett described it in a letter to Mrs Martin of May 1843:

The bed, like a sofa and no bed; the large table placed out in the room, towards the wardrobe end of it; the sofa rolled where a sofa should be rolled—opposite the arm-chair: the drawers crowned with a coronal of shelves [. . .] (of papered deal and crimson merino) to carry my books; the washing table opposite turned into a cabinet with another coronal of shelves; and Chaucer's and Homer's busts in guard over these two departments of English and Greek poetry; three more busts consecrating the wardrobe which there was no annihilating [. . .]

In the window is fixed a deep box full of soil, where are *springing up* my scarlet runners, nasturtiums, and convolvuluses [. . .] among them [. . .] a great ivy root with trailing branches so long and wide that the top tendrils are fastened to Henrietta's window of the higher storey, while the lower ones cover all my panes.

(*Letters of EBB*, i. 143–4.)

The first visit was not the shortest (that, for an unexplained reason, was no. 28, Saturday, 8 November 1845, from 3–4.05); it set the average (between an hour and a quarter and two hours) for the visits of 1845. In February 1846 the visits begin to creep over two hours; by March, two and a half or two and three-quarter hours is standard; the first three-hour visit is no. 74 (Thursday, 24 June 1846); Browning never stayed much after six, because of the return of Elizabeth Barrett's brothers (who would usually come up to see her); Mr Barrett returned from the City at seven.

For the first meetings, Browning sat on a chair, drawn up near the sofa on which Elizabeth Barrett lay; the development of their physical intimacy was focused almost as much on Elizabeth Barrett's increasing freedom to move independently (to rise, for example, when Browning entered or left) as it was on their mutual touching and kissing. We know that, when Browning first entered the room, Elizabeth Barrett looked him in the face, but that for many months after she would not meet his eyes, so that Browning complained of having only the memory of her eyes 'as if one carried dried flowers about when fairly inside the garden-enclosure' (28 Nov. 1845, p. 295); she, for her part, laughed at his 'preposterously wrong way for overcoming anybody's shyness' (28 Nov. 1845, p. 297). At his sixth visit (Saturday, 28 June 1845), and for as long as the season lasted, Browning brought flowers, especially roses, from his parent's garden. This repeated reminder of the living natural world outside her London prison was not lost on Elizabeth Barrett (she gave Browning back his flowers in Sonnet XLIV, the last of *Sonnets from the Portuguese*, in the form of a symbol).

We know that Elizabeth Barrett thanked Browning for his 'kindness' in coming to see her, and Elvan Kintner has plausibly inferred that Browning commented, by means of an analogy which later found its way into his play *A Soul's Tragedy*, on the strange stories which circulated about Elizabeth Barrett's situation (see her letter of 29 Mar. 1846, p. 570 and Kintner's note 4, p. 571); but apart from this we have no knowledge of what was said at the first meeting, and we know equally little of most of the subsequent ones. To a remarkable extent, letters and meetings are self-contained. The letters may carry forward a discussion started at a meeting, but almost always in a way which leaves nothing unaccounted for: only rarely do we come across passages which are obscure because they refer to something discussed at a meeting for which there is no other source. In this sense, the meetings are 'holes' in the texture of the correspondence, through which, you might say, either a very little or a very great deal has slipped. I think not much, at any rate in the early stages; but we have no real means of knowing. Elizabeth Barrett may have remarked that the rooms were growing hot; Browning may have wondered whether she had heard if there was to be another adjournment of the House that night. Mr Kenyon was probably mentioned and praised. But really the significance of the meeting was not what was said at it, but that it took place at all—and what followed it.

We would certainly be unjustified in assuming that Browning and Elizabeth Barrett 'fell in love' as a result of this first encounter. Elizabeth Barrett denied it specifically on her own account. 'I had loved you all my life unawares', she told him later, ' . . that is, the idea of you. [. . .] Yet indeed I did not fancy that *I* was to love *you* when you came to see me . . any more than I did your caring on your side' (23 Feb. 1846, pp. 487–8). The effect he had on her was, so far, indefinite:

Then, when you came . . you never went away—I mean I had a sense of your presence constantly. Yes . . & to prove how free that feeling was from the remotest presentiment of what has occurred . . I said to Papa in my unconsciousness the next morning . . 'it is most extraordinary how the idea of Mr. Browning does beset me [. . .] it haunts me—it is a persecution.' On which he smiled & said that 'it was not grateful to my friend to use such a word.'

(ibid.)

During the course of this same morning, Elizabeth Barrett received the letter which Browning wrote the previous evening. It would not have given her any great cause for alarm; it is not passionate and declamatory, but anxious and solicitous.

I trust to you for a true account of how you are—if tired, if not tired, if I did wrong in any thing,—or, if you please, *right* in any thing (only, not one more word about my 'kindness,' which, to get done with, I will grant is excessive)—but, let us so arrange matters if possible,—and why should it not be?—that my great happiness, such as it will be if I see you, as this morning [sic], from time to time,—may be obtained at the cost of as little inconvenience to you as we can contrive. For an instance—just what strikes me—they all say here I speak very loud [. . .] And did I stay too long?

I would tell *you* unhesitatingly of such 'corrigenda'—nay, I will again say, *do* not humiliate me—do *not* again,—by calling me 'kind,' in that way.

I am proud and happy in your friendship—now and ever. May God bless you!

(20 May 1845, p. 70.)[2]

---

[2] The word 'would' in 'I would tell *you*' is emended from 'will' in both Kintner and the first edition of the letters.

Browning's handwriting gets larger and shakier towards the end of this letter (the last lines are blotted), but his emotion is not (or not directly) to do with his love for Elizabeth Barrett. It is to do with her 'humiliating' thanks for his 'kindness' in coming to see her: 'my "kindness," which, to get done with, I will grant is excessive'. The joke is uneasy; he has not 'done with' the topic by any means; he returns to it, by a kind of compulsion, and this time the tone is much more earnest. But it was, in a sense, his own fault: in his last letter before the visit, *he* had thanked *her* for the 'infinite kindness' with which she had given him leave to call on her (16 May 1845, p. 68), and she had (mildly) ridiculed the extravagance of the phrase (17 May 1845, p. 69).

Elizabeth Barrett did not see how her own gratitude could be 'humiliating' to Browning; and (after assuring him that he did not speak too loudly!) she responded forcefully to this point:

Why deny me the use of such words as have natural feelings belonging to them—and how can the use of such be 'humiliating' to *you*? If my heart were open to you, you cd see nothing offensive to you in any thought there [. . .] but it is hard for you to understand [. . .] what my mental position is after the peculiar experience I have suffered [. . .] a sort of feeling is irrepressible from me to you, when, from the height of your brilliant happy sphere, you ask, as you did ask, for personal intercourse with me. What words but 'kindness' . . but 'gratitude'—but I will not in any case be *un*kind & *un*grateful, and do what is displeasing to you. And let us both leave the subject with the words—because we perceive in it from different points of view; we stand on the black & white sides of the shield,—& there is no coming to a conclusion.

(21 May 1845, p. 71.)

The relationship had now reached its first crisis. We must bear in mind that this exchange of letters, taking place after the stress of the first meeting which had been so long in question, was not an outburst of new feelings, but a culmination of the debate which had been going on ever since the start of the correspondence. Who was the idol, and who the worshipper? who the lover, and who the beloved? who (to put it at its lowest) was conferring a social favour on whom? The same argument as to their respective status as poets is carried over into their personal relation. For Browning at least there was no distinction between literary and personal identity. He thought of Elizabeth Barrett in the same terms whether as a poet or

a person. Her poetry was superior to his because it was the direct
expression of her spirit; that spirit was superior to his own, because
it could so express itself. But Elizabeth Barrett did not experience
herself as Browning envisaged her—integral, self-sustaining, divine.
On the contrary, she felt her identity divided, precarious, and weak.
Her poetry fed on her unhappiness; to her, self-expression did not
seem so wonderful when the self being expressed was in such miserable straits. When she and Browning first met, they were, in a sense,
further apart than they were ever to be again.

Browning, in reply to Elizabeth Barrett's letter protesting at his
denial of her 'natural feelings', which he probably received in the
afternoon or evening of 21 May, wrote her a letter, his sixteenth,
and the only one now missing from the sequence; a letter which
'was read in pain & agitation', as Elizabeth Barrett told him a
year later (19 May 1846, p. 714). Since we cannot read it
directly, we must try to reconstruct it from Elizabeth Barrett's
reply (23 May 1845, pp. 72–3). Let us dispose, first of all, of the
notion that it contained a proposal of marriage. The first thing
Elizabeth Barrett says in her letter is that she is 'disobeying'
Browning by 'speaking [. . .] of your wild speaking'; and
Browning confirms that he asked her not to allude to what he
had written (24 May 1845, p. 76). It is different to see how a
proposal could have gone forward in those conditions. What,
then, was Browning saying? Elizabeth Barrett spoke of 'a generosity from which I recoil by instinct, yet conclusively'; and she
went on:

You have said some intemperate things . . . fancies,—which you will not
say over again, nor unsay, but *forget at once, & for ever, having said at
all*,—& which (so) will die out between *you & me alone*, like a misprint
between you and the printer. And this you will do *for my sake* who am
your friend,—(& you have none truer)—& this I ask, because it is a condition necessary to our future liberty of intercourse. You remember—
surely you do—that I am in the most exceptional of positions; & that, just
because of it, I am able to receive you as I did on Tuesday; and that, for me
to listen to 'unconscious exaggerations,' is as unbecoming to the humilities
of my position, as unpropitious (which is of more consequence) to the
prosperities of yours—Now, if there shd be one word of answer attempted
to this,—or of reference; *I must not . . I* WILL *not see you again*—& you
will justify me later in your heart . . So for my sake you will not say it—I
think you will not—& spare me the sadness of having to break through an
intercourse just as it is promising pleasure to me,—to me who have so
many sadnesses & so few pleasures. You will—!

We have one more piece to add to the jigsaw. When he wrote his letter, Browning later told Elizabeth Barrett, he believed that she was
suffering from 'a spinal injury irremediable in the nature of it' (18
Sept. 1845, p. 206). Again, this rules out marriage as an objective;
the implication is that Browning never expected Elizabeth Barrett to
be in a condition to leave Wimpole Street at all, let alone in his company. Nevertheless he definitely declared his love for her. 'Judge if
the deeps of my heart were not shaken', Elizabeth Barrett later wrote
(19 May 1846, p. 714). But in what terms did Browning speak? In
those 'becoming to the humilities of *his* position, and (what is of
more consequence) the prosperities of *hers*'. For if we reverse Elizabeth Barrett's terms, Browning's declaration begins to make sense.
Given his belief in her supremacy, he was not offering to rescue her,
but to adore her. The word 'love' certainly appeared in the letter, but
in an application *devoid of mutuality*. 'I was eager', Browning
explained to Elizabeth Barrett (months later; his first explanation, as
we shall see, was less considered) 'to get the horrible notion away
from never so flitting a visit to you, that you were thus and thus to
me *on condition* of my proving just the same to you—just as if we
had waited to acknowledge that the moon lighted us till we ascer-
tained within these two or three hundred years that the earth happens to light the moon as well!' (16 Sept. 1845, p. 199.) That was
why he required no answer from her—self-devotion to a person (as
to a cause) is necessarily one-sided, if it is to have any real value. The
notion of *reward* or *return* is as alien to the idea of worship as it is to
that of duty. Just as Browning wrote poetry, he told Elizabeth Barrett, 'from a thorough conviction that it is the duty of me', so that
'the not being listened to by one human creature would, I hope, in
nowise affect me' (11 Feb. 1845, p. 18), so, as he later put it to her, 'I
loved you from my soul, and gave you my life, so much of it as you
would take [. . .] it was, in the nature of the proceeding, wholly
independent of any return on your part' (30 Aug. 1845, p. 176).

  Elizabeth Barrett's reference to Browning's 'unconscious exaggerations' picks up a phrase from a letter written over two months
before, in which she told him: 'you unconsciously exaggerate what I
can be to you' (5 Mar. 1845, p. 35); proof enough that she was responding not just to Browning's 'intemperate' letter, but to everything which led up to it. Browning, in turn, was shocked into a
realization of the distance between his idea of Elizabeth Barrett's
right relation to him, and hers; or rather, he realized that the distance

mattered, and that, by not taking account of it, he was in danger of wrecking their friendship.

What was he to do? He could not, of course, persist in the line he had taken; Elizabeth Barrett had threatened to foreclose if he did, and he had no reason to doubt her word. On the other hand, he had to say something, he had to account for what he had written. 'I did fully believe', he later wrote, 'that you were about to deny me admittance again unless I blotted out,—not merely softened down,—the past avowal' (4 Feb. 1846, p. 434). He wrote under pressure; and his letter (24 May 1845, pp. 74–7) makes excruciating reading.

Browning's argument, like Elizabeth Barrett's, alludes to the history of the relationship, and not just to the immediate event. 'Don't you remember I told you, once on a time, that you "knew nothing of me"?' his letter opened, 'whereat you demurred—but I meant what I said, & knew it was so.' (He is referring to his letter of 27 January, and to her reply of 3 February.) Accordingly, Browning sets out to give Elizabeth Barrett this knowledge—or rather, knowledge of the context in which his offending letter had been written. 'To be grand in a simile,' he explained, 'for every poor speck of a Vesuvius or a Stromboli in my microcosm there are huge layers of ice and pits of black cold water'. These two contrasted images represent opposed faculties of self-expression. The volcanoes represent direct, untrammelled self-expression, whereas the ice and black water represent indirect, inhibited utterance. 'I make the most of my two or three fire-eyes,' Browning continues, 'because [. . .] these tend to extinction—and the ice grows & grows'. The ice (he is thinking of his published work) 'is true part of me, most characteristic part, *best* part perhaps [. . .] only,—when you talked of "*knowing* me"!' What he means is that for Elizabeth Barrett really to know him, she would have to appreciate this balance of forces within his identity; and so 'utterly unused' was he to 'dream of communicating anything about *that* to another person (all my writings are purely dramatic as I am always anxious to say)', that 'when I make never so little an attempt, no wonder if I *bungle* notably'. The syntax understandably confused Elizabeth Barrett, who thought that Browning was, however improbably, claiming that his offending letter was one of these 'purely dramatic' productions. On the contrary; it was 'never so little an attempt' to communicate something of his real self, directly; it was an eruption of one of the 'fire-eyes'. *But*—and this is the crucial point—it had to be understood in the context of all those layers of ice, etc. 'Will you not think me very brutal', Browning begged her, with a ghastly affectation of self-assurance, 'if I tell you that I could almost smile at your misapprehension of what I meant to write?' And now his gestures become a little flustered:

Yet I *will* tell you, because it will undo the bad effect of my thoughtlessness, and at the same time exemplify the point I have all along been honestly earnest to set you right upon . . my real inferiority to you; just that and no more. I wrote to you, in an unwise moment, on the spur of being again 'thanked,' and, unwisely writing just as if thinking to myself, said what must have looked absurd enough as seen apart from the horrible counterbalancing never-to-be-written *rest of me*—by the side of which, could it be written & put before you, my note would sink to its proper & relative place, and become a mere 'thank you['] for your good opinion—which I assure you is far too generous,—for I really believe you to be my superior in many respects, and feel uncomfortable till *you* see that, too [. . .] I do assure you, that had you read my note, *only* having '*known*' so much of me as is implied in having inspected, for instance, the contents, merely, of that [. . .] 'portfolio' there [. . .] you would see in it, (the note not the portfolio) the blandest utterance ever mild gentleman gave birth to [. . .] if you had *not* alluded to my writing, as I meant you should not, you would certainly have understood *something* of its drift when you found me next Tuesday precisely the same quiet [. . .] mild man-about-town you were gracious to, the other morning [. . .]

Browning presumably realized that comparing his letter to one of his 'fire-eyes' would explain it to Elizabeth Barrett, but hardly excuse it: he was, after all, engaged in 'blotting out' and not 'softening down'. He therefore attempted to neutralize the impact of his letter, not only by calling it a 'note', but by claiming that it was not, after all, what it seemed; that the volcano was a 'poor speck' indeed, and that the eruption, considered in its 'counterbalancing' context, was no more than the 'blandest utterance ever mild gentleman gave birth to'. The contradiction between excuse and explanation glares: for the value of any attempt to 'make the most of my two or three fire-eyes'—of 'writing just as if thinking to myself'—is surely not compatible with the process of comparing and reducing-to-scale by which a volcano becomes a pop-gun, and a love-letter 'a mere "thank you" for your good opinion'.

The contrast between the love-letter and the 'horrible counterbalancing never-to-be-written *rest of me*' recalls that between the 'fire-eyes' and the 'huge layers of ice'. Had Elizabeth Barrett known the full range of his feelings, Browning argues, she would not have been surprised at the vehemence of his protestation to her: such vehemence was necessary if his feeling was to make itself felt at all. Elizabeth Barrett would have realized this if she had been able to compare his 'note' with the drafts of poems which Browning kept in his 'portfolio' (about which he had told her in a previous letter, 3 May 1845, p. 56). These poems—despite being *written*—are associated with the 'never-to-be-written rest of me', because both are features of the 'counterbalancing' side of Browning's identity, the side which produces his 'purely dramatic' works and which lives in the world of gestures, masks, and surfaces.

This account, which takes us deep into the psychology of the dramatic monologue, both in what it says and the way it says it, is inconsistent with the one which Browning gave Elizabeth Barrett later on: he told her that, being unable to communicate in one utterance the full extent of his love for her, and 'having to put down some one *point*, so to speak, of it', he 'took any extreme one *first* . . never minding all the untold portion that *led* up to it, made it possible and natural' (16 Sept. 1845, p. 199). Here we have the same contrast between what is said and what is unsaid: the '*point*' corresponds to the 'fire-eye', and the 'untold portion' to the 'layers of ice' or 'never-to-be-written *rest of me*'. But the contrast now has the *opposite implication*: the 'untold portion' is in harmony with, and not opposed to, the 'point' of actual expression. But by the time Browning wrote this later letter, he and Elizabeth Barrett were acknowledged lovers; the avowal had been un-blotted.

The one point which Browning could not give up was 'the point I have all along been honestly earnest to set you right upon . . my real inferiority to you'. Elizabeth Barrett had been shocked at Browning basing his love for her on this presumed inferiority; now, in denying that he had meant any such thing, Browning ingeniously stuck to his opinion: the fact that he had 'bungled' his 'mere "thank you" ' proved his inferiority, since she, of course, would never have made such an ass of herself! And Browning asked her, at the end of his letter, to confirm her 'kind promise to forget the "printer's error" in my blotted proof' by sending him back his letter, 'if you have not inflicted proper and summary justice on it'.

What Elizabeth Barrett made of all this (there is a lot more I have not quoted) is hard to say. The letter stuck in her mind, she told Browning later, especially the image of the 'fire-eyes' and the 'layers of ice' (see her letter of 30 Jan. 1846, p. 430); but she seems not to have understood its application, and, in her immediate reply (25 May 1845, pp. 78–80), she certainly misread Browning's remark about his writings being 'dramatic' as a comment on the love-letter itself. It was not, in fact, necessary for her to read the letter fully in one sense to read it fully in another: she understood perfectly well that Browning was accepting her rebuke, retracting his rash move, and trying to extricate himself with a semblance of dignity. She co-operated with his version and kept a straight face, apologizing (perhaps a touch too profusely) for having mistaken his 'indefinite compliments' as more than they seemed, and soothingly ascribing it to 'a habit of very subtle association' in his writing, 'the effect of which is to throw together on the same level and in the same light, things of likeness & unlikeness— till the reader grows confused as I did, & takes one for another'. She did, however, remark that, if he was right in saying that she had so utterly mistaken his meaning, 'it is scarcely an apposite moment for you to talk, even "dramatically," of my "superiority" to you'; and, amidst the balm of forgiving and forgetting which she poured out in her letter, she allowed herself a single sharp moment: she returned his love-letter, and—while sardonically admitting it, as a 'dramatic composition', to be 'very beautiful, and well worthy of the rest of its kin in the portfolio'—she advised him 'to burn it at once'.

The crisis had passed; Elizabeth Barrett made it clear that Browning would be welcome to call again, and, with a few awkward gestures on either side, the relationship resumed. But it made a profound difference to the course which both Browning and Elizabeth Barrett took. Browning had, as he candidly put it, been 'soundly frightened' (26 May 1845, p. 81), and, for the next few months, he had to ensure that nothing he said or did caused a recurrence of Elizabeth Barrett's anxieties. As for Elizabeth Barrett, her position was, in a way, more difficult. She reflected on it to Browning on the eve of the anniversary of his first visit:

it was not the character of the letter apart from you, which shook me,—I could prove that to you—I received & answered very calmly, with most absolute calmness, a letter of the kind last summer . . knowing in respect to the writer of it, (just as I thought of *you*), that a moment's enthusiasm had carried him a good way past his discretion. I am sure that he was perfectly satisfied with my way of answering his letter . . as I was myself. But *you* . . *you* . . I could not escape so from *you*. You were stronger than I, from the beginning, & I felt the mastery in you by the first word & first look.

(19 May 1846, p. 714.)

Elizabeth Barrett's problem, therefore, was to reconcile her own attraction to Browning with, on the one hand, her conviction that it could not be realistically reciprocated ('the humilities of my position', 'the prosperities of yours'), and, on the other hand, the sense that she 'could not escape' from him—in other words, that she did not want to give him up. She was compelled (against her own better judgement, as she emphasized to him) to continue to see him, while persisting in the belief that the relationship must not develop in certain directions; even though she must have known (or, if she did not, she soon discovered) that successive visits and letters could only confirm and intensify the feelings which they were supposed to ignore.

Elizabeth Barrett had one trump card against her own impulses: the belief, to which she clung when every other reason for not acknowledging Browning as her lover was gone, that she might harm him by doing so, that she might be a burden to him. 'What could I give you,' she asked him, 'which it would not be ungenerous to give?' (31 Aug. 1845, p. 179.) This was not false modesty on her part; it was more even than a pessimistic appraisal of her health and state of mind; it was a fear rooted in the trauma of the loss of Bro, who had stayed in Torquay with her at her desire, and then been drowned. The superstition which flowed from her guilt at this event was so powerful that she categorically refused, at first, to name the days on which Browning was to come for his visits; even the letter in which she gave her reasons (6 June 1845, pp. 85–8) is uncharacteristically nervous and stumbling. And so, through the whole period of the courtship, we find Elizabeth Barrett repeating her fear that, in some way, Browning might be harmed by associating with her. She prayed, for example, on one occasion, 'that I may never have the sense, . . intolerable in the remotest apprehension of it . . of being, in any way, directly or indirectly, the means of ruffling your smooth path by so much as one of my flintstones!' (26 July 1846, p. 137.) Browning found a way to persuade Elizabeth Barrett that the only flintstone in his path was, in fact, her scrupulous refusal to let him love her; but before he could do this, he had to wait through the period in which he was formally prohibited from broaching the topic at all. This period lasted through the summer of 1845; and it was Mr Barrett, paradoxically enough, who helped bring it to a close.

4

'The Offices of Friendship'

1 Bells and Pomegranates

'I am but a very poor creature compared to you and entitled by my wants to look up to you': so Browning, in his letter of excuse for the 'over boisterous gratitude' of his love-letter (24 May 1845, p. 76). Elizabeth Barrett had now forbidden him to apply this principle to their personal relations; but no such prohibition extended to the other, parallel question between them—namely, who was whose superior in poetry. Accordingly, in the summer of 1845, it is this question which takes a central place in the relationship: in and through it, Browning and Elizabeth Barrett continued the debate which she had brought to a halt, but which neither of them felt had been really settled.

In replying to Browning's love-letter, Elizabeth Barrett had spoken of the 'free gifts of thinking, teaching, master-spirits' which she would lose if the friendship were broken: 'Your influence & help in poetry will be full of good & gladness to me' (23 May 1845, p. 73). Browning, in turn, had written a week before his visit, 'you must help me with all my new Romances and Lyrics, and Lays & Plays, and read them and heed them and end them and mend them!' (13 May 1845, p. 63.) His was the more concrete proposal, and he ended by getting his way.

At the beginning of 1845, Elizabeth Barrett was at something of a standstill in her work. She had just published in volume form almost everything of her own which she had written during the past seven years; and her new translation of *Prometheus Bound* (which she had undertaken to expiate the 'sin' of her first version, published in

1833) was finished, as she told Browning, 'except the transcription & last polishing' (27 Feb. 1845, p. 30). She had the first glimmerings of 'a sort of novel-poem' which would be 'completely modern [. . .] running into the midst of our conventions, & rushing into drawing-rooms & the like "where angels fear to tread" '; but it was 'not mature enough yet to be called a plan' (ibid., p. 31). She was 'waiting for a story'—the story, as it turned out, of *Aurora Leigh*. But that was ten years away; and meanwhile, there was nothing for Browning to help her with. In the period of the courtship she wrote nothing except *Sonnets from the Portuguese*, on which she could not, for obvious reasons, ask him to pass judgement. He, on the other hand, had a 'portfolio' of unfinished poems and plays, which eventually made up the last two numbers of his series *Bells and Pomegranates*, and his early letters are full of references to work-in-progress—teasing references, which were meant to (and did) arouse Elizabeth Barrett's curiosity.

Browning had, nevertheless, started on the wrong foot, by a mention in his very first letter of (possibly) 'finding fault' with Elizabeth Barrett's poetry. She was quick to take him up: he would 'confer a lasting obligation' on her if he would point out 'such faults as rise to the surface and strike you as important in my poems, (for of course, I do not think of troubling you with criticism in detail)' (11 Jan. 1845, p. 4). That last phrase has an ironic ring, in view of what followed: it was Elizabeth Barrett, later on in the summer of 1845, who found herself, against her will, supplying Browning with 'criticism in detail' of his poems. Browning replied (with a metaphor which strives to turn the criticism itself into a compliment) that Elizabeth Barrett's style was sometimes a little wordy (13 Jan. 1845, p. 6–7); but this is, I believe, the sole recorded instance of him breathing a single derogatory word against her poetry, either in the correspondence or elsewhere. In his next letter, he announced with resolute jocoseness that 'the said faults cannot be lost, must be *somewhere*, and shall be faithfully brought you back whenever they turn up' (27 Jan. 1845, p. 11); and they seem never to have done so.

Browning did offer to 'pencil [. . .] and annotate, and dissertate upon that I love most and least' (ibid.); but Elizabeth Barrett never required him to do so. Instead, she asked him to go through her new translation of *Prometheus Bound*, and he did so, suggesting a number of changes. But these changes, as he himself emphasized

(7 June 1845, p. 89) were entirely to do with differences of opinion about the Greek text which Elizabeth Barrett was using; he scrupulously refrained from commenting critically on Elizabeth Barrett's style of translation. He was prepared to discuss Greek scholarship (about which, as it happens, she knew a good deal more than he), but not the merits of her own work.

It was probably at their second meeting, on 31 May—the first, that is, after the débâcle of Browning's love-letter—that Elizabeth Barrett asked Browning to make these notes on her *Prometheus*; and he seems to have given them to her in two lots (5 and 11 June). But that, as far as he was concerned, was that. From this moment on, Browning began to press Elizabeth Barrett to adopt the role of critic of his work; and the terms in which he did so make it clear that he had found a means of demonstrating, once again, his 'real inferiority' to her.

He had the advantage, as I have said, of a batch of unfinished work; he was able, for example, to comment on 'a certain "Saul" I should like to show you one day—an ominous liking,—for nobody ever sees what I do till it is printed' (3 May 1845, p. 55). Elizabeth Barrett had 'both hands open for what poems you will vouchsafe to me [. . .] anything you may have in a readable state by you [. . .] I shall be so glad & grateful to you!' (13 June 1845, p. 95.) She appreciated that he was privileging her as a reader, but she did not bargain for Browning's interpretation of the privilege. 'You do not understand what a new feeling it is for me to have someone who is to like my verses or I shall not ever like them after!' he replied (14 June 1845, p. 94). And he made it clear to her that he meant her to correct as well as to admire what she read—to supplement his creativity with her own. 'Do not you be tempted', he warned her, 'by that pleasure of pleasing which I think is your besetting sin— may it not be?—and so cut me off from the other pleasure of being profited' (13 July 1845, p. 123).

When Elizabeth Barrett realized what Browning wanted her to do, she was genuinely shocked. Certainly, she had told him that 'if when your poems come, you persist in giving too much importance to what I may have courage to say of this or of that in them, you will make me a dumb critic'(19 June 1845, p. 99); but she categorically denied that she would be afraid to say what she thought. 'I have a pretention to speak the truth like a Roman, even in matters of literature, where Mr Kenyon says falseness is a fashion', she wrote

(16–17 July 1845, p. 124); and she went on to explain that her diffidence was nothing to do with her 'besetting sin':

I can tell you truly what I think of this thing & of that thing in your 'Duchess'—but I must of a necessity hesitate & fall into misgiving of the adequacy of my truth, so called. To judge at all of a work of yours, I must *look up to it*,—& *far up*—because whatever faculty *I* have is included in your faculty, & with a great rim all round it besides! And thus, it is not at all from an over-pleasure in pleasing *you*, not at all from an inclination to depreciate myself, that I speak & feel as I do & must on some occasions—it is simply the consequence of a true comprehension of you & of me—& apart from it, I shd not be abler, I think, but less able, to assist you in anything. I do wish you wd consider all this reasonably, & consent not to spoil the real pleasure I have & am about to have in your poetry, by nailing me up into a false position with your gold-headed nails of chivalry, which wont hold to the wall through this summer. Now you will not answer this?—you will only understand it & me—& that I am not servile but sincere—but earnest—but meaning what I say—& when I say I am afraid, you will believe that I am afraid, . . and when I say I have misgivings, . . you will believe that I have misgivings—you will *trust* me so far, & give me liberty to breathe & feel naturally . . according to my own nature.

(ibid., p.125.)

The plain passionate eloquence of this plea was lost on Browning: he *could* not accept it, and did not attempt to reply to it. Elizabeth Barrett had touched on exactly the point at issue: the 'true comprehension of you & of me'. Her tone, full of anxious emphasis and reiteration, is hard to account for unless we read into it her perception that the argument about poetry was also an argument about personality; that the 'gold-headed nails of chivalry' were being hammered into the woman as well as the critic. Nevertheless, Elizabeth Barrett did not withdraw from the agreement she had made with Browning: he won the argument and installed her as critic of the poems of his forthcoming volume, *Dramatic Romances and Lyrics*.

In this context, the first poem he submitted to her has a special significance—though not for the reasons which have traditionally been given. 'The Flight of the Duchess' tells the story of a woman, by nature 'active, stirring, all fire', who escapes from the repressive environment created by her loveless, mean-spirited husband. She sickens under his petty tyranny until the arrival, one morning, of an old Gypsy woman. While the Duke is out hunting, the Gypsy entrances the Duchess with a vision of emotional and sexual and social freedom—'liberty to breathe & feel naturally', in fact—and, with the help of the Duke's retainer who narrates the story, the Duchess flees with the Gypsy into this life of renewal and fulfilment.

The resemblance between this story and Browning's relationship with Elizabeth Barrett has led to a firm belief that Browning wrote the whole poem in order to persuade Elizabeth Barrett to elope with him. But the dates do not fit; Browning had the idea for the poem in 1842, and wrote most of it long before he began to correspond with Elizabeth Barrett; and, even if he had not, the early period of the courtship is wholly unsuited to the kind of strategy which he is supposed to have adopted. For the first few months, after all, Browning was not trying to persuade Elizabeth Barrett to leave Wimpole Street, but to let him in; nor could Mr Barrett, who had barely been mentioned so far, have sat for the portrait of the Duke—he was not yet a tyrant in Browning's eyes, but the respectable guardian of a fragile treasure. Moreover, even had Browning conceived of Mr Barrett as an ogrish rival, he would have been an idiot to let Elizabeth Barrett know how he felt, let alone invite her to share the feeling. On the eve of their elopement, long after she had received, as she thought, conclusive proof that her father did not love her, she told Browning that if she loved him 'a little, little less' she would tell him 'that our marriage was invalid, or ought to be', so 'dreadful' did she feel it 'to have to give pain here by a voluntary act—for the first time in my life' (18 Sept. 1845, p. 1087).

So much for the idea that Browning designed the poem as an allegory of Elizabeth Barrett's domestic situation. But what of his own current relationship with her? Here Browning seems to have used 'The Flight of the Duchess', not by design, but opportunistically. Elizabeth Barrett had seen and liked the first part of the poem, which had been published in *Hood's Magazine* in April 1845; and Browning may well have realized, in the aftermath of his disastrous love-letter, just how well suited the poem was to his continuing propaganda campaign on the subject of Elizabeth Barrett's superiority to him.

The poem lent itself to this campaign not because of its subject, but because of its *form*. The narrator of the poem, as I have said, is one of the Duke's retainers—a rough huntsman, who tells the story in picturesque vocabulary and grotesque rhyme. He represents the kind of poet Browning believed himself to be, just as the very struc-

ture of the story, in which everything is filtered through the huntsman's idiosyncratic vision, represents the 'dramatic' as opposed to
the 'lyrical' method. The centre-piece of the story—the Gypsy's
speech of persuasion to the Duchess—is given to us only partially
by the huntsman, who has not managed to catch it all, he tells us,
and who warns us that even the portion he has retained has suffered
from his clumsy paraphrase. And, Browning told Elizabeth Barrett,
it was 'characteristic' of his poetry that it should have turned out so;
characteristic, that is, of his failure to be a true, lyrical poet: for,

of *the poem* [. . .] not a line is written [. . .] as I conceived the poem, it
consisted entirely of the gipsy's description of the life the Lady was to lead
with her future gipsy lover—a *real* life, not an unreal one like that with the
Duke—and as I meant to write it, all their wild adventures would have
come out and the insignificance of the former vegetation been deducible
only—as the main subject has become now—

(25 July 1845, p. 135.)

Moreover, Browning may have seen in the huntsman's relation to
the Duchess a model of his desired relation to Elizabeth Barrett. It is
even possible that, in the period after the failed love-letter, but
before he brought the poem to Elizabeth Barrett for her to criticize,
he added some of the passages which are closest to expressions in
the letters: the lines, for example, where the huntsman, saddling the
Duchess's palfrey in preparation for her escape, says that she

> knew the poor devil so much beneath her
> Would have been only too glad for her service
> To dance on hot ploughshares like a Turk dervise,
> But, unable to pay proper duty where owing it,
> Was reduced to that pitiful method of showing it:

(ll. 749–53.)

The huntsman is a 'poor devil' just as Browning is a 'poor creature'
in relation to Elizabeth Barrett, but the huntsman has better
grounds for saying so. He is (unarguably and of necessity) the
Duchess's social inferior; the social distance between them acts as a
metaphor for their different kinds of identity. The Duchess, like her
unlucky counterpart in 'My Last Duchess', is less an individual than
an embodiment of 'life and gladness'; she lives at a level of direct
experience, whereas the huntsman is confined (by a social convention which articulates his nature) to the responses of alienation and
irony. He is an observer and a story-teller, not a visionary; the

Duchess, riding away with the Gypsy, rewards him with 'a look that placed a crown on me', and a lock of her hair, but leaves him, like the lame child in 'The Pied Piper of Hamelin', irredeemably behind.

Elizabeth Barrett's notes on 'The Flight of the Duchess' are the longest and most detailed on the poems of *Dramatic Romances and Lyrics*, and they set the pattern for the notes which she wrote throughout the summer on the poems which Browning brought to her. As she told him, her notes were 'written after your own example & pattern, when, in the matter of my Prometheus [. . .] you took trouble for me & did me good' (26 July 1845, p. 136). In other words, she steadily refrained from making any comment on the conception of the poem (except to praise it); she pointed out a few grammatical flaws, and some passages where the meaning seemed to her obscure, but, in general, her criticisms concentrated on the versification, the technical correctness of which she felt able to judge. (Alas, her judgement here was poor; she objected to Browning's metrical angularities and abruptnesses, his use of short lines, the twists and turns of his syntax: her intervention made the verse of *Dramatic Romances and Lyrics* blander and smoother than it need have been.) She reminded Browning that her criticisms were the result of his insistence: '*I promised to tell all my impressions*' she wrote after one note of doubt, and again, after suggesting a change of wording, 'but this & ever so much before, is such impertinence that I am quite & really ashamed of it—& should be still more, if it did not come of obedience rather then want of reverence'— obedience, that is, to his injunction to 'tell all her impressions'.

As for Browning, he pursued to its uttermost the strategy which had led him to appoint Elizabeth Barrett the judge of his work in the first place. When he received the last batch of notes on 'The Flight of the Duchess', he began by expressing his gratitude to her for the 'material' service she had rendered him, as distinct from the 'immaterial' benefit which came to him simply from knowing her; how perverse of her, he implied, to allow him to be grateful for the first and lesser gift, when he could not 'make you see the substantiality of those other favours you refuse to recognise, and reality of the other gratitude you will not admit' (25 July 1845, p. 134). This link between the poetic and the personal is carried further by Browning's declaration, in an image of 'natural' eroticism and fertility, that 'The Flight of the Duchess' has been enriched for him (not merely as a work of art) by Elizabeth Barrett's touch; it has become a poem 'which I shall ever rejoice in—wherever was a bud, even, in that strip of May-bloom, a live musical bee hangs now' (ibid., p. 135).

'For the criticism itself,' Browning wrote, enforcing his deference to Elizabeth Barrett's judgement, 'it is all true, except the overrating—all the suggestions are to be adopted, the improvements accepted' (ibid.). He was as good as his word—even to the bizarre extent of refusing to accept Elizabeth Barrett's second thoughts about one of her own suggestions. She wrote to him,

I am delighted to have met your wishes in writing as I wrote; only [. . .] you are surely wrong in refusing to see a single wrongness in all that heap of weedy thoughts [. . .] One of the thistles is the suggestion about the line

'Was it singing, was it saying,'

which you wrote so, & which I proposed to amend by an intermediate 'or.' Thinking of it at a distance, it grows clear to me that you were right, & that there should be and must be no 'or' to disturb the listening pause.

(26 July 1845, pp. 136–7.)

The line in question comes from the passage where the huntsman has just become aware of the Gypsy casting her spell over the Duchess:

> my ear was arrested
> By—was it singing, or was it saying,
> Or a strange musical instrument playing
> In the chamber?

(ll. 511–14.)

Browning's first version was metrically imperfect, but exactly caught the 'listening pause' which Elizabeth Barrett, on reflection, admired; but since her second thought sprang from an impulse to deny the superiority which Browning attributed to her judgement, he ignored it, and the line stands to this day as testimony to his determination to have the last word on her behalf. It is the same story with the other poems of *Dramatic Romances and Lyrics*, and later on with *Luria* and *A Soul's Tragedy*: what Elizabeth Barrett called her 'querulous queries' were accepted without question, and her insistence that they were 'just passing thoughts', 'just impressions, & by no means pretending to be judgments' (25 July 1845, pp. 132–3), went for nothing. In one letter Browning spoke of her 'correcting my verses' (15 Aug. 1845, p. 156), and the word 'correcting' stung Elizabeth Barrett into exclaiming at the 'miserably false position' he was putting her in. 'Do you not see at once what a disqualifying and paralysing phrase it must be, of simple necessity?' (16 Aug. 1845, p. 159.) But Browning did not see. For him, the scraps of paper on which Elizabeth Barrett's notes were scribbled, as if to emphasize their lack of pretension, might as well have been tablets of stone.

2 The Pisa Affair

Elizabeth Barrett was getting better. By the middle of April she was 'getting slowly up from the prostration of the severe cold' (17 Apr. 1845, pp. 48–9), and, three weeks later, although she had 'not been down stairs yet', she was 'certainly stronger & better than I was— that is undeniable' (5–6 May 1845, pp. 59–60). 'I *shall* be better still', she added, with significant emphasis. She had decided to be well. On 9 June she 'went down stairs—or rather was carried', and was 'none the worse' (10 June 1845, p. 93). 'I thank God that you are better,' Browning wrote; 'do pray make fresh endeavours to profit by this partial respite of the weather!' And he sent her a yellow rose, the first of the year, as proof of the hot weather (14 June 1845, pp. 95–96). It was in other respects an unfortunate choice; as Elizabeth Barrett later pointed out to him, in the language of flowers a yellow rose signifies infidelity. Two weeks later Elizabeth Barrett considered going out, but was advised that it was 'too windy . . soft & delightful as the air seems to be' (30 June 1845, p. 108). Browning began to bring flowers with him on his visits, a practice which he continued to such effect that, in the following year, Elizabeth Barrett's brothers knew when he had called on her by the flowers in her room. And perhaps it was his prompting, at a meeting on 5 July, which finally decided her on the great adventure. On Monday 7 July she tottered out of Wimpole Street, to take the air in a carriage; while Browning, writing from New Cross, anxiously awaited the result. 'You will of course feel fatigued at first—but persevering, as you mean to do, do you not?—persevering, the event must be happy' (7 July 1845, p. 115).

'Well—I have really been out,' Elizabeth Barrett wrote, surprised at her own achievement, '—and am really alive after it—which is more surprising still'. She had failed, however, in her 'great ambition of getting into the Park & of reaching Mr Kenyon's door just to leave a card there vaingloriously [. . .] & was forced to turn back from the gates of Devonshire Place' (7 July 1845, p. 116). The round trip was barely half a mile, and Elizabeth Barrett had not found it easy. 'The carriage shook beyond any imagination of my heart or power of my body', she wrote to her brother George. 'Still my strength is returning so fast that I dream dreams of reaching the botanical gardens perhaps [. . .] As it is, I walk as well as most children of two years old!' (*Letters to George Barrett*, 134.) Again Browning encouraged her: 'I am happy and thankful the beginning (and worst of it) is over and so well. The Park, & Mr Kenyon's all in good time'; and he exhorted her to 'GO OUT, without a moment's thought or care', even if it meant that he missed seeing her: 'I shall be as glad as if I saw you or more—*reasoned* gladness, you know' (9 July 1845, p. 118). But Elizabeth Barrett dispensed with such hero- ism. 'If it were necessary for me to go out every day, or most days even, it wd be otherwise—but as it is, I may certainly keep the day you come, free from the fear of carriages' (11 July 1845, p. 119). Around this time, too, we hear of her replacing her sofa with a chair loaned to her by Mr Kenyon, 'to the obvious inconvenience & dejection' of Flush, for whom there was now no room (*Letters to George Barrett*, 133).

'I daresay you think you have some—perhaps many,—to whom your well-being is of deeper interest than to me', Browning wrote (13 July 1845, p. 121); personal expressions were beginning to seep back into his letters. He had 'a way of putting things which I have not,' Elizabeth Barrett later wrote to Mrs Martin, 'a way of putting aside'; and in every one of his letters and visits at this period, she went on, 'there was something which was too slight to analyse and notice, but too decided not to be understood' (*Letters of EBB*, i. 289). Browning was right, however, that others besides himself were watching and reflecting on Elizabeth Barrett's improvement in health. She told him that they 'must make speed' with her reading of his poems,

for I heard to-day that Papa & my aunt are discussing the question of send- ing me off either to Alexandria or Malta for the winter. Oh—it is quite a passing talk & thought, I dare say! and it wd not *be* in any case, until Sep- tember or October; tho' in every case, I suppose, *I* should not be much consulted . .

(16–17 July 1845, p. 127.)

The aunt (on her mother's side) was Mrs Jane Hedley, who was staying in Wimpole Street with her two children at the time (*EBB to*

MRM, 253), and it was probably she, and not Mr Barrett, who started the topic; but however it came up, it was no 'passing talk & thought'. Two weeks later Elizabeth Barrett wrote to Mrs Martin:

Everybody praises me, and I look in the looking-glass with a better conscience. Also, it is an improving improvement, and will be, until, you know, the last hem of the garment of summer is lost sight of, and then—and then—I must either follow to another climate, or be ill again—*that* I know, and am prepared for.

(*Letters of EBB*, i. 267.)

Browning took the prospect of Elizabeth Barrett's absence in his stride; it would, of course, have been impossible for him, according to the convention that what was good for her was best for him, to have expressed any selfish anxiety on the subject, but there is no reason to believe that he did not fully enter into her growing conviction that she must 'follow [the summer] to another climate'. At the same time, the personal note in his letters continued to increase: he wrote to her (as his 'dear, first and last friend'): 'you may if you please get well thro' God's goodness—with persevering patience, surely—and this next winter abroad—which you must get ready for now, every sunny day, will you not?' He thought of the ebb-tide that would take her from England, and, signing his letter, he clinched with a pun the link between her well-being and his: 'did not the prophet write that "there was a tide in the affairs of men, which taken at the E.B.B." led on to the fortune of Your R.B.' (25 July 1845, p. 135; the allusion is to *Julius Caesar*, IV. iii. 217–18.)

For the first time since she had rejected his love-letter, Elizabeth Barrett took note of these protestations. She seized on and satirized the idea that she could get well 'if she pleased', which reminded her 'of what Papa says sometimes when he comes into this room unexpectedly & convicts me of having dry toast for dinner, & declares angrily that obstinacy & dry toast have brought me to my present condition, & that if I *pleased* to have porter & beefsteaks instead, I shd be as well as ever I was, in a month!'(26 July 1845, p. 137.) But there was nothing sarcastic about what followed: it told Browning unequivocally that Elizabeth Barrett had not missed a drop of the balm he had been cautiously infusing into his letters since the beginning of the summer:

What I wished to say was this—that if I get better or worse . . as long as I live & to the last moment of life, I shall remember with an emotion which cannot change its character, all the generous interest & feeling you have spent on me [. . .] I shall never forget these things, my dearest friend; nor remember them more coldly.

(ibid.)

This is the first indication that Elizabeth Barrett had begun, even tentatively, to think of Browning as he thought of her; and, appropriately enough, it comes immediately after a slighting allusion to Mr Barrett. Elizabeth Barrett was just entering (though she did not know it yet) on the first real trial of strength with her father since the argument over whether her brother Edward should stay with her at Torquay, which had ended so disastrously. By the middle of August, there was still 'not a word of Malta!—except from Mr. Kenyon who talked homilies of it last Sunday & wanted to talk them to Papa—but it would not do in any way' (19 Aug. 1845, p. 162). These 'homilies' were part of a growing chorus of opinion among Elizabeth Barrett's friends that a winter abroad was essential to her health; and Mr Barrett's silence was a characteristic response to the pressure which he undoubtedly felt. From far back, in the Hope End days, he had been in the habit of keeping his counsel about such domestic arrangements; the loss of Hope End itself was the subject of a nerve-racking guessing-game among the children.

At this point—and for the first time—her father and his peculiar character became a subject for conversation between Elizabeth Barrett and Browning. Elizabeth Barrett, in a letter of 20–2 August (pp. 167–71) refers to something which she had said at their meeting on 22 August, and which she felt might have prompted an 'unjust opinion' of her father in Browning's mind. That something evidently concerned the fact that the members of Mr Barrett's household were subject to his will in a peculiarly uncomfortable way. 'But then,' Elizabeth Barrett remarked, '[. . .] no one cares less for a "will" than I do [. . .] for a will in the common things of life'. Nevertheless, the picture which she went on to give of life in Wimpole Street must have given Browning a shock. While stressing that 'my own sense of right & happiness on any important point of overt action, has never run contrariwise to the way of obedience required of me', Elizabeth Barrett had to admit that it was an accident that things turned out so easy for her (her sister Henrietta had not been so lucky); and she went on to describe how Mr Barrett's children (herself included) deceived him when they could, 'forced into concealments from the heart naturally nearest to us'; only the previous month a whole party of them had gone on an illicit picnic to Miss Mitford's cottage, while Elizabeth Barrett had waited for their return, 'walking on hot coals, all day with terror, lest there shd be a discovery', as she wrote to George (*Letters to George Barrett*, 134). As a result, 'disingenuousness' and 'cowardice'—the 'vices of slaves'—were, she told Browning, 'the worst of it all'. 'And everyone you see . . all my brothers, . . constrained *bodily* into submission . . apparent submission at least . . by that worst & most dishonoring of necessities, the necessity of *living*: everyone of them all, except myself, being dependent in money-matters on the inflexible will . . do you see?'

Then comes a striking change of tone. What Browning did *not* see, Elizabeth Barrett emphasized, was 'the deep tender affection behind & below all those patriarchal ideas of governing grownup children [. . .] and there never was (under the strata) a truer affection in a father's heart . . no, nor a worthier heart in itself . . a heart loyaller & purer, & more compelling to gratitude & reverence, than his, as I see it!' As long as Elizabeth Barrett saw it this way, her father could do more or less what he liked. Love—the presumption of it, if not the proof—excused the arbitrary actions of Mr Barrett as it did those of the Protestant God whom he and his daughter worshipped. But Elizabeth Barrett turned atheist when, for reasons which we shall come to, she decided that the presumption of her father's love had been unfounded. (Unlike Jehovah, he did not have unlimited credit.) When that happened, it was Browning who usurped those titles of loyalty and purity of heart, and laid claim to Elizabeth Barrett's 'gratitude & reverence'.

'The evil is in the system', Elizabeth Barrett maintained; 'he takes it to be his duty to rule like the Kings of Christendom, by divine right. But he loves us through & through it—& *I*, for one, love *him*!'

Even this—as Browning must have been aware in the course of reading—was the mark of an exceptional confidence on Elizabeth Barrett's part. It was the fruit of three months (to the day, almost) of meetings, in which friendship had gradually, and almost unawares on Elizabeth Barrett's side, ripened into intimacy. But there was more to come—indeed, Elizabeth Barrett was about to take one of the crucial steps in the whole courtship. In the flow of revelation about her father, struggling to mediate his complex character, she recalled the most traumatic episode of her life, the death of Bro at Torquay in 1840, for which she blamed herself. It was in the context of her father's forbearance 'in that hour of bitter trial' that she related the event to Browning: he 'never reproached me as he might have done & as my own soul has not spared—never once said to me then or since, that if it had not been for *me*, the crown of his house wd not have fallen'. Mr Barrett, if he had any knowledge of his daughter's character, would have known that he had no need to say anything to reproach her; she would do the job for him. Still, Elizabeth Barrett chose to give him credit for his silence, and to offer it to Browning as evidence of his fundamental affection. She did so at a moment when she needed, again, to summon her faith in the actuality of that affection. The next two months would cause that faith to shatter.

Browning was fully alive to the opening which Elizabeth Barrett had made for him in the most private and painful of her feelings. He did not comment directly, except to say how grateful he was for 'this admission to participate, in my degree, in these feelings' (27 Aug. 1845, p. 172); but he brought with him, at his next visit, the manuscript of his unfinished poem 'Saul'. Again, as with 'The Flight of the Duchess', there is no sense in which he wrote the poem on purpose (it was in the 'portfolio' long before); but by choosing this moment to show it to Elizabeth Barrett, Browning may well have meant it to convey his sympathy and his consolation. The story of how the young David, playing on his harp, drove an 'evil spirit' out of King Saul, is elaborated in Browning's poem from its bare origins in 1 Samuel 16: 23 to a brilliant lyrical celebration of 'the wild joys of living', addressed to a despairing sufferer whose condition ('drear and stark, blind and dumb') strikingly resembles that of Elizabeth Barrett after Bro's death ('I, who could not speak or shed a tear, but lay for weeks & months half conscious, half unconscious, with a wandering mind'.) 'The whole conception of the poem, I like', Elizabeth Barrett wrote, ' . . & the execution is exquisite'; 'I cannot tell you how the poem holds me & will not let me go until it blesses me' (27 Aug. 1845, p. 173).

Elizabeth Barrett's letter about Bro's death gave Browning more assurance than he had ever had before that his love for her was close to being returned. But it also contained a renewed expression of her melancholy sense of the unreality of their situation: 'it is gravely true, seriously true, sadly true, that I am always expecting to hear or

to see how tired you are at last of me!' (20–2 Aug. 1845, p. 167.)
Later on Elizabeth Barrett, not having heard from Browning for a
couple of days, became anxious lest he had taken offence at this
apparent distrust of him (29 Aug. 1845, pp. 174–5). Browning
seized the opportunity to renew his declaration of love for her, in
defiance of her prohibition, which was nominally still in force. 'Can
you understand me *so*, dearest friend, after all?' his letter opened.
'Do you see me [. . .] "taking offence" at words, "being vexed" at
words, or deeds of yours, even if I could not immediately trace
them to their source of entire, pure kindness—, as I have hitherto
done in every smallest instance?' (30 Aug. 1845, pp. 175–6.) For
Browning, too, had his notion of love as a justifying motive. He
went on to make his feelings explicit, in order, as he claimed, 'to put
an end to possible misunderstanding—to prevent your henceforth
believing that because I *do not write*, from thinking too deeply of
you, I am offended, vexed &c &c'. With this cover, he allowed himself the luxury (after three months!) of plain speaking:

I loved you from my soul, and gave you my life, so much of it as you would
take,—and all that is *done*, not to be altered now [. . .] the assurance of
your friendship, the intimacy to which you admit me, now,—make the
truest, deepest joy of my life [. . .] what you could and would give me, of
your affection, you would give nobly and simply and as a giver—you
would not need that I tell you—(*tell* you!)—what would be supreme happiness to me in the event—however distant—

Elizabeth Barrett's reply to this outburst (31 Aug.–1 Sept. 1845,
pp. 177–9) brought her to the brink of an open declaration of her
own—to the brink, but not quite beyond. She refused to accept
Browning's assurance of the permanence of his feelings; she would
not 'suffer you to hold to words because they have been said [. . .]
Why, if a thousand more such words were said by you to me, how
could they operate upon the future or present, supposing me to
choose to keep the possible modification of your feelings, as a probability, in my sight & yours?' And she did so choose: 'Can you help
my sitting with the doors all open if I think it right?' At the same
time, she admitted that she had been surprised and touched—'more
than I dare attempt to say'—that he had persisted as far as he had: 'I
thought [. . .] that the feeling on your part was a mere generous
impulse, likely to expend itself in a week perhaps'. Nevertheless, she
stuck fast to the one principle which Browning could not yet get

round: her belief that she would not do him good if she allowed herself to accept his love. 'My dearest friend', she wrote sadly, '—you have followed the most *generous* of impulses in your whole bearing to me [. . .] Yet I cannot help adding that, of us two, yours has not been quite the hardest part'. In this way Elizabeth Barrett revealed to Browning the temptation that his love represented for her, a temptation to take advantage of his 'generous nature', and against which she struggled, in 'the effort to recover the duty of a lost position'. It was a struggle which Elizabeth Barrett (forlornly, it seems to us now) believed she could win.

Meanwhile, there was movement on the question of Elizabeth Barrett spending the winter abroad. Mr Barrett had broken his silence: he wrote Elizabeth Barrett a 'hard cold letter', in which, apparently, he gave his grudging consent to her plan. She showed the letter to her aunt, Mrs Hedley, who 'exhorted' her to act: '[she] saw with her eyes how the change came with the sun, and how, from a feeble colourless invalid, I strengthened and brightened as the season advanced' (*EBB to MRM*, 255). Her brother George, who was away on circuit, sent her a 'strong & full' opinion, which 'has had its right weight with me [. . .] I have turned my face steadily towards the south' (*Letters to George Barrett*, 135). Mr Kenyon sent 'the kindest of letters [. . .] urging it' (6 Sept. 1845, p. 184). There had also been a change in destination, from Malta to Pisa. Late in August (perhaps in the letter he wrote to her, and as a condition of his consent) Mr Barrett had requested that Elizabeth Barrett should get a medical opinion about her proposed trip. If it was a delaying tactic, it backfired. Elizabeth Barrett saw Dr Chambers on Saturday, 30 August; and, writing to her brother George four days later, she gave the following account: 'He said, after using the stethoscope, that a very slight affection of the left lung was observed but which threatened no serious result whatever, if I did but take precautions [. . .] and he not merely *advised* but ENJOINED the trial of a warm climate . . *naming Pisa*. It is the very best thing I could do, he said—& everything in the way of res- toration was to be expected from it' (*Letters to George Barrett*, 136). She made the same emphatic point in a letter to Miss Mitford:

Papa wished me to see Chambers and have his advice—and I sent for him, and was examined with that dreadful stethoscope, and received his com- mand to go without fail *to Pisa by sea*. He said that it was the obvious thing to do—and that he not merely advised but enjoined it—that there was nothing for me but *warm air* . . no other possible remedy. [. . .] You see there is nothing for me in England during the winter, but to be shut up as I have been:—and the cold kills me and the seclusion exhausts me . . and there is no possible alternative here.

(*EBB to MRM*, 255–6.)

Curiously enough, although Elizabeth Barrett frequently expressed her impatience with the bumblings of the medical profession, she seems to have taken Dr Chambers's word for gospel in this instance; and so did everyone else. Browning added his voice to the chorus: 'I trust you see your . . dare I say . . your *duty* in the Pisa affair, as all else *must* see it' (30 Aug. 1845, pp. 176–7); and again, three days later: 'Surely the report of Dr Chambers is most satisfactory,—all seems to rest with yourself [. . .] try, dearest friend!' (2 Sept. 1845, p. 180.) Elizabeth Barrett agreed: 'the Pisa-case is strengthened all round by his [Dr Chambers's] opinion & injunction' (4 Sept. 1845, p. 182). There is, of course, no way of proving the case one way or another; all we know is that the following winter in England (a mild one, admittedly) did not kill Elizabeth Barrett, and that she seems to have been somewhat inconsistent in her claim that there was 'no other possible remedy'; Miss Mitford had commented two years before that she was 'so foolish still as to cling to London, and so obstinate as to pretend that there is no difference between the air of Wimpole Street and that of the country'; her fault was 'not choosing to do that which everybody advises for her health' (Taplin, 155). It seems clear that she decided to take 'everybody's advice' now because she wanted to; because she had, at last, a real motive for wishing to leave her father's house. The nature of this motive is revealed in a letter which Elizabeth Barrett wrote to Mrs Martin in October, when her departure, she thought, was imminent (*Letters of EBB*, 267–70). She already knew that her father opposed the trip, but she was 'thrown so on my own sense of duty as to feel it right, for the sake of future years, to make an effort to stand by myself as I best can'. Again she repeated 'the unhesitating advice of two able medical men (Dr Chambers, one of them), that to escape the English winter will be *everything for me*, and that it involves the comfort and usefulness of the rest of my life'; and then she gave her reason for taking this advice so seriously:

The cold weather, they say, acts on the lungs [. . .] whereas the necessary shutting up acts on the *nerves* [. . .] And thus, without any mortal disease

[. . .] I am thrown out of life, out of the ordinary sphere of its enjoyment and activity, and made a burden to myself and to others. Whereas there is a means of escape from these evils, and God has opened the door of escape, as wide as I see it!

In all ways, for my own *happiness's sake* I do need *a proof* that the evil is irremediable. And this proof (or the counter-proof) I am about to seek in Italy.

The tone of this is unmistakable. Elizabeth Barrett saw in Robert Browning (not just in going abroad) the 'door of escape' into 'the ordinary sphere' of life from which she had been so long an exile. She knew that Browning would follow her; he had dropped several heavy hints to that effect, and she did nothing to dissuade him. But before she could allow herself to accept Browning's love, she had to be sure that she was in a fit condition to reciprocate it. That is why she seized so eagerly on the idea of wintering abroad: it was a kill-or-cure test of her own principle that she would only do Browning harm by encouraging his affection. If she did not recover in Italy, it would prove her ill health to be 'irremediable', and she would there-fore be justified in continuing to refuse Browning—for his own sake. But if Italy gave her the 'counter-proof'—

Mr Barrett, meanwhile, had relapsed into silence after his 'hard cold letter'. 'Growing gravity in Papa's eyes, & perhaps displeasure deeper within him', Elizabeth Barrett reported to George. 'Perhaps he has relented in his thoughts of me—or perhaps, George (which I conjecture sometimes) perhaps he takes for granted that I have given up my scheme, & his good nature is meant for my compensation— However this may be, I am making every preparation' (*Letters to George Barrett*, 135–6). Despite these preparations (concerning the timetable of steamers to Leghorn, for example, on which she con-sulted Browning), she felt a sense of foreboding: 'in this dead silence of Papa's . . it all seems impossible, . . & I seem to see the stars *con-stellating* against me, and give it as my serious opinion to you that I shall not go' (6 Sept. 1845, p. 184).

By the middle of September, her feeling on the subject was turn-ing sour. The problem was that she could not go entirely alone; she needed one of her brothers and one of her sisters to accompany her, and, without Mr Barrett's goodwill, she did not feel justified in ask-ing them. She plucked up courage to confront her father:

All I asked him to say [. . .] was that he was not displeased with me–& *he wouldn't*; & for me to walk across his displeasure spread on the threshold of the door, & moreover take a sister & brother with me, & do such a thing for the sake of going to Italy & securing a personal advantage, were altogether impossible, obviously impossible! So poor Papa is quite in disgrace with me just now—if he would but care for *that*!

(18 Sept. 1845, p. 205.)

A week later, she made an even more determined effort, with an even more negative result.

I have spoken again, & the result is that we are in precisely the same position,—only with bitterer feelings on one side. If I go or stay they *must* be bitter: words have been said that I cannot easily forget, nor remember without pain [. . .] he complained of the undutifulness & rebellion (!!!) of everyone in the house—& when I asked if he meant that reproach for ME, the answer was that he meant it for all of us, one with another. And I could not get an answer. He would not even grant me the consolation of thinking that I sacrificed what I supposed to be good, to HIM. I told him that my prospects of health seemed to me to depend on taking this step, but that through my affection for him, I was ready to sacrifice those to his pleasure if he exacted it—only it was necessary to my self-satisfaction in future years, to understand definitely that the sacrifice *was* exacted by him & *was* made to him, . . & not thrown away blindly & by a misapprehension. And he would not answer *that*. I might go my own way, he said—*he* would not speak—*he* would not say that he was not displeased with me, nor the contrary:—I had better do what I liked:—for his part, he washed his hands of me altogether—

(25 Sept. 1845, pp. 210–11.)[1]

Even so the matter was not finally concluded; George, now back in Wimpole Street, advised Elizabeth Barrett to continue with her preparations for the voyage, and promised to speak to their father at the last minute. So the charade continued into October, with Elizabeth Barrett finally deciding to travel by a steamer to Gibraltar on the 17th. Both her sisters were willing to accompany her; but Elizabeth Barrett steadfastly refused to involve them, just as she did a year later when it came to the actual knowledge of her marriage. Mr Barrett, for his part, took action to show his disapproval of his daughter's conduct: he stopped paying her his regular nightly visit. Elizabeth Barrett took the point:

he used to sit & talk [. . .] & then *always* kneel & pray with me & for

---

[1] The word 'go' in 'I might go my own way' is emended from 'do' in Kintner.

me—which I used of course to feel as a proof of very kind and affectionate sympathy on his part, & which has proportionably pained me in the withdrawing. They were no ordinary visits, you observe, . . & he could not well throw me further from him than by ceasing to pay them—the thing is quite expressively significant.

(10–11 Oct. 1845, p. 227.)

George spoke to his father on the evening of 12 October, and right up to that time Browning was willing to co-operate in the fiction that Mr Barrett was merely making a 'surprizing and deplorable mistake of mere love and care' (12 Oct. 1845, p. 228); but, on the following day, Elizabeth Barrett reported the outcome of George's attempt, and the whole tone of the discussion changed:

Do not be angry with me—do not think it is my fault—but I *do not go to Italy* . . it has ended as I feared. What passed between George & Papa there is no need of telling: only the latter said that I 'might go if I pleased, but that going it would be under his heaviest displeasure.' George, in great indignation, pressed the question fully . . . but all was vain . . & I am left in this position . . to go, if I please, with his displeasure over me, (which after what you have said & after what Mr. Kenyon has said, and after what my own conscience & deepest moral convictions say aloud, I would unhesitatingly do at this hour!) and necessarily run the risk of exposing my sister and brother to that same displeasure . . from which risk I shrink & fall back & feel that to incur it, is impossible. [. . .] And so, tell me that I am not wrong in taking up my chain again & acquiescing in this hard necessity.

(11–13 Oct. 1845, pp. 232–3.)

This really was the end of the 'Pisa affair'. It had two main features. First Elizabeth Barrett's luck ran out: an issue finally arose in which her 'sense of right' ran 'contrariwise to the way of obedience' required by Mr Barrett. The result was a decisive alienation. 'The bitterest "fact" of all', she told Browning, 'is, that I had believed Papa to have loved me more than he obviously does—: but I never regret knowledge . . I mean I never would *un*know anything . . even were it the taste of the apples by the Dead sea—& this must be accepted like the rest' (11–13 Oct., p. 233). The forbidden fruit is associated here, as in *Paradise Lost* (x. 566–7), with the punishment of the rebel angels, compelled to eat Dead Sea fruit; for Elizabeth Barrett, too has rebelled against a paternal deity ('he complained of the undutifulness & rebellion of everyone in the house'), and, child of Romanticism as she is, bravely refuses to '*un*know anything'.

The second feature followed from the first: Elizabeth Barrett transferred her affection to Browning. The process was straightforward. In the aftermath of her first, abortive confrontation with her father, on 25 September, Browning, for the first time, let Elizabeth Barrett know how he felt about Mr Barrett's conduct. He virtually called Mr Barrett a madman, who ought to be prevented for his own good from injuring his daughter; as for that daughter herself, resistance was her moral and religious duty. 'All passive obedience and implicit submission of will and intellect is far too easy, if well considered, to be the course prescribed by God to Man in this life of probation', he declared; 'stifle your reason altogether and you will find it is difficult to reason ill'. 'The hard thing', he insisted, '[. . .] is to act on one's own best conviction—not to abjure it and accept another will' (25 Sept. 1845, pp. 213–14). Nor did Browning flinch from what was, for him, the personal sting in the whole business. 'You are in what I should wonder at as the veriest slavery—and I who *could* free you from it, I am here— scarcely daring to write'. But he did dare: 'I would marry you now and thus—I would come when you let me, and go when you bade me—I would be no more than one of your brothers [. . .] I deliberately choose the realization of that dream (—of sitting simply by you for an hour every day) rather than any other, excluding you, I am able to form for this world, or any world I know'. These last were among the words which Elizabeth Barrett most cherished: she cited them in her letters of self-justification after her marriage, both to Mrs Martin and to Miss Mitford.

To Browning himself, in her immediate reply (26 Sept. 1845, pp. 215–16), she felt bound to reply that she could not accept his proposal, 'on pain of sinking me so infinitely below not merely your level but my own, that the depth cannot bear a glance down'. But the refusal was a mere formality, which applied simply to Browning's far-fetched idea that he might marry Elizabeth Barrett in her present condition. She went on to give him the open acknowledgement of her love for which he had waited so long. When it came, it was whole-hearted:

to receive such a proof of attachment from YOU, not only overpowers every present evil, but seems to me a full and abundant amends for the merely personal sufferings of my whole life. [. . .] Henceforward I am yours for everything but to do you harm [. . .] none, except God & your will, shall interpose between you & me, . . I mean, that if He should free me within a moderate time from the trailing chain of this weakness, I will then be to you whatever at that hour you shall choose . . whether friend or more than friend . . a friend to the last in any case.

At the end of this letter, Elizabeth Barrett tried (but was too embarrassed) to ask for the return of Browning's first love-letter—the one she had sent back to him and told him to burn. (She plucked up courage to ask for it in November, but Browning had obeyed her and burnt it.) The wheel had come full circle: the crisis of Browning's mistimed declaration in May had, thanks in part to Mr Barrett's unknowing intervention, turned into the cherished memory of love's beginning.

So much, then, for the catalytic effect which Elizabeth Barrett's alienation from her father had on the block which she had established between herself and Browning. But what of Mr Barrett himself? In Part Two (pp. 237–51), I give an account of the way in which Browning and Elizabeth Barrett came to construe Mr Barrett as a selfish tyrant, a process in which the Pisa affair played a leading role, since it seemed to indicate not only that Mr Barrett was dictatorial, but that he was irrational and dangerous as well. Was he? I think not. It is hard to like Mr Barrett, but it is not hard, given a little imagination, to construct a human—if not an attractive—reason as to why he should have objected to Elizabeth Barrett's proposed journey.

It was a reason which Elizabeth Barrett ought perhaps to have appreciated. She might have remembered her own distress when, in September 1843, two of her brothers had gone on holiday abroad: 'it was a hard, terrible struggle with me to be calm and see them go' (*Letters of EBB*, i. 151); or when, a year later, two of her brothers again left England on one of Mr Barrett's merchant ships, the *Statira*, taking a cargo of coal to Alexandria. The proposed trip had been kept from her until the last moment, and, though she gave herself credit in a letter to Miss Mitford for having had 'strength to avoid any scene or weak demonstration', she was bitterly upset; the pleasure to her brothers of a few days in the exotic ports of the Near East was, she thought, 'disproportionate to the long anxiety of those left at home' (*EBB to MRM*, 219). Why should she have been so anxious, on both occasions? She was remembering Torquay, and the drowning of her brother. On the first occasion, she was relieved when she heard that the travellers had crossed the Channel safely: it meant that 'the fatal influences of *my star*' had not operated as they

had with Bro. On the later occasion, she thought in vain of 'the fine
bright weather, and the favorable wind'; Bro had drowned in a sudden squall: 'when the sun shone brightest I was near my greatest
woe'. It had been Mr Barrett's 'greatest woe' too, she believed; his
eldest son, 'the crown of his house', had been lost—and all because
she had *divided the household*. Now she was proposing to do it
again—to take two of her siblings with her and leave England, by
sea. No wonder Mr Barrett loathed the idea. The precedent of his
eldest daughter's absence from home was not encouraging.

His silence on the subject was, in one respect, the counterpart of
Elizabeth Barrett's own; neither of them could bear to refer to the
incident. Perhaps Mr Barrett assumed that his daughter would
understand his feelings without his having to explain them; in any
event, he was unwilling to give such explanations. Here he was
undoubtedly to blame—not for motiveless malignity, but for
obstinate sulkiness. His whole tone of voice, as Elizabeth Barrett
renders it in her report of the argument in which he 'washed his
hands of her', is full of that injured grandeur which seems so high-
minded to most men and so ridiculous to most women. But then,
Elizabeth Barrett's own conduct on that occasion, with its priggish
assumption of moral superiority, might have been especially
designed to try her father's patience—which was not that of a
saint. Mr Barrett was used to getting his own way, and unused to
being put so loftily in the wrong. He was, in the end, the victim of
his own bad temper.

So the lovers, as they now were, settled down to await the
approaching winter. 'Be sure, my own, dearest love, that this is for
the best,' wrote Browning. 'It is hard to bear now—but *you* have to
bear it; any other person could not,—and you will, I know, knowing you—*will* be well this one winter if you can' (14 Oct. 1845,
p. 234). Elizabeth Barrett replied, 'You may be quite sure that I
shall be well this winter [. . .] & that I *will not* be beaten down, if
the will can do anything' (15 Oct. 1845, p. 238). She attributed her
new-found resolution entirely to him; and, in the aftermath of her
alienation from her father, she began to think of safeguarding the
future. From this time forward, she and Browning were conspira-
tors as well as lovers. 'We must be wise', she told him, '[. . .] &
abstain from too frequent meetings, for fear of difficulties. I am
Casandra [*sic*] you know, & smell the slaughter in the bathroom'
(17 Oct. 1845, p. 240). Perhaps it would be unfair to point out that

Mr Barrett was a better candidate than anyone else in Wimpole Street for the role of Agamemnon.

At any rate, a better omen was soon forthcoming. On 6 November, Browning's *Dramatic Romances and Lyrics* appeared; and a presentation copy went to the poet Walter Savage Landor, whom Browning greatly admired, and who in turn had been a friend and supporter of his since the days of *Paracelsus*. 'What a profusion of imagery,' Landor replied, 'covering what a depth of thought. You may stand quite alone, if you will: and I think you will'. But Landor did more than this. He wrote a poem, 'To Robert Browning', which was published in the *Morning Chronicle* on 22 November, in which he compared Browning to Chaucer for his energy, his powers of observation, his 'tongue / So varied in discourse'. But then, picking up an allusion to the 'isles of the siren' in 'The Englishman in Italy', and reflecting on Browning's interest in the foreign and the exotic, and in the past (both history and myth), Landor swerved away from Chaucer and the English tradition, and placed Browning in a different and magical setting:

> But warmer climes
> Bring brighter plumage, stronger wing; the breeze
> Of Alpine heights thou playest with, borne on
> Beyond Sorrento and Amalfi, where
> The Siren waits thee, singing song for song.

To Browning and Elizabeth Barrett, as Elvan Kintner says, these lines 'came to sound like prophecy'; and, in the months which followed the breakthrough of the 'Pisa affair', they gradually consolidated the idea that they were to marry, to elope, to go to Italy. It was Browning's doing that matters advanced beyond the theoretical stage, but there were no great decisive moments; rather, Browning took a step whenever he saw his opportunity, and Elizabeth Barrett was willing to let him do so. At a meeting in January 1846, for example, Browning upset Elizabeth Barrett by asking her whether, in the event that she no longer cared for him, she would go to Italy anyway, for the sake of her health. It was 'the most unkind & hard thing you ever said to me', she lamented; 'That you should have the heart to ask such a question!' When she first knew him she had been 'tired of living . . unaffectedly tired'; her only motive for living was him: 'take away the motive . . & I am where I was'. 'To put it in plainer words . . (as you really require information),' she concluded almost angrily, 'I should let them do what they liked to me till I was dead—only I *wouldn't go to Italy* . . if anybody proposed Italy out of contradiction' (13 Jan. 1846, pp. 384–5). The logical inference of this did not escape Browning: he wanted Elizabeth Barrett to get well whether he were with her or not, but she only wanted to get well for his sake; she must, therefore, agree to an early elopement. 'So begin thinking—,' he told her in his reply, 'as for Spring, as for a New Year, as for a new life' (15 Jan. 1846, p. 388). With this decided, Browning judged that Elizabeth Barrett would be at the peak of her physical strength at the end of the summer; a fortnight later, he wrote to her fixing this deadline. 'I claim your promise's fulfilment—say, at the summer's end [. . .] We can go to Italy for a year or two and be happy as day & night are long' (28 Jan. 1846, p. 425). That, indeed, is what they did. But Italy, and the creative miracle which Landor's verses promised them, were not yet within their reach. There was the London winter for Elizabeth Barrett to get through; and, as the prospect of their marriage became real and near, a whole host of practical considerations began to assail them. How were they to live? What would people say? And what about Mr Barrett? The taste of him which Browning had had in the Pisa affair was nothing compared to what he was going to have to swallow.

5

Secret Lovers

1 Selves and others

And now, my love—I am round you . . my whole life is wound up and down and over you . . I feel you stir everywhere: I am not conscious of thinking or feeling but *about* you, with some reference to you—so I will live, so may I die!

(16 Nov. 1845, p. 271.)

I saw Mr. K., last night at the Amateur Comedy—and heaps of old acquaintances—and came home tired and savage—and *yearned* literally, for a letter this morning, and so it came and I was well again.

(ibid., p. 272.)

From the very beginning, Browning had emphasized to Elizabeth Barrett his hatred of 'society'. At first, his motive was the same as that which prompted him to deny the value of foreign travel—an impulse to depreciate any 'advantages' which were denied to Elizabeth Barrett. But as the two passages above show, his feeling developed in a different direction—towards a contrast between the intimate seclusion which he now shared with Elizabeth Barrett, and the whole of his 'outside' life. Desire created two selves, one of which frequented literary London and the other Elizabeth Barrett's room; the first, the public self, being devalued in comparison with the second. Even 'dear Mr Kenyon' is reduced to an initial, and as for the 'heaps of old acquaintances', they are jumbled together in undignified anonymity. The public self, 'tired and savage', is contrasted with the private self whose feeling is so delicately noted. As always, in Browning, the sense of touch is primary: even the abstract word 'about' ('I am not conscious of thinking or feeling but *about* you') is alive with his sense of being 'round' Elizabeth Barrett, of feeling her 'stir everywhere'. 'For, love, what is it all, this love for you, but an earnest desiring to include you in myself, if that might be,—to feel you in my very heart and hold you there for ever, thro' all chance and earthly changes?' (21 Nov. 1845, p. 283.)

This 'earnest desiring' stems in part from what Browning described to Elizabeth Barrett as a 'primitive folly of mine, which I shall never wholly get rid of, of desiring to do nothing when I cannot do all; seeing nothing, getting, enjoying nothing, where there is no seeing & getting & enjoying *wholly*' (3 May 1845, pp. 53–4). Love of Elizabeth Barrett, therefore, meant, ideally, both total inclusion (of self in self), and total exclusion (of other selves). 'We two, one another's best': Christopher Ricks (*The Brownings: Letters and Poetry*, 8–9) rightly draws attention to the presiding figure of John Donne, Browning's 'revered and magisterial' predecessor: love, which 'makes one little room, an every where', duly performed the miracle in Wimpole Street.[1]

Browning was aware, from an early stage, of a luxury in the absolute distinction between public and private identity: what he called

the deep delight of playing the Eastern Jew's part here in this London— they go about, you know by travel-books, with the tokens of extreme destitution & misery, and steal by blind ways & by-paths to some blank dreary house, one obscure door in it—which being well shut behind them, they grope on thro' a dark corridor or so, and then, a blaze follows the lifting a curtain or the like, for they are in a palace-hall with fountains and light, and marble and gold, of which the envious are never to dream!

(9 July 1845, p. 118.)

Elizabeth Barrett, too, felt the pleasure of Browning's visits in contrast with her 'other' existence (though in her case the 'tokens of extreme destitution & misery' signified something tangible enough); and she was not above savouring the ignorance of those around her. At the same time, there were other considerations which qualified, for her, the 'deep delight' of secrecy. In seeing Browning, to begin with, she was implicitly breaking faith with several other literary men (in particular Richard Horne and Henry

---

[1] The first Donne quotation comes from 'The Ecstasy', l. 4, the second from 'The Good Morrow', l. 11; Browning calls Donne 'revered and magisterial' in l. 912 of *The Two Poets of Croisic*.

Chorley) with whom she had corresponded, but whom she had declined to see 'because she saw nobody'. She was anxious simply on that score for news of Browning's visits to be kept quiet; when she and Browning became lovers, the threat of domestic discovery redoubled her anxiety. She and Browning were enclosed in their private bliss, but they were also locked in it; they were committing a kind of adultery, breaking their 'vows', respectively, of sociableness and invalidism; and she, in particular, was concealing what her father thought of as a real crime.

Accordingly, as Browning and Elizabeth Barrett relaxed in each other's company during the winter of 1845–6, their attitude towards the outside world sharpened into suspicion and apprehension. They began to tell each other of the need for alertness, for caution, in their dealings with other people, even as their dealings with each other became increasingly open and playful. This need for vigilance, as they saw it, also made them chafe. Being forced to wear a mask took the fun out of disguise. Neither Browning nor Elizabeth Barrett, by the end, got much pleasure out of the hypocrisy and deceit they were forced (and forced themselves) to practise. Browning, in this respect, was far better placed than Elizabeth Barrett, since he was able to confide in his immediate family, his mother and father and his sister Sarianna. Elizabeth Barrett, on the other hand, though she could confide in Arabel and Henrietta that she was in love with Browning, dared not expose them to Mr Barrett's anger by telling them that she planned to elope with him, and her brothers were even less in her confidence. As for old friends like Mary Russell Mitford, with whom Elizabeth Barrett had discussed Browning's talent and character long before she knew him, and whom she had begun by telling of Browning's letters and his first visit, Elizabeth Barrett systematically kept them at arm's length. She congratulated herself on her 'good fencing' when Miss Mitford came to see her (31 Oct. 1845, p. 254): 'Your name was not once spoken today', she told Browning; 'when I saw you at the end of an alley of associations, I pushed the conversation up the next'.

Miss Mitford, admittedly, did not like Browning and was not renowned for her tact (though she later kept from Elizabeth Barrett her dismay at the marriage); but no such stigma attached to John Kenyon, and yet Elizabeth Barrett nursed the absurd fear that he, her closest male friend (and a close friend of Browning's, too) would discover and somehow thwart the relationship which he had done so much to bring about. Under the pressure of her jealous insecurity, Kenyon metamorphosed from a benevolent patron into a lynx-eyed moralist, snooping out and condemning her and Browning's rash conduct. His spectacles (which we first hear of in the letter from which I have just quoted, describing Miss Mitford's visit) became a recurrent image for Elizabeth Barrett both of Kenyon's detective powers, and of his presumed disapproval. Her accounts of his visits in the latter part of the courtship are portentous: 'Today Mr. Kenyon came, spectacles & all. He sleeps in those spectacles now, I think. Well, & the first question was . . "Have you seen Mr. Browning? And what did he come for again, pray?" ' (17 Apr. 1846, p. 633.) And on the day after their marriage: 'He came with his spectacles, looking as if his eyes reached to their rim all the way round; & one of the first words was, "*When did you see Browning?*" ' (13 Sept. 1846, p. 1065.) She made Browning promise never to yield to the temptation to confide in Kenyon; she was convinced that he would attempt to persuade him to give her up—for her own good, of course. 'Oh, what a vision, *that* is! [. . .] it takes away my breath—the likelihood of it is so awful that it seems to *promise* to realize itself, one day!' (29 July 1846, p. 914.) And her anxiety on this occasion made her really intemperate: 'But *you promised*. I have your solemn promise, Robert!—If ever you should be moved by a single one of those vain reasons, it will be an unfaithful cruelty in you—You will have trusted *another*, against *me*' (ibid., p. 915).

In the event, it was Browning who more correctly anticipated Kenyon's response. 'Ours is the only thoroughly rational match that ever came under my notice,' Browning asserted, 'and he [Kenyon] is too clever not to see *some* justification in it' (30 July 1846, p. 916). Even this was an underestimate: 'I know no two persons so worthy of each other', Kenyon wrote to Elizabeth Barrett after the marriage; 'if the thing had been asked of me, I should have advised it'. So much for the spectacles! But the real point lies in Elizabeth Barrett's emphatic injunction to Browning about trusting '*another*, against *me*'; it sums up the closed circle (closed even against Kenyon) which they drew around themselves as the courtship progressed.

The threat from within Wimpole Street, of course, was both more realistic and more difficult to deal with. The 'Pisa affair' merely demonstrated Mr Barrett's selfishness and injustice; now Elizabeth

Barrett had to make her lover aware of her father's—'peculiarity' was the word she fixed on. Apparently Browning found it hard to take in. Elizabeth Barrett told him as early as September 1845 that her father 'never *does* tolerate in his family (sons or daughters) the development of one class of feelings' (16 September 1845, p. 196), and a month later she was reiterating her point, 'that if you came too often & it was *observed*, difficulties & vexations wd follow as a matter of course' (21–2 Oct. 1845, pp. 242–3); but in reply to this, Browning blithely remarked, 'For your friends [he is using the archaic term for 'relations'] . . whatever can be "got over," whatever opposition may be rational, will be easily removed, I suppose' (23 Oct. 1845, p. 246). He still did not appreciate that the opposition was singular (in every sense); 'In relation to WHOM, however,' as Elizabeth Barrett put it, 'there will be no "getting over"—you might as well think to sweep off a third of the stars of Heaven with the motion of your eyelashes' (24 Oct. 1845, p. 248). Browning's incredulity outlasted even this: as late as December he was proposing to write a letter to Mr Barrett which Elizabeth Barrett was to give to him if she and her father had an argument about him! 'No', said Elizabeth Barrett; 'it would seem like a prepared apology for something wrong—And besides, . . the apology would be nothing but the offence in another form' (12 Dec. 1845, p. 319).

Besides the central fact of her father's intransigence, there were a number of other annoyances with which Browning and Elizabeth Barrett had to come to terms. Some of them sprang directly from the main obstacle. When she was planning to go to Pisa, Browning wanted to give her a travelling-cloak; but 'do you consider', wrote Elizabeth Barrett, ' . . how many talkers there are in this house, & what would be talked—or that it is not worth while to provoke it all? And Papa, knowing it, would not like it' (1 Oct. 1845, p. 219). It was equally out of the question, Elizabeth Barrett told Browning, for him to be formally invited to Wimpole Street to meet other members of the family; Mr Barrett did not allow his children to issue such invitations (26 Jan. 1846, p. 423). Later on still, in the summer of 1846, Browning proposed an outing to New Cross to meet *his* parents. Elizabeth Barrett again refused. Not, of course, that she wanted to neglect 'even the forms of respect & affection towards your family'; but, as it happened, it was not 'the usual worldly form' for a lady to pay such a call, and so its omission could not be construed as neglect; and, she went on, 'Your father &

mother would be blamed (in this house, I know, if not in others) for not apprizing my father of what they knew' (12 June 1846, pp. 773–4). She and Browning nearly quarrelled on this point. 'What possible harm can follow from their knowing?' Browning burst out. 'Why should I wound them to the very soul and for ever [. . .] As to any harm or blame that can attach itself to *them*,—it is too absurd to think of!' (12 June 1846, p. 775.) 'You think that nothing can be said—I wish *I* could think so', Elizabeth Barrett replied (12 June 1846, p. 778). Her caution, whether justified or not, prevailed; she and Browning left England without her having met any member of Browning's family. (They had not yet returned when, in March 1849, Browning's mother died; neither he nor Elizabeth Barrett ever met the parent who was most dear to the other.)

The one member of Elizabeth Barrett's family whom Browning did meet a number of times was her brother George, at evening parties at Mr Kenyon's house. They got on reasonably well: Browning, of course, could only say, after the first meeting, 'I like him very much and mean to get a friend in him' (21 Nov. 1845, p. 283); as for the lawyer (who was laughed at in Wimpole Street for his stuffiness), he found the poet 'unassuming' (22 Nov. 1845, p. 286). On a later occasion, and without being prompted, he compared Browning's conversation favourably with that of Tennyson; for which Elizabeth Barrett forgave him the 'barristerially' pompous manner in which he delivered his opinion (1 May 1846, p. 667). She built a false foundation of hope on these fragments of acquaintance: George was furious at the elopement, and it took several years before the breach was healed.

On Browning's side, the secret of his visits to Elizabeth Barrett was kept watertight. Wimpole Street was, of course, a good deal less secure: there were many more Barretts, they were great gossips, especially the men, and they soon latched on to Elizabeth Barrett's new visitor as a fertile source of amusement. Not in front of Mr Barrett, of course; they all knew better than that. 'I told you once', Elizabeth Barrett wrote to Browning, 'that we held hands the faster in this house for the weight over our heads' (15 Jan. 1846, p. 395). It was fortunate, nevertheless, that Mr Barrett, in his daughter's graphic phrase, '*never* draws an inference of this order, until the bare blade of it is thrust palpably into his hand' (12 Dec. 1845, p. 319); for the house was filled with 'suspicions & conjectures', not just about Elizabeth Barrett, but about her sister Henrietta's romance with Captain Surtees Cook, whom she eventually married (to be rejected and disinherited like her sister). A Barrett cousin from Jamaica came to stay, 'an intimate friend of my brothers besides the relationship, & they talk to him as to each other,' Elizabeth Barrett reported; and this cousin made her afraid to venture downstairs:

Think of his beginning to attack Henrietta the other day . . 'So Mr. C. has retired & left the field to Surtees Cook. Oh . . you needn't deny . . it's the news of all the world except your father. And as to *him*, I don't blame you—he never will consent to the marriage of son or daughter.—Only you should consider, you know, because he won't leave you a shilling, &c &c . . . ' You hear the sort of man. And then in a minute after . . 'And what is this about Ba?' 'About Ba' said my sisters, 'why who has been persuading you of such nonsense?' 'Oh, my authority is very good,—perfectly unnecessary for you to tell any stories, Arabel,—a literary friendship, is it?' . . . and so on . . after that fashion!

(6 Mar. 1846, p. 521.)

On a later occasion, her brothers were teasing her about a rumoured engagement between Browning and a certain 'Miss Campbell'; and when she denied it, one of them remarked

that 'of course Ba must know, as she & Mr. Browning are such VERY inti-·mate friends,' & a good deal of laughter on all sides: on which, without any transition & with an exceeding impertinence, Alfred threw himself down on the sofa & declared that he felt inclined to be very ill, . . for that then perhaps (such things being heard of) some young lady might come to visit *him* [. . .]

(24 May 1846, p. 727.)

Elizabeth Barrett conveys this with a story-teller's relish; but you wonder how she felt, knowing her brothers were nearer to the truth than they realised. It is likely, however, that such teasing meant the opposite of what it appeared; that her brothers could not conceive of their eldest sister, at forty years of age, *seriously* conducting a clandestine romance, let alone defying their father and leaving home. Elizabeth Barrett surprised them; but then, she surprised herself.

2 Money

How to keep the relationship secret was one problem; but how it would look when it was no longer secret was another. Browning and Elizabeth Barrett, of course, disagreed as to which of them would be thought to have taken advantage of the other. When this disagreement concerned their own self-opinion, it took its place in the familiar debate about who was whose superior, and there is no need to document it here. But there was one aspect of the relationship on which they both knew 'the world' would comment. A clandestine marriage meant no 'settlement'—no legal and financial transaction between the parties or their families. That was one of the reasons why Elizabeth Barrett thought that Mr Kenyon would be against the idea: 'a marriage without lawyers would be an abomination in his sight' (9 June 1846, p. 772). This is not as unreasonable as it sounds. Mr Kenyon would not have been objecting to the absence of merely formal documents, but to the absence of safeguards for Elizabeth Barrett. Without a legal settlement, all her property would pass to Browning after marriage, and he could then do what he liked with it. She was effectively putting herself in his power.

This would not have mattered so much, but for the added circumstance that Browning had no money of his own, and no immediate prospect of getting any. He was living with his parents, he had no employment, and his books, which were published at his father's expense, brought in virtually nothing. In other words, not only did a clandestine marriage mean that Elizabeth Barrett's property was unsecured, it meant that Browning was laying himself open to the charge of marrying for money. And the charge was in fact made—by the Barretts. The sums involved, in terms of annual income, were relatively small, as we shall see, and the whole idea seems absurd at this distance; but it did not seem absurd to some at the time. It was undoubtedly the most unpleasant question which Browning and Elizabeth Barrett had to face besides the opposition of her father. The fact that they both, as they reaffirmed to each other, despised mercenary considerations in marriage, did not free them from the necessity of considering what would be said by those who did not.

Browning had, in a sense, made a brave decision to be a professional poet and live off his parents. Novelists in the 1830s and 40s could make enough money to live on; so could playwrights (this partly accounts for Browning's long and vain pursuit of success in the theatre); so could journalists, essayists, pamphleteers . . . but not poets. Not without another profession (such as Matthew Arnold) or a public pension (such as Tennyson). Browning had neither. He had not even the dignity of doing hackwork in the reviews. As a result, his status among other writers and in London 'society' was equivocal. There was admiration (from Kenyon, from Richard Monckton Milnes, and from Elizabeth Barrett, even before she knew him), but there was also criticism, and the criticism was tinged with contempt.

Both Browning and Elizabeth Barrett were acutely aware of all this. Browning, to begin with, was eager to assure Elizabeth Barrett that he *could* find work if he wanted to, and that he *would* if it were necessary (that is, for securing her father's consent; it took him a while to understand that Mr Barrett's opposition had no such motive, and even when he was released from this worry, there was still the question of what everyone else would think and say). As soon as he saw Elizabeth Barrett beginning to return his affection (during the 'Pisa affair' in the late summer of 1845), he began to make what he felt were the required gestures:

My whole scheme of life, (with its wants, material wants at least, closely cut down,) was long ago calculated—and it supposed *you*, the finding such an one as you, utterly impossible—because in calculating one goes upon *chances*, not on providence—how could I expect you? So for my own future way in the world I have aways refused to care [. . .] but now I see you near this life, all changes—and at a word, I will do all that ought to be done,—that everyone used to say could be done [. . .]

(13 Sept. 1845, pp. 193–4.)

Elizabeth Barrett, in her reply, of course refused to speak this 'word'. And, in the course of a letter which was supposedly devoted to persuading him to abandon the idea of marriage, she let him know that marriage was financially feasible! 'You must leave me', she wrote, '—these thoughts of me [. . .] & force your mind at once into another channel'. Further on:

I will say, in reply to some words of yours, that you cannot despise the gold & gauds of the world more than I do, & should do even if I found a use for them. And if I *wished* to be very poor, in the world's sense of poverty, I *could not*, with three or four hundred a year of which no living will can dispossess me. And is it not the chief good of money, the being free from the need of thinking of it?

(16 Sept. 1845, pp. 196–7.)

There is a clear enough signal; even so, the tone of Browning's reply is still nervous and defensive:

One final word on the other matters—the 'worldly matters'—I shall own I alluded to them rather ostentatiously, because—because *that would be* the *one* poor sacrifice I could make you—one I would cheerfully make,—but a sacrifice, and the only one; this careless 'sweet habitude of living'—this absolute independence of mine, which, if I had it not, my heart would starve and die for, I feel, and which I have fought so many good battles to preserve—for that has happened, too—this light rational life I lead, and know so well that I lead; this I could give up for nothing less than—what you know—but I *would* give it up, not for you merely, but for those whose disappointment might re-act on you—and I should break no promise to myself—the money getting would not be for the sake of *it* [. . .] one must not be too old, they say, to begin their ways: but, in spite of all the babble, I feel sure that whenever I make up my mind to that, I can be rich enough and to spare [. . .]

(16 Sept. 1845, p. 200.)

But Browning did not have to fight any 'good battles' with Elizabeth Barrett to preserve his 'absolute independence', his 'light rational life' (he chooses these terms because they challenge the notion that he was dependent on his parents and unreasonable in following his vocation without money); she was as eager as he was to maintain his self-respect:

if I were in a position to accept sacrifices from you, I would not accept *such* a sacrifice . . amounting to a sacrifice of duty & dignity as well as of ease & satisfaction . . to an exchange of higher work for lower work . . & of the special work you are called to, for that which is work for anybody. I am not so ignorant of the right uses & destinies of what you have & are.

(17 Sept. 1845, p. 203.)

Elizabeth Barrett, with unearned income of 'three or four hundred a year', could afford her high-mindedness; but both she and Browning were forced to acknowledge that others might see it differently. Elizabeth Barrett, who had already argued the point with Miss Mitford before she knew Browning (*EBB to MRM*, 115, 172), heard from her again in July 1845 on the subject, and had to defend Browning against an anonymous 'visitor and family friend' of the Brownings, who had reported that Browning's family were unhappy with his 'want of masculine resolve to work like common men'. (Miss Mitford was curiously insistent on Browning's supposed effeminacy.) Elizabeth Barrett rejected the imputation: Browning was 'eminently masculine and downright—strikingly so I think!' As for his family, they 'may regret perhaps that he does not, by means of his talents, climb the woolsack rather than Parnassus Hill—*that* sort of regret is possible enough!—but I feel quite confident that if his position had required him to work, he is the last man under sun to shrink from it—I would throw down my silken gauntlet to maintain that point' (ibid., pp. 250–1).

She kept this particular piece of malicious gossip from Browning; but in April 1846 she was further irritated by Mr Kenyon, who reported the opinion of one of Browning's society acquaintances, Mrs Anne Procter (wife of B. W. Procter, the lawyer and minor writer who published under the name 'Barry Cornwall') that 'it was a pity he [Browning] didn't have seven or eight hours a day of occupation'. 'I really *could* SAY something to *that*', Elizabeth Barrett told Browning. 'And I did say that you "did not *require* an occupation as a means of living . . having simple habits & desires—nor as an end of living, since you found one in the exercise of your genius! & that if Mr. Procter had looked as simply to his art as an end, he would have done better things' (12 Apr. 1846, p. 615). Browning could only agree with Elizabeth Barrett's conclusion that 'to put race horses into dray carts, was not usually done nor advised': 'Mrs. Procter is very exactly the Mrs. Procter I knew long ago', he replied. 'What she says is of course purely foolish. The world does seem incurably stupid on this, as other points' (14 Apr. 1846, p. 622). But in a meeting which took place the day after this letter was written, Browning apparently felt impelled to justify himself further, with 'profusions of confusions of speech about Mrs. Procter and her wise notions' (16 Apr. 1845, p. 627). And Elizabeth Barrett, too, was perhaps not quite so confident of outfacing the Mrs Procters of this world; for, in the same letter in which she reported her spirited reply to Mr Kenyon, she proposed to Browning that they conceal the fact that they were marrying on her money, a proposal which, she said, had been in her mind for a long time:

The peculiarity of our circumstances will enable us to be free of the world . . of our friends even . . of all observation & examination, in certain respects: now let us use the advantage which falls to us from our misfortune,—&, since we must act for ourselves at last, let us resist the curiosity of the whole race of third persons [. . .] & put it into the power of nobody to say to himself or to another, . . 'She had so much, & he, so much, in worldly possessions—or she had not so much & he had not so much.' Try to understand what I mean. As it is not the least importance to either of us, as long as we can live, whether the sixpence, we live by, came most from

you or from me . . & as it will be as much mine as yours, & yours as mine,
when we are together . . why let us join in throwing a little dust in all the
winking eyes round—oh, it is nonsense & weakness, I know—but I would
rather, rather, see winking eyes than staring eyes. What has anybody to do
with us? Even my own family . . why should they *ever* see the farthest
figure of *our* affairs, as to mere money?

(12 Apr. 1846, p. 616.)

The anxious emphasis of this passage clearly implies that Elizabeth
Barrett did worry that people would think it unmanly of Browning
to live off her money, and for once her common sense deserted her;
there was no way in which she and Browning could have disguised a
difference in their incomes which too many people already knew
about or could easily discover. Browning, too, later admitted to
having had 'a few misgivings at first', but declared that 'I am not
proud, or rather, am proud in the right place' (26 Aug. 1846,
p. 1005); and he seems to have been much more upset by the idea
that his lack of money would be attributed to weakness or incompe-
tence on his part than that he was not conforming to the convention
of the male being the provider.

This point arose again in June 1846, when Browning, in spite of
what she had told him several times in the past, mistakenly understood Elizabeth Barrett to imply that his suit would be objected to
in Wimpole Street because of his financial position. 'Does anybody
doubt that I can by application in proper quarters obtain quite
enough to support us both in return for no extraordinary expendi-
ture of such faculties as I have?' he wrote (12 June 1846, p. 775).
And he came up with a concrete proposal to demonstrate that he
meant what he said: he would write to Lord Monteagle (former
Chancellor of the Exchequer), 'who reads and likes my works, as he
said at Moxon's two days ago on calling there for a copy to give
away', and say to him: 'When you are minister next month, as is
expected, will you give me for my utmost services about as much as
you give Tennyson for nothing?' This Browning affirmed, 'would
be rational and easy as all rationality. *Let me do so, and at once, my
own* Ba!' She, for her part, was to 'transfer your own advantages to
your brothers or sisters [. . .] So shall the one possible occasion of
calumny be removed and all other charges go for the simple absur-
dities they will be' (ibid., p. 776). The tone of this is shrill and
uneasy, particularly in the rankling remark about Tennyson's Civil
List pension. It does not say much for Browning's practical good

sense, either, since Lord Monteagle was in retirement and had no prospect of returning to office; moreover, as Elizabeth Barrett gently pointed out, if Browning were thinking of a diplomatic post, 'how do you know that you may not be sent to Russia, or somewhere impossible for me to winter in?' (12 June 1846, p. 779.) As to the proposal that she should divest herself of her income, Elizabeth Barrett turned it down:

you are generous & noble as always—but, no, . . I shall refuse steadily for reasons which are plain, to put away from me God's gifts . . given perhaps in order to this very end . . & apart from which, I should not have seen myself justified [. . .] to cast the burden of me upon you. *No.* I care as little for money as you do—but this thing I will not agree to because I ought not. [. . .] I should laugh to scorn all *that* sort of calumny . . even if I could believe it to be possible. Supposing that you sought *money*, you would not be quite so stupid, the world may judge for itself, as to take hundreds instead of thousands, & pence instead of guineas.

(ibid., p. 778.)

Browning gave in to her judgement: 'I will care nothing about diplomatism or money-getting extraordinary', he promised (13 June 1846, p. 780). His letter crossed with Elizabeth Barrett's next, in which she reaffirmed her refusal to give her money away, her incredulity at the idea of Browning being thought of as a fortune-hunter, and that fortune's small size. She was no great catch, she assured him. 'People are more likely to say that *I have taken you in*' (13 June 1846, p. 782).

In fact, as she went on to tell him, Elizabeth Barrett did not know exactly how much money she had. Mr Barrett managed her money: 'I am not "allowed" to spend what I might—but the motive is of course a kind one . . there is no mistaking *that*. Poor Papa!—He attends just to those pecuniary interests which no one cares for, with a scrupulous attention'. Later on, with the prospect of marriage nearer, Browning realized that he, too, ought to pay some attention to this point; so, with some embarrassment, he asked Elizabeth Barrett to 'ascertain what you certainly possess—what is quite yours, and in your sole power, to take or to let remain—what will be just as available to you in Italy as in England' (5 Aug. 1846, p. 933). Elizabeth Barrett replied (5 Aug. 1846, pp. 935–7) that she had about £8,000 in government stocks, from which she drew a quarterly income of between £40 and £45, and £200 annually from what she called 'the ship money', that is shares in the *David Lyon*, a merchant ship trading with the West Indies. She never touched this 'ship money'; it was always reinvested, currently in safe railway stock. 'Whatever I have, is mine', she emphasized, ' . . & for use in Italy, as in England'; her father 'could not for a moment think of interfering with an incontestable right of property'. The only problem was that her situation made it difficult for her to ask for a large cash sum without arousing suspicion; and the actual elopement, in the end, was financed by a loan of £100 from Browning's father.

Browning, who had travelled widely in Italy, must have known that Elizabeth Barrett's income was more than enough for two people with reasonable tastes. On this point, too, the lovers had several discussions. During a visit in March 1846, Browning mentioned the luxury in which his friend, the journalist and writer Henry Chorley, lived, and remarked that, although he did not care for such things, other people might. Elizabeth Barrett immediately realized that he meant her; she could not bring herself to say anything at the time, but poured out her feelings in her next letter (15 Mar. 1846, pp. 535–6), assuring Browning that he need not worry about her having expensive tastes or longing for luxuries which he would, of course, be unable to provide. 'All I meant was,' wrote Browning, 'to express a very natural feeling—if one could give you diamonds for flowers, and if you liked diamonds,—then, indeed!' (16 Mar. 1846, p. 539.)

This was one of a number of occasions on which Browning and Elizabeth Barrett assured each other of their preference for a plain style of living. At a meeting in July 1846, for example, they discussed 'house-rents and styles of living' in Italy, and Browning, in his letter the following day (22 July 1846, p. 893), had again to overcome his embarrassment to beg Elizabeth Barrett 'to consult my feelings on the only point in which they are sensitive to the world', by living 'as simply and cheaply as possible, down to my own habitual simplicity and cheapness'—so that no one could accuse him, if they lived in a large house or kept a carriage, that he was spending his wife's money on himself. Elizabeth Barrett promptly agreed: 'The more simply we live, the better for *me*!' (22 July 1846, p. 895.) All this made it slightly awkward for her to explain to Browning how it came about that, living in Wimpole Street at her father's charge, she was far from emulating Browning's 'habitual simplicity and cheapness'; on the contrary, she managed to spend (and at times overspend) her quarterly income of £40, a considerable sum, given that she had virtually no living expenses. It was not on dress, she hastened to say: 'Never in any one year of my life, even when I was well, have my expenses in dress [. . .] exceeded twenty pounds' (5 Aug. 1846, p. 936). The gown she wore at their last meeting had cost five shillings. 'My greatest personal expense lately has been *the morphine*' she said; for the rest, she was vague enough: 'the money flows out of window & door . . you will understand how it flows like a stream. I have not the gift (if it is a gift) of making dykes . . in my situation, here. Elsewhere, all changes, you know—You shall not call me extravagant—you will see.'

It was Browning's anxiety about money, in the end, which produced the oddest document to be found in the correspondence. In his eagerness to demonstrate that he was not fortune-hunting, he took up a suggestion originally made by Elizabeth Barrett that her money should revert to her family after their deaths, if Browning so wished (12 June 1846, p. 778). He asked her, at a meeting on 25 July 1846, to put this in writing, and so, with a proper sense of the ridiculous at this exercise of her 'legal genius', she sent with her next letter (26 July 1846, pp. 901–4) the following declaration, written on a separate slip of paper:

In compliance with the request of Robert Browning, who may possibly become my husband, that I would express in writing my wishes respecting the ultimate disposal of whatever property I possess at this time, whether in the funds or elsewhere, . . I here declare my wishes to be . . that he, Robert Browning, . . having, of course, as it is his right to do, first held & used the property in question for the term of his natural life, . . should bequeath the same, by an equal division, to my two sisters, or, in the case of the previous death of either or both of them, to such of my surviving brothers as most shall need it by the judgement of my eldest surviving brother.

Elizabeth Barrett Barrett
Wimpole Street: July, 1846.

George would have been proud of her. However, she and Browning had neglected one vital point in their discussion of this arrangement. It suddenly struck Browning that 'There may even be a *claimant*, instead of a recipient, of whatever either of us can bequeath—who knows?' (27 July 1846, p. 906.) In other words, he and Elizabeth Barrett might have a child.

3   The nature of love

Although Browning and Elizabeth Barrett refer often enough in their letters to the physical side of their relationship, they do so casually, for the most part; they almost never discuss it directly. They chose to write about other things, probably because there was more to say. This does not mean that there was no physical contact between them, or that the subject embarrassed them; simply that they agreed about it, and found nothing to refine upon or analyse. They took each other physically for granted, in part because each of them fitted the other's ideal type—down to the colour of Browning's hair, as Elizabeth Barrett told him. They were alone in her room for the duration of their meetings, but there was no possibility—even had there been any likelihood—of the physical contact between them going further than embracing and kissing. It got that far in stages, if Sonnet XXXIX of *Sonnets From the Portuguese* is to be believed: first a kiss on 'The fingers of this hand wherewith I write'; then a kiss which 'sought the forehead, & half missed, / Half falling on the hair'; then a kiss on the lips, 'since when, indeed, / I have been proud, and said, . . "My Love, my own." ' One of the few direct comments on these kisses comes from Browning, and it connects with one of the topics which, as we shall see, was uppermost in the lovers' minds. 'I would not have dared to take the blessing of kissing your hand, much less your lip', Browning told Elizabeth Barrett, ' . . but that it seemed as if I was leading you into a mistake,—as did happen—and that you might fancy I only felt a dreamy, abstract passion for a phantom of my own creating out of your books and letters, and which only took your name' (3 June 1846, p. 753). This makes it clear that it was Browning who initiated the kissing, and in fact almost all the references in the letters to these kisses are his (they begin in the aftermath of the 'Pisa affair', and go on increasing in frequency in the letters of 1846); but there is no sense that Elizabeth Barrett was less passionate than he, only that their kisses had a greater meaning for Browning, both for the reason he gave, and as a displacement or evasion of language, or even of the inferior medium of sight (like the lovers in 'Love Among the Ruins' who 'extinguish sight and speech, / Each on each').

It was in language that the lovers had most of their contact, and even here it is their letters which survive, not, except for a few traces, the words they spoke at their meetings. Our view of the courtship is influenced by the fact that we have access only to the kinds of experience which are susceptible of being recorded. The letters tell us that Browning and Elizabeth Barrett were preoccupied by a number of topics of feeling, which they discussed seriously or playfully, simply or elaborately, literally or metaphorically—but, in any event, minutely and at length. These topics, in turn, preoccupy us, and we tend to discount or ignore what is *not written*. But we can be fairly sure, even from the little we know, that the subjects explored in the letters were not those which were spoken of in the meetings. Browning several times remarked on his being awkward or tongue-tied during his visits, and Elizabeth Barrett spoke of 'the curious double feeling I had about you . . you personally, & you as the writer of these letters', and how, at first, 'I could not help but that the writer of the letters seemed nearer to me [. . .] than did the personal visitor' (4 Jan. 1846, pp. 359–60). It seems that the visits were less taken up with talk *about* love, at first because of the lovers' diffidence or caution, and then because of their increasing intimacy.

In part, this implies that the long and complex discussions in their letters about the nature of their feelings for each other were a substitute for each other's silent and passionate presence in their meetings. But the nature of these meetings must have been in part determined by what had been and was being said in the letters. Though Browning, in particular, repeatedly stressed the inadequacy of writing as a medium of feeling, there is no doubt that the correspondence developed an energy and momentum of its own, that Browning and Elizabeth Barrett loved each other *in* their letters. They were both subject to the process by which the act of writing generates at least some, if not all, of its own material. Their feelings for each other did not exist, objectively, in a given quantity which they gradually discovered and mined out like a seam of ore; the letters created the seam as they advanced.

Browning and Elizabeth Barrett both had fixed ideas (long before they met) about love and their own place in an ideal relationship. Their love language is in part the product of these ideas, so that at times they seem like two prima donnas on the same stage, singing simultaneous and separate arias. In this sense, the element of interchange in the letters, the way in which phrases and images and subjects are picked up and exchanged, is sometimes deceptive; the mutuality it suggests exists in appearance only, while the difference in point of view remains as great as ever.

Nor were these fixed ideas altered by the actual process of the courtship. On the contrary, they were strengthened; both Browning and Elizabeth Barrett married each other proclaiming their firm belief that their partner's love was a providential and miraculous blessing, which they did not deserve but were determined to do their best to justify by their future conduct. This exactly corresponded with their own preconceived notions of what an ideal match would be, and with their attitudes throughout the whole preceding twenty months, going back to the very first letters they wrote; and Browning, for one, was emphatic that there had been no change in his feelings, but only development.

Nevertheless, though there may be no dialogue in the letters, they comprise an *encounter* between Browning and Elizabeth Barrett which is vital to our understanding of how the relationship developed. After the 'Pisa affair', over the winter of 1845–6 and most of the following spring and summer, very little 'happened' in the courtship. There were no further confrontations between Elizabeth Barrett and her father. Browning finished his two plays, *Luria* and *A Soul's Tragedy*, for which Elizabeth Barrett adopted without question her role of critic. Her health continued to improve. There was nothing, of course, comparable with the crisis of Browning's first, abortive declaration. The only 'event' of any importance was the actual decision to marry and go to Italy, which was made in late January 1846, when Browning claimed the fulfilment of Elizabeth Barrett's promise 'at the summer's end' (28 Jan. 1846, p. 425). But (as I will be showing in the next chapter) it took Elizabeth Barrett a tremendous mental effort, an effort of realization and concentration, to carry the decision out; and in the end Browning had to take advantage of an opportunity (again, provided unwittingly by poor Mr Barrett) to precipitate her into marriage and flight.

In this context, the discussions of love in the letters had a function quite separate from that of coming to any conclusions. They were a means of affirming, or rather demonstrating, the reality of the love which they described. Given the static character of the relationship and its physical limitations, rhetoric was the one resource which was equally available to both lovers. Their love language, with all its searching and discriminating analysis of shade upon shade of feeling, is like a dance, which displays to the other person, in a pattern of corresponding gestures, the rhythm of the silent music to which it is performed.

At this point, however, we need to discriminate between the effect on Browning and Elizabeth Barrett of each other's love language. Browning could and did assimilate Elizabeth Barrett's declarations of love into the design of the relationship of which he was the architect. Such declarations 'proved' the divine superiority of her nature to his own, even (or especially) when she was attributing to *him* the qualities of generosity and goodness which he identified with *her*. In one letter (19 Apr. 1846, pp. 637–9) he tried to explain to her 'why the *wrongness* in you should be so exquisitely dear to me, dear as the *rightness*, or dearer, inasmuch as it is the topmost grace of all'; the 'wrongness' consisting in her 'strange unconsciousness of how the love-account really stands between us,—*who* was giver altogether and who taker'. And after passionately restating the true balance of the account from his side ('I solemnly assure you I cannot imagine any point of view wherein I ought to appear to any rational creature the benefitting party and you the benefitted [. . .] you are immeasurably my superior [. . .] I *know* and could prove you are as much my Poet as my Mistress' etc.), Browning concludes: 'I love your inability to feel it in spite of right and justice and rationality. [. . .] So Shakespeare chose to "envy this man's art and that man's scope" in the Sonnets'. The allusion is to Sonnet XXIX ('When in disgrace with fortune and men's eyes'), l. 7: 'Desiring this man's art, and that man's scope'. Browning argues that Shakespeare is the more admirable for not, as it were, knowing that he was Shakespeare; his obliviousness is proved by his envy of other writers (if he knew he was 'Shakespeare' he would know he was better than they), and we, his readers, have the satisfaction of conferring on him as a reward the title which was his by right, but which he was too modest to claim for himself. In the same way, Elizabeth Barrett, in her 'unconsciousness' of being the 'giver' and not the 'taker' in her relationship with Browning, displays the 'topmost grace of all', the grace of humility, which actually demonstrates the superiority which it denies. Browning's analogy works well provided you take as your premiss the real (i.e. factual, objectively established) supremacy of the unknowing subject of your praise, and of course the comparison with Shakespeare implicitly puts Elizabeth Barrett on exactly this kind of pedestal. By the mid-nineteenth century, the 'right and justice and rationality' of

Shakespeare's pre-eminence were undisputed. Elizabeth Barrett might well have retorted that Browning had no warrant, in the case of their debate as to who was the other's superior, for usurping the role of posterity.

She, for her part, did not have Browning's resource of incorporating whatever she said into a pre-determined scheme; on the contrary, the effect on her of his protestations of love and devotion was complex and ambivalent, and it took her a long time to find a way of reconciling the two conflicting emotions which they aroused in her. You might say that Browning's rhetoric did him nearly—but not quite—as much harm as good. It compelled Elizabeth Barrett to believe in the reality of his feelings, but it stimulated her doubts about herself as the object of such feelings. Browning's language constructed, in front of her eyes, an image of herself with which she could not identify.

Her sense of this emerges early in the relationship. During their argument over the propriety of her acting as critic of his poems, when she was writing her notes on 'The Flight of the Duchess', Browning claimed that he would be 'one glow of gratitude [. . .] if you can warm your finger-tips and so do yourself that much real good, by setting light to a dozen "Duchesses": why ought I not to say this when it is so true?' (13 July 1845, p. 121.) This was too much for Elizabeth Barrett; she expostulated in her next letter:

it is difficult to thank you, or *not* to thank you, for all your kindnesses [. . .] Only Mrs. Jameson told me of Lady Byron's saying 'that she knows she is burnt every day in effigy by half the world, but that the effigy is so unlike herself as to be inoffensive to her'—and just so, or rather just in the converse of *so*, is it with me & your kindnesses. They are meant for quite another than I, or are too far to be so near. The comfort is . . in seeing you throw all those ducats out of the window, . . (& how many ducats go in a figure to a 'dozen Duchesses,' it is profane to calculate) the comfort is that you will not be the poorer for it in the end; since the people beneath, are honest enough to push them back under the door. Rather a bleak comfort & occupation though!

(16–17 July 1845, p. 126.)

The allusion to Lady Byron has a wider application than the personal one which Elizabeth Barrett makes here; like Byron's 'Princess of Parallelograms', Elizabeth Barrett was famous without being known—the legend of her seclusion had established for her an identity separate from her own. 'Half the world' as well as Browning worshipped her 'every day in effigy'. 'Once I had this proposition', she later lamented, '—"If we mayn't come in, *will you stand up at the window that we may see?*" ' (21 May 1846, p. 720.) But this enthusiasm was uncomfortably close to Browning's before he was allowed in, and afterwards it did not diminish, but became more intense and, to Elizabeth Barrett's eyes, more unreasonable. In that last remark about the 'bleak comfort & occupation' of restoring to Browning all the praise he wasted on her, there is a pathos which Elizabeth Barrett was eventually to overcome; but her complaint got worse before it got better.

Like Browning, Elizabeth Barrett claimed to know herself, her own real worth; and on that basis, Browning's admiration of her seemed not only perverse, but ill-omened. 'You see in me what is not:—*that*, I know', she remarked; '& you overlook in me what is unsuitable to you . . *that* I know, & have sometimes told you' (16 Sept. 1845, p. 195); and again, in her next letter: 'That *you* should care at all for *me* has been a matter of unaffected wonder to me from the first hour until now—& I cannot help the pain I feel sometimes, in thinking that it would have been better for you if you never had known me . . May God turn back the evil of me!' (17 Sept. 1845, p. 203.) The 'evil' concerns Elizabeth Barrett's superstition, arising from her guilt at Bro's death, that she harmed whomever she touched. When Browning wrote to her that she made him happy, she was disconcerted almost in the measure that she was pleased: 'If I only knew certainly, . . more certainly than the thing may be known by either me or you;—that nothing in me could have any part in making you *un*happy . . , would it not be enough . . *that* knowledge . . to content me, to overjoy me?' (2 Dec. 1845, p. 303.) Some of the most forceful passages in her letters are those in which she recoils from Browning's persistent assertion that she, and not he, was *responsible* for their relationship, that it was her will which had predominated in its course and would direct its outcome. Browning wrote to her: 'If any of it had been *my* work, my own . . distrust and foreboding had pursued me from the beginning,—but all is *yours*—you crust me round with gold and jewelry like the wood of a sceptre' (3 Dec. 1845, pp. 301–2). 'What an omen you take in calling anything my work!' Elizabeth Barrett retorted. 'If it is my work, woe on it—for everything turns to evil which I touch. Let it be God's work & yours, & I may take breath & wait in hope' (4 Dec. 1845, p. 305).

But Elizabeth Barrett's most enduring anxiety concerned the very nature of Browning's love—the fact (indubitable to her) that it was based on a false image, that he was 'liable [. . .] to such a set of small delusions, that are sure to break one by one, like other bubbles, as you draw in your breath' (16–17 July 1845, p. 126). She had thought at first that he would change his mind after their first meeting: 'I am deeply touched now,' she wrote to him in the letter in which she gave him permission to call, '—& presently, . . I shall understand' (15 May 1845, p. 65). But Browning's mind did not change, and Elizabeth Barrett's alarm continued to increase. Of the several explanations which she gave to herself for Browning's love, she was forced (under the pressure of his rhetoric) to abandon two. 'I thought besides sometimes', she told Browning, ' [. . .] that you were selfdeceived as to the nature of your own feelings. [. . .] What was *I* that I should think otherwise? I had been shut up here too long face to face with my own spirit, not to know myself, &, so, to have lost the common illusions of vanity' (17 Nov. 1845, pp. 274–5). Sheer length of time, combined with Browning's repeated assertions, convinced Elizabeth Barrett that he knew his own mind. Her second idea was that Browning cared for her because of one or other of her attributes—her poetry, for example, or her invalidism. We have seen Browning's claim that he 'dared' to kiss her in order to persuade her that he was not in love with 'a phantom of my own creating out of your books and letters', and he was right in thinking that this thought had crossed Elizabeth Barrett's mind. But she was perhaps more sensitive still to the idea that Browning cared for her because of her condition: 'really & truly I have sometimes felt jealous of myself . . of my own infirmities, . . and thought that you cared for me only because your chivalry touched them with a silver sound—& that, without them, you would pass by on the other side:—why twenty times I have thought *that* & been vexed—ungrateful vexation!' (24 Oct. 1845, p. 247.) Even when the 'vexation' had gone, Elizabeth Barrett claimed 'the right of remembering to my last hour, that YOU, who might well have passed by on the other side if we two had met on the road when I was riding at ease, . . *did not* when I was in the dust' (26 Mar. 1846, p. 565.) (She wittily inverts the parable of the Good Samaritan: those who 'passed by on the other side' were the uncaring priest and the Levite in Luke 10: 30–7, who refused to tend to the man who 'fell among thieves'.) Here, however, she was genuinely mistaken; for, although there was something attractive to Browning in Elizabeth Barrett's vulnerability, it was not for the reason she supposed. It came from his idea that, if she were ill, he would have something to do for her, some way of demonstrating his love and subjection. 'My uttermost pride & privilege and glory above all glories would be to live in your sick-room and serve you', he told her; but he was not 'so selfish' as to wish for this, rather than seeing her 'in a condition to need none of my service' (4 June 1846, p. 757). He was as good as his word here: from the moment in which he glimpsed the possibility of her getting well, Browning (coach, crowd, and team-mate in one) urged Elizabeth Barrett towards her goal.

In a sense, however, Elizabeth Barrett's conviction that Browning loved her for herself made things worse, because she felt that self so unworthy of being loved. Another, and greater fear possessed her: that Browning loved 'a phantom of his own creating' which bore no relation to her at all, not even the tenuous of one of bearing the same name as the poet, or the mythical invalid of popular legend. 'So you think that I meant to complain when we first met, of your "*loving me only for my poetry*"!' she wrote to him. 'Which I did not, simply because I did not believe that *you loved! me for any reason*. [. . .] I thought you did not love me at all—you loved out into the air, I thought—a love *a priori*, as the philosophers might say, & not *by induction*, any wise! [. . .] I did not believe in miracles *then*' (11 May 1846, p. 696). And the reality of Browning's love never ceased to seem precarious to Elizabeth Barrett. She, who had been 'in the desert', was now 'among the palm-trees'; she had 'come to the end of the sand & within sight of the fountain'; but 'even in that case . . to doubt whether it may not all be *mirage*, would be the natural first thought . . the recurring dream-fear! now would it not?' (15 Dec. 1845, p. 323.) 'Good Heavens!' she wrote to him again, in the aftermath of their quarrel about the morality of duelling, '—how dreadfully natural it would be to me, seem to me, if you DID leave off loving me! How it would be like the sun's setting . . & no more wonder!' (8 Apr. 1846, p. 608.) Repeatedly, she applies to Browning the imagery of dreams and visions, of supernatural beings and events, stressing their fleetingness and fragility. 'Oh—you do not understand how with an unspeakable wonder, an astonishment which keeps me from drawing breath, I look to this Dream, & "see your face as the face of an angel," and fear for the vanishing, . . because dreams & angels *do* pass away in this world' (12 Mar.

1846, p. 532). The dream matched her own past desires, it came from sources of feeling long since buried; that was part of its equivocal power. 'Dearest—I feel to myself sometimes, "Do not move, do not speak—or the dream will vanish"! So fearfully like a dream, it is!—Like a reflection in the water of an actual old, old dream of my own, too, . . touching which, . . now silent voices used to say "That romantic child"!' (12 Aug. 1846, p. 958.)

Elizabeth Barrett's anxiety reached its height, not surprisingly, whenever Browning's praise of her was particularly fulsome. 'When you overpraise me (*not* over*love*) I must be frightened', she told him (21 Dec. 1845, p. 338); but Browning was not deterred. Once he compared her to 'the Queen-diamond they showed me in the crown of the Czar' (31 Jan. 1846, p. 428; Browning had been to Russia in 1834), and Elizabeth Barrett replied:

Seriously . . gravely . . if it makes me three times happy that you should love me, yet I grow uneasy & even saddened when you say infatuated things such as this & this [. . .] I shall end by being jealous of some ideal Czarina who must stand between you & me . . I shall think that it is not *I* whom you look at [. . .]

(30 Jan. 1846, p. 432.)

Elizabeth Barrett's strong and primitive self-consciousness here directly challenges Browning's image and reverses its connotations. She did not want the dream-identity which she felt Browning was foisting upon her, even though it was notionally 'better' than her own; she could not experience it, and therefore it could give her no pleasure. Moreover, it was liable to shatter when Browning 'woke up'—as she was convinced he would. Both her rejection of Browning's error, and her conviction that it would end badly, are what give her longest and most earnest remonstrance on the subject its edge of pain and fear. Browning had, as usual, written 'ever so much foolishness' to her, and she replied:

There is no use, no help, in discussing certain questions: some sorts of extravagance grow by talking of [. . .] Only I PROTEST, from my understanding . . from my heart . . and besides I do assert the truth [. . .] that you always make me melancholy by using such words. It seems to me as if you were in the dark altogether, & held my hand for another's—let the shutter be opened suddenly . . & the hand . . is dropped perhaps . . must I not think such thoughts, when you speak such words?—I ask you if it is not reasonable. No, I do not ask you. We will not argue whether eagles creep, or worms fly. [. . .] Ah,—if you could know . . if you could but know for a full moment of conviction, how you depress & alarm me by saying such things, you would never say them afterwards, *I* know. [. . .] Is it not enough that you love me?—Is there anything greater? And will you run the risk of ruining that great wonder by bringing it to the test of an 'argumentum ad absurdum' such as I might draw from your letter? Have pity on me, my own dearest, & consider how I must feel to see myself idealized away, little by little, like Ossian's spirits into the mist . . till . . 'Gone is the daughter of Morven'! And what if it is mist or moon-glory, if I stretch out my hands to you in vain, & must still fade away farther? Now *you will not any more*.

(21 Apr. 1846, pp. 639–40.)

And so on: what I have quoted is not complete, and she had not finished. She was wasting her ink, of course; that last injunction went the way of all the others. Browning *could not*, according to the imperative of his own nature, take it for real; and, as I have shown, he had a ready-made framework of interpretation by which such protests on Elizabeth Barrett's part became further proof of her supremacy.

How was Elizabeth Barrett to resolve the problem? Not by giving up her point: she was comically in earnest 'that for *me* to be too good for *you*, & for *you* to be too good for *me*, cannot be true at once, both ways'; and she 'could discern & prove, from the beginning of the beginning, that *you* were too good for *me*—it is too late therefore to take up the other argument' (8 June 1846, p. 768). Her ingenuity found another way: she defined the 'love' which Browning offered her as an irrational and overpowering force which created and sustained its own order of reality. Browning's delusion became a merit for him and a security for her.

It was Browning, in fact, who gave her the hint by remarking, in one letter (23 Oct. 1845, p. 245), 'I love you because I *love* you'— that is, absolutely, without reference to their respective circumstances. But later on, recalling the phrase, Elizabeth Barrett took it to mean something different, something to do with the motive for love itself:

The first moment in which I seemed to admit to myself in a flash of lightning the *possibility* of your affection for me being more than dream-work . . the first moment was *that* when you intimated [. . .] that you cared for me not for a reason, but because you cared for me. Now such a 'parceque' ['because'] which reasonable people wd take to be irrational, was just the only one fitted to the uses of my understanding on the particular question we were upon [. . .] for I could understand that it might be as you said, &, if so, that it was altogether unanswerable . . do you see?—If a fact includes its own cause . . why there it stands for ever—one of 'earth's immortalities'—*as long as it includes it.*

(12 Nov. 1845, pp. 265–6.)

It was this principle of love's 'irrational' self-justification which enabled Elizabeth Barrett to reconcile herself to Browning's adoration of her. She never really lost her unease at its unstable footing, as her allusion to 'Earth's Immortalities' suggests. (This short poem, recently published in *Dramatic Romances and Lyrics*, tells us that the title-phrase is a contradiction in terms: neither earthly fame nor earthly love endure.) Despite her misgivings, however, Elizabeth Barrett felt herself safer as the object of an arbitrary feeling. 'It has been only your love for me, . . which I believe in perfectly as love . . & which, being love, does not come by pure logic, as the world itself may guess . . it has been only, wholly & purely your love for me which has made a level for us two to meet & stand together' (21 Apr. 1846, p. 640). She, who had been so reluctant for Browning to 'see' her, and who had then been so disturbed at his not seeing her truly, wrote to him at last: 'Once I used to be more uneasy, & to think that I ought to *make* you see me. But Love is better than Sight, & Love will do without Sight' (15 July 1846, pp. 87–9). It is curious, in the light of this epigram, to look forward ten years to the blinding of Romney in *Aurora Leigh*. For although there, too, 'love does without sight'—indeed, the marriage of Aurora and Romney depends in every way on his blindness—the implication is the reverse of what it is in the letter. Only when Romney is blind can he 'see' Aurora for what she is—acknowledge her genius, her nobility of spirit, her supremacy to him—everything which Elizabeth Barrett considered to be a delusion when Browning 'saw' it in her. 'I stand by a miracle in your love,' she told him '& because I stand in it & it covers me, just for *that*, you cannot see me—!' (1 May 1846, p. 670.) Her solution was simple: 'May God grant that you NEVER *see me*'.

6

Marriage and Elopement

1 Triumphs of the will

Browning made much of the abnegation of his will to Elizabeth Barrett. The man who, when she was facing up to her father in the 'Pisa affair', told her that 'all passive obedience and implicit submission of will and intellect' was morally wrong, who inveighed equally against 'the direction of an infallible church, or private judgment of another', and pronounced that one's duty was 'to act on one's own best conviction—not to abjure it and accept another will' (25 Sept. 1845, pp. 212–14), changed his tune, apparently, when it came to his own relation to her. 'I should like to breathe and move and live by your allowance and pleasure' (23 Apr. 1846, p. 648); 'instead of fruitless speculations how to give you back your own gift, I will rather resolve to lie quietly and let your dear will have its unrestricted way' (1 May 1846, p. 668); 'I wish your will to be mine, to originate mine, your pleasure to be only mine' (4 June 1846, p. 757); '*I* feel it delicious to be free when most bound to you, Ba,—to be able to love on in all the liberty of the implied subjection' (14 June 1846, p. 784); 'My own will has all along been annihilated before you,—with respect to you—I should never be able to say "she shall dine on fish, or fruit,"—"She shall wear silk gloves or thread gloves"—even to exercise in fancy that much "will OVER YOU" is revolting—I *will* THIS, never to be "over you" if I could' (26 June 1846, p. 815).

Browning represented this subjection of his will to Elizabeth Barrett's as the necessary and desired condition of his future life, and especially of his work. This theme was announced early in the correspondence, when he spoke of himself as 'going to try' to write a different kind of poetry from the 'dramatic' work he had produced hitherto, a poetry of direct self-expression like that of Elizabeth Barrett herself: 'so it will be no small comfort to have your company just now,' he remarked (13 Jan. 1845, p. 7). As the courtship progressed, Browning shifted the time of his new work into the future which he was to share with Elizabeth Barrett. 'I look forward to a real life's work for us both: *I* shall do all,—under your eyes and with your hand in mine,—all I was intended to do' (6 Feb. 1846, p. 439); and again (these are only two among many similar passages), 'I seriously hope and trust to shew my sense of gratitude for what is promised my future life, by doing some real work in it,—work of yours, as thro' you' (29 March 1846, p. 568).

What are we to make of these continual protestations? According to Betty Miller (*Portrait*, 103–18), they signify Browning's evasion of adult sexuality, with all that it implies of mutual responsibility; his desire to regress into (or rather, perpetuate) what he called the 'prolonged relation of childhood' which he enjoyed at New Cross (13 Aug. 1846, p. 960). Certainly it is true that Browning told Elizabeth Barrett, 'I hope if you want to please me especially, Ba, you will always remember I have been accustomed, by pure choice, to have another will lead mine in the little daily matters of life' (ibid.); but Miller does not lay enough stress on the phrase 'by pure choice'; nor does she draw the right conclusion from a passage she quotes from another letter, which explicitly challenges her interpretation of Browning's attitude. 'I hate being *master*, and alone, and absolute disposer in points where real love will save me the trouble', he wrote, ' . . because there are infinitely more and greater points where the solitary action and will, with their responsibility, cannot be avoided. [. . .] Moreover, I should be perhaps more refractory than anybody, if what I cheerfully agree to, as happening to take my fancy, were forced on me, as the only reasonable course' (21 Aug. 1846, p. 982).

More important, however, is Miller's failure to distinguish between the psychology of Browning's rhetoric, and that of his actions. Her account of him explains why he wrote as he did; but if he meant what he wrote, he and Elizabeth Barrett would probably never have met, let alone eloped together. After all, to look at the process of the courtship is to see Browning acting, step by step, to impose his will on Elizabeth Barrett; initiating every significant stage in their relationship, from the writing of the first letter to the decision about the date of the wedding; willing (if not compelling) her, in the division of her feelings between the desire for life and the desire for death, to choose life.

Elizabeth Barrett herself was aware that, for all his demonstrative humility, Browning exercised his will over her. 'You shall have it your own way, as you have everything', she wrote to him on one occasion, '—which makes you so very, very, exemplarily submissive, you know!' (21 Jan. 1846, p. 409.) After their argument about the ethics of duelling (see below), when Browning deferred to her opinion, she wrote: 'ah, you are so fond of dressing me up in pontifical garments! [. . .] but because they are too large for me, they drop off always of themselves [. . .] After all, too, you, . . with that præternatural submissiveness of yours, . . you know your power upon the whole, & understand, in the midst of the obeissances, that you can do very much what you please, with your High priest' (12 Apr. 1846, p. 614). Her letters are filled with the sense of his power, and it is nonsense of Miller to claim that she was disappointed at finding him weak. 'I felt as if you had a power over me & meant to use it,' she wrote to him, '& that I could not breathe or speak very differently from what you chose to make me' (23 Feb. 1846, p. 489); and again, 'You were stronger than I, from the beginning, & I felt the mastery in you by the first word & first look' (19 May 1846, p. 714). Her expressions to her friends after the marriage were equally unequivocal: 'he persisted and overcame me', she wrote to Miss Mitford, 'with such letters, and such words, that you might tread on me like a stone if I had not given myself to him, heart and soul' (*EBB to MRM*, 273). Nor was she deceived by her own humorous sense that, as she wrote to him two days after their wedding, Browning had 'acted throughout too much "the woman's part," '; she knew it was *acting*. 'And now, you still go on—you persist—you will be the woman of the play, to the last; let the prompter prompt ever so against you' (14 Sept. 1846, p. 1073). But who had written the script?

Browning himself realized that he must offer some explanation to Elizabeth Barrett for doing what he was continually claiming he would not do. Whenever he made a forcing move, therefore, he covered himself by a characteristically ingenious excuse. In late January, he set the limit date for their departure; and this is how he did it:

You know that when I *claim* anything, it is really yourself in me—you *give* me a right and bid me use it, and I, in fact, am most obeying you when I appear most exacting on my own account—so, in that feeling [. . .] I claim your promise's fulfilment—say, at the summer's end: it cannot be for your good that this state of things should continue.

(28 Jan. 1846, p. 425.)

And again, in deciding that the time had come for them to take the plunge: 'See the *tone* I take, the way I write to *you* . . but it is all thro' you, in the little brief authority you give me' (10 Sept. 1846, p. 1060). But unlike Angelo in *Measure for Measure* (II. ii. 117–18: 'man, proud man, / Dressed in a little brief authority'), he bends a woman to his will only because she has willed him to do so.

The motive for such rhetoric must be sought in Browning's long-held beliefs about the nature of the will itself, especially the creative will, the energy which conceives and acts. These beliefs are profoundly ambivalent. The hero of *Sordello* (1840), for example, turns out, in the end, to need 'A soul [. . .] above his soul, / Power to uplift his power' (vi. 41–2), a need which corresponds to what Browning appeared to require from Elizabeth Barrett; but what of the *author* of *Sordello*, who has willed the whole poem into being, whose implied audience is 'Summoned together from the world's four ends, / Dropped down from heaven or cast up from hell, / To hear the story I propose to tell' (i. 32–4)? The spirit of mastery wrestles with the spirit of submission; the quintessential Browning poem, in this light, is 'The Bishop Orders His Tomb at St. Praxed's Church' (written during the period of the courtship), whose speaker, powerless on his death-bed, attempts to impose his will by sheer force of rhetoric on his uncaring children, and, failing in one respect (for the magnificent tomb he 'orders' will never be built) succeeds, beyond his knowledge, in another. The poem is his tomb: he is, as he desired, indistinguishable from his monument.

Browning knew perfectly well that Elizabeth Barrett, though she wanted to leave Wimpole Street in the aftermath of the 'Pisa affair', would not do so without being drawn by a power which she felt she could not resist. He claimed to have borrowed her will, rather than used his own, because that was the psychological position from which he felt able to act; but act he undoubtedly did. 'Take time, take counsel if you choose', he wrote to her; 'but at the end tell me what you will do for your part—thinking of me as utterly devoted, soul and body, to you, living wholly in your life, seeing good and ill, only as you see,—being yours as your hand is,—or as your Flush, rather' (15 Jan. 1846, p. 388). (No doubt Flush would have enjoyed eating as many cakes as he liked and attributing his greed to Elizabeth Barrett's will!) As we have seen, Browning chose in late January 1846 to fix the prospect of their marriage at the end of the summer: Elizabeth Barrett was to think of it, he wrote, 'as *ordained*, granted by God [. . .] not to be put in doubt *ever again*' (28 Jan. 1846, p. 425).

He was equally emphatic on the subject of her health. The winter of 1845–6 was exceptionally mild: 'Is it not a warm summer?' wrote Elizabeth Barrett. 'The weather is as "miraculous" as the rest, I think' (15 Jan. 1846, p. 390), and Browning took every opportunity to encourage her to be active. In a passage about his love of small wild creatures, he used the Italian verb 'guizzare' to describe the lively darting motion of 'the English water-eft'; two paragraphs later, he applied it to her: 'Now, *walk*, move, *guizza, anima mia dolce*' (4 Jan. 1846, p. 357). '*Vo guizzando* . . & everything else that I ought to do', Elizabeth Barrett dutifully replied (7 Jan. 1846, p. 371). As the spring season advanced, and Elizabeth Barrett prepared to venture outside (many months earlier than she would have thought of doing the year before), Browning offered her a lyrical description of renewal and rebirth in his own surroundings:

I expect everything from your going out of doors, that is to be—what a joy to write it, think of it, expect it! Oh, why are you not here,—where I sit writing,—whence, in a moment, I could get to know why the lambs are bleating so, in the field behind—I do not see it from either window in this room—but I see a beautiful sunshine ($2\frac{1}{2}$ p.m.) and a chestnut tree leafy all over, in a faint trembling chilly way, to be sure—and a holly hedge I see, and shrubs, and blossomed trees over the garden wall,—were you but here, dearest, dearest—how we would go out, with Flush on before, with a key I have, I lock out the world, and then look down on it; for there is a vast view from our greatest hill—did I ever tell you that Wordsworth was shown that hill or its neighbour;—someone saying 'R.B. lives over *there* by that HILL'—'Hill'? interposed Wordsworth—'*we* call that, such as that,—a *rise*'!

(16 Apr. 1846, p. 627.)

Of course the poet of the Lake District could not recognize the pretensions of a London suburb; but really it is Browning who gets a rise out of Wordsworth here, for he knows that he is offering Elizabeth Barrett the beautiful and not the sublime—the contours of a civilized idyll, combining the pleasure of locking out the world with the pleasure of looking down on it, commanding it with a 'vast view' from an enclosure, like Eden, of private erotic bliss. And again Elizabeth Barrett responded as the rhetoric required: 'I may see the "hill" or the "rise" at some distant day. Shall I, do you think? I would rather see it than Wordsworth's mountains' (16 Apr. 1846, p. 628).

When the subject of her use of morphine came up—Elizabeth Barrett was anxious to emphasize that it was not a dependence—Browning showed consummate tact and delicacy in his encouragement of her 'experiment' in reducing the daily dose. He accepted her explanation that it must be done by degrees, and then went on to pour out for her his sense of the natural world outside the room in which she had been taking her artificial 'elixir':

All the kind explaining about the opium makes me happier. 'Slowly and gradually' what may *not* be done? Then see the bright weather while I write—lilacs, hawthorn, plum-trees all in bud,—elders in leaf, rose-bushes with great red shoots; thrushes, whitethroats, hedge sparrows in full song— there can, let us hope, be nothing worse in store than a sharp wind, a week of it perhaps—and then comes what shall come—

(6 Feb. 1846, pp. 438–9)

As the year went on, his encouragement became tinged with warning. 'Care for everything—if you should have taken cold last night, for instance! Talk of a sword suspended by a hair!—what is the feeling of one whose priceless jewel hangs over a gulf by a hair?' (12 Apr. 1846, p. 618.) 'Tell me, write of yourself, love', he urges her, in the 'fierce heat' of June; '*never* go up the long stairs—or, at least, *rest* at proper intervals. I think of the Homeric stone [of Sisyphus] heaved nearly to the hill-top and *then*! . . an accident now would be horrible,—think, and take every precaution—because it is *my* life, (if that will influence you) my whole happiness you are carrying safely or letting slip' (7 June 1846, p. 765).

And Elizabeth Barrett did as he said. Throughout the winter of 1845–6, we hear of her walking about her room or even going downstairs (something unheard of the year before, when she was totally insulated in her room for the duration of the cold weather); as soon as the weather allowed, she began to make expeditions in the carriage and on foot, until there was a seat reserved for her at Hodgson's, the bookshop in Great Marylebone Street (now New

Cavendish Street) where she and Browning were to meet on the day of their elopement. She, who had written to Browning that her fear of the east wind kept her shut up until past May, wrote to him in the May of 1846 that she had been out, and that 'the little breath of wind could do nobody harm, I felt' (28 May 1846, p. 738). More even than this, she began to take an interest in life outside, both the life of Nature and the life of the city, to which she had been so indifferent in her isolation. The experience of having a religious tract thrown into her carriage as she drove down Oxford Street delighted her—especially as it was on 'the enormous wickedness of frequenting plays & balls!!' (13 July 1846, p. 874.) Driving in Hyde Park, 'close by the Serpentine', in the twilight of a day in June, she noticed 'by the ruffling of the water that there was a breath of wind more than we felt', and that, as the shadows closed in, 'the silvery water seemed to hold all the light left, as on the flat of a hand'. 'Very much I liked & enjoyed it', she exclaimed. 'And, as we came home, the gas was in the shops . . another strange sight for me—and we all liked everything' (16 June 1846, p. 791). The note of childlike wonder and pleasure is struck again and again in these descriptions. She gathered laburnum blossom for Browning in Regent's Park: 'It hung quite high up on the tree, the little blossom did, and Arabel said that certainly I could not reach it—but you see!' It was 'the strangest feeling' for her to 'put both my feet on the grass', with 'all those strange people moving about like phantoms of life,—How wonderful it looked to me!' (11 May 1846, pp. 695–6.) In late May, she stole a pansy for him from the Botanical Gardens, despite Arabel's scandalized objection that 'all gathering of flowers in these gardens is highly improper'; in fact, she made Arabel 'finish her discourse, standing between me & the gardeners' (29 May 1846, p. 740). But she was moved, on this same outing, by 'the green under the green . . where the grass stretches under trees. *That* is something unspeakable to me, in the beauty of it'. Once she drove as far as *Hampstead* (she underlined the achievement), and gathered 'a great branch [. . .] starred over with dog-roses' (8 June 1846, pp. 766–7); of course one went to Browning, who, realizing that it was in fact eglantine (or sweetbriar, *rosa rubiginosa*, and not *rosa canina*), magnanimously allowed it to be ' "*dog*-rose" for Flushie's sake!' (9 June 1846, p. 769.) She was 'vainglorious' about her improvement: of the first letter she had written outside her room for five years, of carrying a letter to the post herself, of walking upstairs without being carried; or of her heroism on the evening when, realizing that she had not been out during the day, and that there was no one to accompany her (her maid, Wilson, 'had taken holiday', and the family were at dinner), 'I put on my bonnet, as a knight of old took his sword . . & called Flush, & walked down stairs & out into the street, all alone—*that* was something great!— And, with just Flush, I walked there, up & down in glorious independence' (18 June 1846, p. 799).

There were premonitions of Italy in the interest which she began to take in painting and sculpture and famous buildings, subjects on which, as she told Browning several times, she felt her ignorance and the need of his guidance. An invitation to visit the studio of John Graham Lough (sculptor of the Trafalgar Square lions) came to nothing because of Browning's hypersensitivity (on Elizabeth Barrett's behalf) about the publicity which might result; but she did go, in the company of Mrs Jameson, to see the famous art collection of the banker and poet Samuel Rogers, where she saw works by Michaelangelo and Raphael, Titian, Rubens, and Rembrandt, as well as Milton's contract for the sale of *Paradise Lost*. Her description of the visit (22 June 1846, pp. 806–8) is almost pathetically exclamatory. 'How was it possible not to feel giddy with such sights!—Almost I could have run my head against the wall, I felt, with bewilderment'. She was equally moved by a visit to Westminster Abbey in July; the sound of the organ so affected her 'that I hurried & besought my companions out of the door after a moment or two' (30 July 1846, p. 918); but she had time for a glimpse of Poets' Corner, where the link between religious faith and poetic genius in the epitaph of Edmund Spenser particularly struck her.

Not that art was the only object whose 'excitement & newness' she experienced that summer. In June Mr Kenyon took her to see 'the strange new sight (to *me*!) of the Great Western . . the train coming in: & we left the carriage & had chairs—& the rush of the people & the earth-thunder of the engine almost overcame me . . not being used to such sights & sounds in this room, remember!!' (13 June 1846, p. 781.) But she was not overcome; two months later she made another expedition to 'some bridge, whence to look at the Birmingham train'; and again, 'we saw the great roaring, grinding Thing . . a great blind mole, it looked for blackness. We got out of the carriage to see closer—& Flush was so frightened at the roar of it, that he leapt upon the coach-box. Also it rained,—& I had ever so many raindrops on my gown and in my face even, . . which pleased me nearly as much as the railroad sight. It is something new for me to be rained upon, you know' (15 Aug. 1846, p. 967).

It is that last comment, perhaps more than any other in the correspondence, more even than the repeated imagery of graves and prisons, which gives the clearest and most poignant sense of the seclusion which Elizabeth Barrett had undergone; but it is another episode, which took place two weeks later (almost on the brink of her marriage), which gives the surest sign of the extent of her recovery. She and Arabel were out on a shopping expedition, and they were just getting into their carriage when Flush, who had lingered on the road, was snatched by the 'dog-stealers'—a gang of professional thieves, who stole and ransomed back the pets of the wealthy classes. He had been stolen and ransomed twice before (a fact which Virginia Woolf suppressed, for the sake of artistic effect, in her biography of him) and Elizabeth Barrett, though naturally upset, dealt with the situation coolly enough. Indeed, it gives you a curious glimpse of how comfort and privilege took for granted the existence of a predatory lower class in the London of those days. 'Henry went down for me directly to the Captain of the banditti, who evidently knew all about it,' Elizabeth Barrett told Browning matter-of-factly (Henry *knew where to go*!); '& after a little form of consideration & enquiry, promised to let us hear something this evening [. . .] Henry told him that I was resolved not to give much—but of course they will make me give what they choose—I am not going to leave Flush at their mercy' (1 Sept. 1846, p. 1031). The next day, 'the chief of the Confederacy came to call on Henry & to tell him that the "Society had the dog," having done us the honour of tracking us into Bond Street & out of Bond Street into Vere Street where he was kidnapped—Now he is in Whitechapel (poor Flush)—And the great man was going down there at half past seven to meet other great men in council & hear the decision as to the ransom exacted, & would return with their *ultimatum*' (2 Sept. 1846, p. 1035).

Elizabeth Barrett, 'learned in the ways of the Philistines', was prepared to pay; but others saw it differently. Henry was 'angry'—his temper was not improved by finding 'the great man' smoking a cigar in the drawing-room—and found it hard to obey his sister's injunction to be 'civil & respectful'. Her old friend Hugh Boyd sent a letter to her saying that it would be 'awful sin' to give in to the

blackmail. And Browning, too, vented his outrage when he thought
(mistakenly) that Flush had already been returned; he himself, he
declared 'would not have given five shillings on that fellow's application'. He was under some strain at the time, as we shall see; but
the bluster of what follows does him little credit:

I would have said,—and in entire earnestness '*You* are responsible for the
proceedings of your gang, and *you* I mark [. . .] I will spend my whole life
in putting you down, the nuisance you declare yourself—and by every
imaginable means I will be the death of you and as many of your accom-
plices as I can discover [. . .] now try my sincerity, by delaying to produce
the dog tomorrow. And for the ten pounds—see!' Whereupon I would give
them to the first beggar in the street.

                                                (3 Sept. 1846, p. 1037.)

For the only time in the courtship (it must have given him an
unpleasant shock when he realized it) Browning found himself on
Mr Barrett's side. For Papa had taken a hand in the matter, as Elizabeth Barrett woefully explained: the 'great man' (whose name was
Taylor) had indeed come with the ransom demand the previous
evening ('six guineas, with half a guinea for himself, considering the
trouble of the mediation'), but 'Papa desired Henry to refuse to pay,
& not to tell me a word about it—all which I did not find out till
this morning' (3 Sept. 1846, p. 1039). Elizabeth Barrett was
furious. The unhappy Henry 'talked of Papa' (you can sympathize
with his feelings) and declined to resume negotiations with Taylor.
'All this time he [Flush] is suffering & I am suffering', Elizabeth
Barrett wrote. And now, here was Browning, 'most pattern of citi-
zens', going on about 'abstract principles of justice'. How, she
demanded, would he react if *she* were to be kidnapped by 'banditti'?
In his reply, Browning strongly maintained the principle of resistance to blackmail. He wrote at length and with great skill; but he
could not, of course, offer more than a lame and sophistical answer
to Elizabeth Barrett's pointed question. He would resist extortion
on his own account, of course, and take the consequences: 'I sacrifice *myself* . . all that belongs *to me*—but there are some interests
which *I* belong to—I have no right, no more than inclination, in
such a case, to think of myself if your safety is concerned' (4 Sept.
1846, p. 1043). Elizabeth Barrett came back with relish: 'Does not
Flush's condition assimilate to my own among the banditti?—for
you would not, after all, leave me to the banditti—and I, *exactly on*

the same ground, will not leave Flush. It seems to me that you and I are *at one* upon the whole question,—only that *I* am *your* Flush, and *he* is mine. You, if you were "consistent" . . dearest! . . would not redeem me on any account [. . .] But Flush is not to be sacrificed—nor even is Ba, it appears. So our two weaknesses may pardon one another, yours & mine!' (4 Sept. 1846, p. 1046.)

Meanwhile, in defiance of lover and father both, Elizabeth Barrett took action on her own account. Since none of her brothers would engage in what Browning called 'the burlesque dignities of mediation' with 'the lowest of the vile', Elizabeth Barrett got in a cab with Wilson and went herself in search of 'the archfiend Taylor'. And indeed, this venture into the slums might have had the character of a descent into Hell for our sheltered, middle-aged, middle-class heroine; except that Elizabeth Barrett, alive and kicking with her new strength, kept not just her wits but her sense of humour about her. As she had told Browning long before, she was *'very fond of romances'*. Here was one of her own; Dickens could hardly have done it better:

We got into obscure streets,—& our cabman stopped at a public house to ask his way. Out came two or three men, . . 'Oh, you want to find Mr Taylor, I dare say'! (mark that no name had been mentioned!) & instantly an unsolicited philanthropist ran before us to the house, & out again to tell me that the great man 'wasn't at home!—but wouldn't I get out?' Wilson, in an aside of terror, entreated me not to think of such a thing—she believed devoutly in the robbing & murdering, & was not reassured by the gang of benevolent men & boys who 'lived but to oblige us' all round the cab— 'Then wouldn't I see Mrs. Taylor,' suggested the philanthropist:—and, notwithstanding my negatives, he had run back again and brought an immense feminine bandit, . . fat enough to have had an easy conscience all her life, . . who informed me that 'her husband might be in in a few minutes, or in so many hours—wouldn't I like to get out & wait' (Wilson pulling at my gown) (the philanthropist echoing the invitation of the feminine Taylor.)—'No, I thanked them all—it was not necessary <to get> that I should get out, but it *was*, that Mr. Taylor should keep his promise about the restoration of a dog which he had agreed to restore—& I begged her to induce him to go to Wimpole Street in the course of the day, & not defer it any longer'—To which, replied the lady, with the most gracious of smiles— 'Oh yes certainly!—and indeed she *did* believe that Taylor had left home precisely on that business'—poising her head to the right & left with the most easy grace—'She was sure that Taylor would give his very best attention' . . . . . .

So, in the midst of the politeness, we drove away, and Wilson seemed to be of opinion that we had escaped with our lives barely. Plain enough it was, that the gang was strong there. The society . . the 'Fancy' . . had their roots in the ground. The faces of those men!—

(6 Sept. 1846, p. 1049.)

Passages like this make you feel that Elizabeth Barrett missed her vocation in becoming a portentous, high-minded poet (even her verse satire is *bardic*); she should have been a novelist. The vividness of her observation here is shaped both by a sense of the strangeness of the experience (those back-to-back parentheses segregating Wilson's genteel terror from the 'philanthropist's' amiability), and by the narrator's distance (she scrupulously corrects the direct 'not necessary to get out' to the reported 'not necessary that I should get out'). There is no empathy with the lower class, but there is no false sentiment either. Only the final exclamation reveals the personal shudder which, in *Aurora Leigh*, makes the indignant descriptions of the London slums sound so strained.

There was a further fracas in Wimpole Street later that day, when Taylor came for his money, and was greeted by Alfred in the hall as 'a swindler and a liar & a thief'. 'Which no gentleman could bear, of course', Elizabeth Barrett conceded; and Taylor rushed out of the house swearing that Flush would never be seen again. This time, Elizabeth Barrett lost her temper, and yet another brother, Septimus, agreed to undertake the mission of pacifying the offended 'gentleman' and taking him his money. Flush was restored at eight o'clock that evening, and Elizabeth Barrett watched him, dirty and thin, drinking bowl after bowl of water; reflecting that she had now, over the three occasions, paid the enormous sum of twenty guineas for him to the dog-stealers (6 Sept. 1846, pp. 1050–1). What neither she nor Browning remarked on, curiously enough, was the strength of mind and body which she had displayed in the adventure. Browning merely exclaimed, 'it *was* very imprudent to go to those disgusting wretches yourself—they have had a pretty honour without knowing it!' (7 Sept. 1846, p. 1846.) He seems to have taken for granted that Elizabeth Barrett had accomplished something which, a little over a year ago, would have seemed as easy to her as going to the moon—or to Italy.

1. First page of Browning's first letter, 10 January 1845.

But you are the real deep wonder of a
creature — and I sail these paper-boats on you
rather impudently. But I always mean to be very
grave one day — when I am in better spirits and can go
fuori di me.

And one thing I want to persuade you of, which is that
all you gain by travel is the discovery that you have gained nothing,
and have done rightly in trusting to your innate ideas — or not
rightly in distrusting them, as the case may be: you get, too, a
little .. perhaps a veritable wealth, good in finding the world's accepted
moulds everywhere, into which you may run & fix your own
fused metal, — but not a grain Troy-weight do you get of
new gold, silver or brass. After this, you go boldly on your own
resources, and are justified to yourself, that's all. True enough,
with a pen, even with this pen, and you have the green
little Syrenuses where ... out and heard the quails
sing. One of these ... I think describe a country I
have seen in my travels only, ... flowers, birds and
all. —

ever yours ... Miss Barrett —
R Browning.

2. Page 4 of Browning's ninth letter, 15 April 1845.

3. Portrait of Browning from the engraving by J. C. Armytage in R. H. Horne's *A New Spirit of the Age* (London 1844), which hung in Elizabeth Barrett's room before she met Browning. She wrote to him subsequently that it 'has not your character, in a line of it . . something in just the forehead & eyes & hair, . . but even *that*, thrown utterly out of your order, by another bearing so unlike you' (4 Dec. 1845, p. 306).

4. Portrait of Browning by D. G. Rossetti, 1855.

5. Portrait of Elizabeth Barrett by Field Talfourd, 1859.

6. The Barrett House at 50 Wimpole Street, as it would have been in the 1840s; it is no longer standing.

No.	When Married.	Name and Surname.	Age.	Condition.	Rank or Profession.	Residence at the Time of Marriage.	Father's Name and Surname.	Rank or Profession of Father.
117	12th September 1846	Robert Browning	Of Full age	Bachelor	Gentm	Saint Paul Deptford	Robt Browning	Gentm
		Elizabeth Barrett Moulton Barrett	Of age	Spinster	—	St Marylebone	Edwd Moulton Barrett	Gentm

Married in the _Parish Church_ according to the Rites and Ceremonies of the Established Church, _by Licence_ by me,

Jas I Stratten Curate

| This Marriage was solemnized between us, | Robert Browning Elizabeth Barrett Moulton Barrett | In the Presence of us, | James Silva Jones Elizabeth Wilson |

2   A lovers' quarrel

Their disagreement over yielding to blackmail was not the first argument between Browning and Elizabeth Barrett. That had occurred in April 1846. It was on the morality of duelling. The subject came up because of Browning's allusion to a sensational trial then taking place in Paris, in which a man who had killed his opponent in a duel was being tried for murder. 'Being fired at by a duellist is a little better [. . .] than being struck on the face by some ruffian', he commented 4 Apr. 1846, p. 588); and, when he and Elizabeth Barrett met two days later, Browning repeated his opinion that duelling was justifiable in some circumstances. Elizabeth Barrett was genuinely shocked: 'I thought you as wrong as possible', she wrote to him the next day, ' . . wonderfully wrong on such a subject, for YOU . . who, only a day or two before, seemed so free from conventional fallacies . . so free!' (7 Apr. 1846, p. 595.) She went on to affirm that, even setting aside 'all Christian principle' and going on 'the bare social rational ground', 'I cannot conceive of any *possible combination of circumstances* which could . . I will *not* say *justify*, but even *excuse*, an honourable man's having recourse to the duellist's pistol, either on his own account or another's'. Her argument was direct and forceful:

A man calls you 'a liar' in an assembly of other men. Because he is a calumniator, & on that very account, a worse man than you, . . you ask him to go down with you on the only ground on which you two are equals . . the duelling ground, . . & with pistols of the same length & friends numerically equal on each side, play at lives with him, both mortal men that you are. [. . .] At best, what do you prove by your duel? . . that your calumniator, though a calumniator, is not a coward in the vulgar sense . . & that yourself, though you may still be a liar ten times over, are not a coward either!

Browning's reply (8 Apr. 1846, pp. 601–6; his letter is nearly three times as long as Elizabeth Barrett's) is a brilliant casuist's display: a sequence of positions held (to show that they could be held) and then abandoned, and then retaken, with the ultimate safeguard that he, Browning, held none of them personally, but was only arguing on what Elizabeth Barrett called 'the bare social rational ground'. Briefly, his main argument was that if 'society' is admitted to be a good, then that good may be defended. Elizabeth Barrett was requiring 'the ordinary multitude of men' to live in society, but not to defend their place in it by the only means which society allowed them. If a man refused a challenge, or refused to send one, 'on conventionally sufficient ground', he would be 'infallibly excluded from a certain class of society thenceforth & forever'—a 'terrible wrong', assuming that social life was held to be a primary value. It was irrelevant that the method by which society compelled men to vindicate themselves from certain kinds of attacks—the method of duelling—was irrational and proved nothing either way: it was the *effect* which mattered.

To this, Elizabeth Barrett's reply was succinct. 'There is a certain class of sacrifice which men who live in society, should pay willingly to society . . the sacrifice of little or indifferent things, . . in respect to mere manners & costume. There is another class of sacrifice which should be refused by every righteous man though ever so eminently a social man, & though to the loss of his social position' (8 Apr. 1846, p. 607). Duelling, it was clear to her, belonged in the second class, and she reiterated her distress that Browning, 'my poet of of the Bells & Pomegranates', should take the opposite view: 'I shut my eyes, & have the heartache [. . .] only to think of it'.

Two considerations arise from this disagreement. One concerns its outcome. Even before he received her letter, Browning sent Elizabeth Barrett a note in which he wrote: 'I submit, unfeignedly, to you, there as elsewhere'; again emphasizing that his argument did not concern him personally (9 Apr. 1846, p. 608). Elizabeth Barrett was bewildered: 'you cannot, you know [. . .] "submit" to me in an *opinion*, any more than I could to you, if I desired it ever so anxiously' (9 Apr. 1846, p. 609). She was right, of course; it was Browning's own position, after all, as we have seen in his strong-minded recommendation to her to act on her own convictions in the 'Pisa affair'. In fact there is no reason to think that Browning was persuaded by Elizabeth Barrett's arguments. His retraction comes in the middle of a further explanation of why he had written as he had done: he pulls himself up short, and says, 'but I won't repeat the offence, dear: YOU ARE RIGHT and I am wrong and will lay it to heart' (10 Apr. 1846, p. 612.) This is demonstrative, but it is not convincing; and we need to ask why Browning behaved with what looks like abject inconsistency. The reason is simple. He had a motive for retraction which overrode anything so unimportant as maintaining his ground in an argument. For he was not the only one who was anxious. After Elizabeth Barrett wrote accusing him of advocating 'the pitiful resources of this corrupt social life', she grew alarmed at her own temerity. 'Tell me if you are angry, dearest!' she pleaded, in another letter sent on the same day. 'I *ask* you to tell me if you felt (for the time even) vexed with me . . I want to know . . I NEED to know' (7 Apr. 1846, p. 600). This was before she had received his letter rebutting her arguments; and then she was still more shaken. 'Why should we see things so differently, ever dearest?—If anyone had asked me, I could have answered for you that you saw it quite otherwise' (8 Apr. 1846, p. 607). Into this unexpected gap in their relationship rushed all her 'old fears and misgivings': 'I know that if I went on to write disagreeing disagreeable letters, you might not help to leave off loving me at the end [. . .] how dreadfully natural it would be to me, seem to me, if you DID leave off loving me!' She spoke in her next letter of having gone downstairs to take her daily exercise, but in a tone of despondency which recalls the letters of the previous year: 'I went down to the drawing-room, I & Flush, & found no one there . . & walked drearily up and down the rooms, &, so, came back to mine. May you have spent your day better. There was sunshine for you, as I could see' (9 Apr. 1846, p. 610)—implying that there was none for her. And at the end of the letter she reverted to the thought Browning most dreaded: 'I think of you, bless you, love you—but it would have been better for you never to have seen my face perhaps'. It was to this recurring anxiety that Browning's 'admission and retraction' were really addressed. His whole suit to Elizabeth Barrett was based on the premiss, which he had persuaded her to take as objective, indisputable fact, that she was entirely and exclusively what he desired in a woman, and that there was (as he had put it in a letter written only the day before they quarrelled) a 'tremblingly exquisite exactness' in their accord: 'In this House of Life—where I go, you go,—where I ascend you run before,—where I descend, it is after you' (5 Apr. 1846, p. 591). At the slightest sign of this accord breaking down, Elizabeth Barrett was liable to relapse into the 'low spirits' which characterized her former state. No wonder, then, that Browning was so eager to recant. Elizabeth Barrett had the fortitude to maintain her conviction despite her fear that Browning would 'leave off loving' her; he did not have the courage to take an equivalent risk.

The second consideration which arises from the argument over

duelling is the difference which it reveals in the attitude of Browning
and Elizabeth Barrett towards 'society'. Curiously enough, in terms
of principle versus pragmatism, this was the reverse of the attitudes
they took up later on about Flush's kidnapping. For all its princi-
pled integrity, Elizabeth Barrett's notion of right and wrong was, as
Browning saw, based on a narrow and theoretical understanding of
how real people actually think and behave. It assumed standards of
conduct based on pure moral imperatives, unendorsed by social
codes. She herself had admitted to Browning that her knowledge of
'life & man' was damagingly limited; here was an example of just
that limitation. Browning, on the other hand, showed in the twists
and turns of his protracted and subtle argument a fierce underlying
grasp of the necessity of social experience for himself, both as
human being and as artist. 'There are uses in it, great uses, for purposes quite beyond its limits—you pass thro' it, mix with it, to get
something by it: you do *not* go into the world to live on the breath
of every fool there, but you reach something *out* of the world by
being let go quietly, if not with a favourable welcome, among them'
(8 Apr. 1846, p. 602). Browning's desire to 'mix with' the world, in
its acceptance of the compromises and corruptions which that process entails, has an honesty which undercuts Elizabeth Barrett's
doctrine of absolute obedience to an abstract principle. The figure
of the ring in *The Ring and the Book* illustrates Browning's point:
the ring is created by a mixture of pure gold and corrupt alloy; the
alloy 'flies in fume' at the end of the process, while 'the shape
remains [. . .] Gold as it was, is, shall be evermore' (i. 25–8). In
the same way, Browning's great circle of truth is shaped with the
help of lies, his vindication of purity and chivalry is forged out of a
sordid history of greed and violence. *The Ring and the Book* was
dedicated to Elizabeth Barrett; but she, when Browning was planning it before her death, 'never took the least interest in the story, so
much as to wish to inspect the papers' (*RB & JW* 168). For her part,
she had ended *Aurora Leigh* with a jewel-figure of her own: the precious stones that make up, in Revelation 21: 19–20, the foundations of the New Jerusalem.

To Elizabeth Barrett herself, Browning consistently maintained
that he, personally and on his own account, had seen enough of
society for his own purposes, and was looking forward to a life of
intimate communion with her in the 'Siren's Isle' of their eventual
marriage. It was just as essential for him to make this point as it was

for him to reassure her about the harmony of their opinions, since she worried about taking him away from the social pleasures in which he was so steeped when she first knew him. Their difference of opinion as to the poet's right relation to society was one which emerged in the light of marriage and Italy; for the moment, it was obscured by the conditions of the courtship. In these conditions, Browning felt it his primary task to persuade Elizabeth Barrett to take, in practice, the step on which they had resolved.

3 Two failures

There might be 'worse poets in their way than painters', Browning reflected, after seeing a collection of 'execrable' pictures; but at least bad poets could use language 'to do a hundred other things', whereas 'the painter has spent the best of his life in learning even how to produce such monstrosities as these, and to what other good do his acquisitions go?' (27 Feb. 1846, p. 500.) It was a thought which came home with a vengeance four months later, on the morning of 23 June. Just the previous day, Elizabeth Barrett had been to see Samuel Rogers's collection of Old Masters, and had written enthusiastically to Browning about her visit; she did not mention then, but remembered later, that she had also seen a copy of Benjamin Robert Haydon's *Napoleon at St. Helena*. On the same day, the self-styled 'historical painter' ended the long struggle of his vain ambition against his own mediocrity and the public's indifference by committing suicide. He—at one time the companion of Wordsworth and Keats, both of whom wrote sonnets in praise of his genius—had been ground down by repeated failures, by privation (including imprisonment for debt), and by public ridicule of his bombast; the last straw seems to have been the spectacle of 'General' Tom Thumb, the American dwarf, attracting a hundred times the number of visitors to Haydon's own latest grandiose exhibition. He killed himself in the belief that he was about to be arrested for debt, and that his suicide would arouse public sympathy for his wife and family.

Browning read the news in *The Times*—which hinted with gruesome restraint at Haydon's suicide by calling him 'the unfortunate gentleman', and saying that 'his decease was hastened by pecuniary embarrassment'—and hurriedly wrote to Elizabeth Barrett, fearing to shock her, yet unable to write a 'cold letter' as though he were unaware of what had happened. The reason for his anxiety was that Haydon and Elizabeth Barrett were friends—in the sense that they had corresponded for several years—and that Haydon had, a week before his death, sent 'quantities of studies—sketches and portraits [. . .] together with paints, palettes, and brushes' to Wimpole Street, in order to avoid their seizure by the bailiffs. The words are Browning's, recalling the event long afterwards (Anne Thackeray Ritchie, *Records of Tennyson, Ruskin and Browning* (London, 1892), p. 139, quoted in Kintner, p. 809); and Browning also recorded Haydon's pathetic bravura in his accompanying note, 'they may have a right to my goods; they can have none of my mere tools and necessaries of existence'. Haydon had sent his 'necessaries of existence' to Wimpole Street once before, and Elizabeth Barett did not realize the gravity of his action on this second occasion. Now, replying to Browning's letter (23 June 1846, pp. 811–14), she confessed that she was shaken by the thought that 'a man so high hearted & highly endowed . . a bold man, who has thrown down gauntlet after gauntlet in the face of the world—that such a man should go mad for a few paltry pounds!'; and she worried that she might be to blame for not having offered to lend Haydon money, even though she had been 'told again & again [. . .] that to give money *there*, was to drop it into a hole of the ground'. But it would be wrong to say that she was personally affected, as she might have been the year before; indeed, the suicide of Haydon marks a significant point in the courtship precisely because of the reaction it did *not* provoke in Elizabeth Barrett. Her reply to Browning's letter, in which he broke the news with tender concern for her feelings, opens not with her thoughts about Haydon, but about him: 'In this world full of sadness, of which I have had my part . . full of sadness & bitterness & wrong . . full of most ghastly contrasts of life & death, strength & weakness side by side . . it is too much, to have *you* to hold by'. Browning's solicitude was in stark contrast to the conduct of her brother Alfred, who, 'seeing the Times at the Great Western Terminus, wrote out the bare extract & sent it to me by the post [. . .] he did not perhaps think how it would shock me'. But Browning *had* thought; and Elizabeth Barrett may have contrasted him with Haydon in her mind—Haydon, whom she had refused to see, and from whose correspondence, even, she had 'receded'—'notwithstanding the individuality and spirit of his letters, & my admiration for a certain fervour & magnanimity of genius, no one could deny to him'. At any rate, her letter closes with a remarkable burst of feeling, in which, half-wondering at her own callousness, she reassures Browning that she has not been too deeply troubled:

Best in the world!—Oh—you help me to live—I am better & lighter since I have drawn near to you even on this paper—already I am better & lighter. And now I am going to dream of you [. . .] in order to be quite well tomorrow. Oh—we are so selfish on this earth, that nothing grieves us very long, let it be ever so grievous, unless we are touched in *ourselves* . . in the apple of our eye . . in the quick of our heart . . in *what* you are, & WHERE you are . . my own dearest beloved! So you need not be afraid for *me*!

The contrast between Browning and Haydon which is implicit in this letter, becomes explicit in Elizabeth Barrett's next (26 June 1846, pp. 817–18), in which, after characterizing Haydon as a man 'who carried his whole being & sensibility on the outside of him [. . .] he could not live without reputation, & he wrestled for it, struggled for it, *kicked* for it, forgetting grace of attitude in the pang', her thoughts turned to another artist whom the world neglected, but who bore the neglect with all the 'grace of attitude' which Haydon lacked:

It is hope & help, to be able to look away from all such thoughts, to YOU, dearest beloved, who do not partake of the faults & feeblenesses of these lower geniuses. There is hope & help for the world in you—& if for the world, why for me indeed much more. You do not know . . ah, you do not know . . how I look up to you & trust perfectly in you. You are above all these clouds—your element is otherwise—men are not your taskmasters that you should turn to them for recompense.

This was not the last which Browning and Elizabeth Barrett had to do with Haydon. Among the effects which he had sent to Wimpole Street was his journal, and in his will he requested Elizabeth Barrett to supervise its (unexpurgated) publication. This was out of the question, of course, and eventually the journal was returned to Haydon's family; but meanwhile Elizabeth Barrett was subjected to some unfortunate gossip, and Browning was forced, for once in the whole courtship, to mention his 'acquaintance' with her in public, in the full glare of a dinner party, in order to deny that she had known or approved of Haydon's request. Of course Browning only went as far as saying that they corresponded occasionally, but even so the incident was alarming; and Browning was angry with

Haydon's ghost for causing all the trouble. Moreover, he was horri-
fied at Haydon's plan to publish such a journal; it recalled his own
fear of exposure, and his thoughts leapt from Haydon's posthu-
mous action to what might happen, in the future, to himself: 'Even
in this life,—imagine a proficient in an art or science,—who, after
thirty or sixty years of progressive discovery, finds that some book-
seller has disinterred and is about publishing the raw first attempt at
a work which he was guilty of in the outset!' (6 July 1846, p. 850.)
Browning himself, of course, had been 'guilty' of just such a 'raw
first attempt' in his youth, in the anonymous poem *Pauline* (1833);
and thirty years after its publication, exactly the same threat of
unauthorized publication arose to haunt him.

If Haydon's artistic and human failure moved Elizabeth Barrett
to contrast him with Browning, there was another figure in her life
in this summer of 1846 with whom the contrast was even more
striking. Elizabeth Barrett had met the Reverend George Barrett
Hunter (despite his middle name, they were not related) when he
was minister of an Independent chapel at Sidmouth, where the Barretts moved in 1832, after the sale of Hope End. Hunter was a
widower, several years older than Elizabeth Barrett; an eloquent
preacher, a man of some talents and quality of mind, but morbid,
frustrated, and with a violent temper. He fell in love with Elizabeth
Barrett; but, though she felt a certain regard for him, she did not
return his love, and she was less and less inclined to do so as the
years went by. Hunter left Sidmouth in 1835, after which his career
declined; he came to London in 1844 to attempt to make a living as
a private tutor, and paid regular visits to Wimpole Street, where
Elizabeth Barrett saw him for the sake of their old friendship.
Hunter was neurotically jealous of Elizabeth Barrett's increasing
fame as a poet, and bitter at his own failures; he made his bitterness
felt in extreme terms, both in his letters and in his visits, to such an
extent that Elizabeth Barrett felt afraid of him and asked Arabel to
remain in the room while he was there.

For a long time, Browning was unaware of Hunter's existence, let
alone his privileged access to Elizabeth Barrett. She refers to him
(not by name) as the author of an angry letter (16–17 July 1845, p.
124), and, again anonymously, as 'an old friend in rather an ill temper' who followed Browning upstairs one day (20–2 Aug. 1845,
p. 171). Later on, she identified this old friend as Hunter (1 Oct.
1845, p. 219), but without implying anything more about his

character or relation to her; then, in April 1846, she compared Hunter to the character of Chiappino in Browning's play *A Soul's Tragedy*, a neurotically self-centred man who brings about his own downfall and is left out in the cold at the end of the play; but still she refused to tell his name, so that Browning may not even have guessed that she was referring to the same person (5 Apr. 1846, pp. 589–90). It was only in August that the connection flashed upon him, when he and Elizabeth Barrett discussed Hunter's persecution of her, and Browning offered to intervene. 'Can this person be the "old friend in an ill humour" who followed me upstairs one day?' he asked (9 Aug. 1846, p. 947). Elizabeth Barrett admitted that it was.

Hunter, on the other hand, being jealous of every friend of Elizabeth Barrett, and particularly the literary ones, was quick to realize that the admission of a new visitor to Elizabeth Barrett's sick-room was an ominous event. On the day he followed Browning upstairs (Elizabeth Barrett later reported) he was 'white with passion', and there was 'an explosion that day among the many—and I had to tell him as a consequence that if he chose to make himself the fable & jest of the whole house, he was the master, but that I should insist upon his not involving my name in the discussion of his violences' (10 Aug. 1846, p. 952). Hunter was the only person, besides Elizabeth Barrett's old friend and mentor, the blind scholar Hugh Boyd (to whom, in any case, she dropped a heavy hint) who guessed the secret of Elizabeth Barrett's relationship with Browning. He nicknamed Browning 'the New Cross Knight', in a sardonic allusion to the Red Cross Knight, St. George, the hero of Spenser's *Faerie Queene*. This 'joke' shows that Hunter grasped what Browning meant to Elizabeth Barrett, and what the outcome was likely to be. It is strange, therefore, to think of this irascible, unstable, and embittered man, throwing his tantrums on paper and in person, but all without a thought of doing what he really could have done to damage Elizabeth Barrett's relationship with Browning—namely, telling Mr Barrett.

It was not a forbearance for which Browning gave him any credit. As soon as he became aware of Hunter's pestering of Elizabeth Barrett, he urged her 'not [to] carry toleration too far in this case, nor furnish an ungenerous, selfish man with weapons for your own annoyance'; and he offered to interfere, assuring her that he would always be '*quietly* firm, and never violent nor exasperating' (9 Aug.

1846, p. 947). But Elizabeth Barrett, in her reply (10 Aug. 1846, pp. 951–2), saw 'nothing for your goodness to do in that badness I told you of'; once again, as in the case of Haydon, she was working out an implied contrast between this failed, rancorous, unwanted lover, and the man who had supplanted him and all others in her affections; she was abandoning a 'miserable man', to whom life was 'a long moan', the 'slave of himself . . of his own passions', for a man who represented the reverse of all this. At the same time, as with Haydon again, there is a disturbing, distorted likeness at the heart of the contrast. When Elizabeth Barrett says of Hunter, 'There is a fine nature too, under those ruins of the will'; or when she calls him 'a sort of dumb Rousseau,—with the Confessions *in* him, pining evermore to get out': we recognize, not Browning himself, but a nightmare image of him. A month before her elopement, when Hunter wrote to ask for a 'last interview', Elizabeth Barrett was as callous about his distress as she had been about Haydon's death, only with less compunction. 'Oh—such stuff! Am I to hold a handkerchief to my eyes & sob a little?' She refused 'to condole with him in lawn & weepers, on the dreadful fact of [Browning's] existence in the world'. And then, Elizabeth Barrett applied to this Browning *manqué* the same worldly judgement which she had so indignantly rejected when it was applied to the real Browning by Mrs Procter. 'Poor Chiappino!—A little occupation would be the best thing that could happen for him [. . .] When a man spins evermore on his own axis, like a child's toy I saw the other day, . . what is the use of him but to make a noise? No greater tormentor is there, than selflove, . . even to self. And no greater instance of this, than *this*!' (16 Aug. 1846, pp. 970–1.) The very next sentence speaks of Elizabeth Barrett turning away from the whole world to Browning. In part, her rejection of Hunter represents the discarding of the 'child's toy' to which she compares him; like St. Paul (1 Corinthians 13: 10–11), when 'that which is perfect is come', she 'puts away childish things'. But part of Browning lies in that 'child's toy'; the dismissal of Hunter is also an exorcism.

4   Summer's end

It was not that Elizabeth Barrett did not want to go; it was not, even, that she could not make up her mind. The thing was settled: she assured Browning, over and over again, that she would not fail him.

Nevertheless, as the year went by, Browning became increasingly anxious, increasingly restless. As early as March, he quoted to Elizabeth Barrett the text (Matthew 24: 20) which warns of the coming of the Last Days: 'Pray ye that your flight be not in the winter' (10 Mar. 1846, p. 527). In June another prophetic lament came into his mind, from Jeremiah 8: 20: 'The harvest is past, the summer is ended, and we are not saved' (8 June 1846, p. 766). He did not quote the following two verses, though they may well have been in his mind: 'For the hurt of the daughter of my people am I hurt [. . .] Is there no balm in Gilead; is there no physician there? why then is not the health of the daughter of my people recovered?'

It depends on what you mean by 'health'. As we have seen, Elizabeth Barrett did get well and strong; by June she was probably strong enough to stand the journey. But the required 'balm' was not just physical. One after another, Browning met her objections, her doubts, her hesitations—mainly those which she expressed on his own behalf. At the beginning of June, Elizabeth Barrett suggested (in the most roundabout and tentative fashion, to protect herself from the charge of its being her actual wish) that it might be better for them to wait 'until next year's summer or autumn' (2 June 1846, p. 748). She left the decision up to him, and, armed with this permission, Browning was prompt and decisive. If *she* thought it best, he would of course wait 'twenty years instead of one'; but since she wanted *his* opinion—'Every day that passes before *that day* is one the more of hardly endurable anxiety and irritation, to say the least; and the thought of another year's intervention of hope deferred—altogether intolerable!' (3 June 1846, p. 752.) He dealt in the same ruthless manner with all other such suggestions; but what remained was something less tangible, but much more potent than all of them; something which lay at their root. Yet again, the shadow of the death of Bro at Torquay fell across Elizabeth Barrett's sense of purpose. The last time she had imposed her will; the last time she had taken a decision which affected the life of a human being who was dear to her: it had ended in catastrophe, in death and guilt. How, she wondered, would Browning feel if *she* were to die as a result of their elopement? Browning's reply was emphatic: 'I would "run the risk" [. . .] and if the result after all *was* unfortunate, it would be far easier to undergo the extremest penalty with so little to reproach myself for,—than to put aside the adventure,— waive the wondrous probability of such best fortune, in a fear of the

barest possibility of an adverse event, and so go to my grave' (17
Mar. 1846, p. 542).

At the same time, Browning must have realized that he could not
force Elizabeth Barrett to act if her heart was not in it. The most he
could do was to act himself as if the whole thing were a foregone
conclusion. Accordingly, passages about Italy and travel begin to
fill the letters, from June 1846 onwards. The two lovers assiduously
discussed the merits of various places (Florence, Ravenna, Salerno)
in terms of their climate and their infestation by colonies of 'the
English', who were more to be avoided than mosquitoes or bad
water; Elizabeth Barrett made enquiries among her acquaintances,
and sent Browning extracts which she had copied from travel-
books; he responded with information picked up on his own two
journeys to Italy. They went thoroughly, too, into the relative
advantages of a direct sea-voyage (more expensive, Browning
pointed out, but with no unforeseen extras) as against crossing the
Channel and travelling overland; and then, what about diligences,
railways, and river-steamers? Eventually, they decided to go cross-
Channel and travel through France, ending up at Pisa (poetic justice
for the failure of the preceding year). They even discussed the best
time to leave London,and which port to travel from. 'How inex-
pressibly charming it is to me to have a pretext for writing thus',
Browning told Elizabeth Barrett, ' . . about such *approaches* to the
real event—these business-like words, and names of places! If at the
end you should bring yourself to say "But you never seriously
believed this would take place"—what should I answer, I wonder?'
(30 June 1846, p. 825.)

Meanwhile, Elizabeth Barrett's resolution was being strengthened by other hands than Browning's. Mr Kenyon continued to
urge her to go, though he was puzzled as to how she was to manage
it without getting her sisters into trouble with their father; in
answer to this, she received practical offers of travel companionship
from Kenyon's friend Sarah Bayley, an energetic and independent-
minded woman whom both Browning and Elizabeth Barrett
admired, and also from Anna Jameson, who was leaving for the
Continent in September, and offered to take Elizabeth Barrett with
her. The lovers were strongly tempted to confide in Mrs Jameson,
so taken were they with her openness, her good sense, and her evident affection for both of them (she met them without realizing that
they knew one another). It was to Mrs Jameson that they were to

turn after their elopement, when they arrived in Paris; but meanwhile they decided that she, like their other friends, would be better
off not knowing. However, Elizabeth Barrett found it hard to conceal from those close to her that she was on the brink of departure;
and when Mrs Jameson 'pressed gently to know "on what I
counted" ', Elizabeth Barrett replied: 'Perhaps on my own courage'
(1 July 1846, p. 832).

Her courage did not impel her to take the plunge in June, in July,
in August; September was agreed on, but at times she seemed to be
looking further into the autumn, reminding Browning that it had
been October when she was to have gone to Pisa the year before.
Browning himself (according to Elizabeth Barrett) conceded that
'October or November would do as well' when she offered to go in
August (31 Aug. 1846, p. 1028); but he was under increasing
strain, and his letters are filled with foreboding. In his letter of 26
June, he sent her a handful of brown leaves; with the same quiet
symbolism, he noted the decline of the season in his next letter: 'all
roses fast going, lilies going . . autumnal hollyhocks in full blow . .
and now to count three months over before summer is to end!' (27
June 1846, p. 819.) He thought of the 'dismal, obscure months' of
separation which might be caused 'by a caprice where the power is'
(5 July 1846, p. 845); 'the ground is crumbling from beneath our
feet,' he warned her, with its chances & opportunities—do not talk
about "four months,"—till December, that is—unless you mean
what *must* follow as a consequence' (29 July 1846, p. 912).

Browning's nervousness communicated itself to Flush, who bit
Browning twice, at the meetings of 8 and 21 July. Browning bore
bravely with Elizabeth Barrett's darling (unless he made a private
arrangement with Mr Taylor?), but at the meeting of 1 August an
event occurred which confirmed his greatest fears. London was
struck, that Saturday afternoon, by a violent thunderstorm, and Mr
Barrett, who was not expected back until seven o'clock, came home
early from the City—anxious, as it turned out, about the condition
of his eldest daughter, for Elizabeth Barrett was terrified of storms,
and this one was the worst in three decades. Mr Barrett arrived in
Wimpole Street to find that Browning was with her. He sent Arabel
up with a message: 'He took up the fancy that I might be ill perhaps
with fear . . & only Mr. Browning in the room!!—which was not to
be permitted. He was *peremptory* with Arabel'. Elizabeth Barrett,
meanwhile, informed of her father's return, was 'most sorely

frightened—uneasy the whole time'. She did not care about the lightning and thunder, and she hardly noticed Browning: 'I was looking at Papa's face as I saw it through the floor' (2 Aug. 1846, pp. 921–2). Browning left at six, in a lull of the storm; it was to be the only time he and Mr Barrett were ever in the same house at the same time. Elizabeth Barrett waited for the other storm to break:

Dearest, he came into the room about seven, before he went to dinner—I was lying on the sofa & had on a white dressing gown, to get rid of the strings . . so oppressive the air was [. . .] He looked a little as if the thunder had passed into him, & said, 'Has this been your costume since the morning, pray?' 'Oh no'—I answered—'only just now, because of the heat.' 'Well,' he resumed, with a still graver aspect . . (so displeased he looked, dearest!) 'it appears, Ba, that *that man* has spent the whole day with you.' To which I replied as quietly as I could, that you had several times meant to go away, but that the rain would not let you,—& there the colloquy ended. Brief enough!—but it took my breath away [. . .] And think how it must have been a terrible day, when the lightning of it made the least terror . .

(ibid., p. 922.)

She was forty years old, remember! but to Mr Barrett, all his children were below the age of consent. Browning, deprived of news till Monday, chafed at home, wondering 'How many of these unfortunate Sundays are in store for me' (2 Aug. 1846, p. 926); and when he did get Elizabeth Barrett's letter, 'See!' he burst out, '*Now* talk of "three or four months"! And is not the wonder, that this should wait for the eighty-second visit to happen?' (3 Aug. 1846, p. 926; the visit was in fact the eighty-third.) The circumstances in which Mr Barrett had found them, Browning pointed out, were the most '*mitigating*' it was possible to imagine: 'in spite of all which, see what comes and is likely to come!'

But even this was not enough to persuade Elizabeth Barrett; she hurriedly qualified the violence of her father's reaction in her next letter: 'It was an unpleasant impression, & that is all, . . & nothing, I believe, has been thought of it since' (3 Aug. 1846, p. 929). There was no need to panic; there was plenty of time; and so the situation continued, with plans and preparations being made, but in such a frame of mind that the journey they envisaged seemed to be less in prospect than ever. Browning took it into his head that Mr Barrett, now that no one wanted or expected him to do anything, might suddenly send his daughter away; but no, Elizabeth Barrett reassured him sadly, 'Papa seems to have no more idea of my living beyond these four walls, than of a journey to Lapland' (28 Aug. 1846, p. 1016). Nor would her brothers or other members of the family do anything for her. She evaded all their ineffectual questions; and her aunt, Mrs Hedley, 'with her usual acuteness in such matters, observing my evasion, said, "Ah Ba, you have arranged your plans more than you would have us believe. But you are right not to tell us—Indeed I would rather not hear" ' (ibid., p. 1017). Mrs Hedley's 'acuteness' did not, however, extend to the truth; she thought that Elizabeth Barrett was going to go away in the company of Henrietta and Surtees Cook.

At their meeting of 30 August, Browning pressed the issue, and Elizabeth Barrett again talked of delay. Browning could not contain himself: 'I would not have believed it of you', he said (reported by Elizabeth Barrett, 30 Aug. 1846, p. 1020). The visit was interrupted, short of its usual time, by Mr Kenyon, and the lovers were forced to part as though they were mere acquaintances. On top of all this, Browning had just learnt of the Reverend George Barrett Hunter's sneering epithet for him, 'the New Cross Knight' (see above). He wrote Elizabeth Barrett a letter whose anger is sufficiently announced by the bare word 'Ba' in the opening sentence, devoid of any endearment:

I wonder what I shall write to you, Ba—I could suppress my feelings here, as I do on other points, and say nothing of the hatefulness of this state of things which is prolonged so uselessly. There is the point—show me one good reason, or show of reason, why we gain anything by deferring our departure till next week instead of to-morrow, and I will bear to perform yesterday's part for the amusement of Mr. Kenyon a dozen times over without complaint. But if the cold plunge *must* be taken, all this shivering delay on the bank is hurtful as well as fruitless. [. . .] You tell me you have decided to go—then, dearest, you will be prepared to go earlier than you promised yesterday—by the end of September at very latest. In proportion to the too probable excitement and painful circumstances of the departure, the greater amount of advantages should be secured for the departure itself. How can I take you away in even the beginning of October? We shall be a fortnight on the journey—with the year, as everybody sees and says, a full month in advance . . cold mornings and dark evenings already. Everybody would cry out on such folly when it was found that we let the favorable weather escape, in full assurance that the Autumn would come to us unattended by any one beneficial circumstance.

(30 Aug. 1846, pp. 1022–3.)

Elizabeth Barrett was upset by this letter. She understood that Browning 'should endure painfully and impatiently' his humiliating position, but not that he should doubt her own resolution. Once again (how Browning must have felt frustrated at these repeated affirmations which led nowhere!) she declared, 'I never wavered from the promise I gave freely'; once again she promised to go 'within a week of any time you choose' (31 Aug. 1846, p. 1028). The trouble was, she gave Browning the power to take the decision without the security that would come from her own expressed desire. She made her acceptance depend simply on his will; she abdicated from her share in the responsibility. 'So if September shall be possible, let it be September', she went on. 'I do not object nor hold back.' But nor did she press forward. Browning was really unwell for a couple of days at the beginning of September; it was like a shout of frustration to Elizabeth Barrett, but it cannot have helped her to make up her mind to go.

   It is uncertain how long things would have dragged on like this, had Mr Barrett not made his second unknowing intervention in the courtship—the decisive one, this time. For some weeks, Browning and Elizabeth Barrett had canvassed the unsettling possibility that the household at Wimpole Street might be moved to the country, while the house was cleaned and redecorated. Elizabeth Barrett thought that nothing would come of it, as nothing had come of it in previous years. She was wrong. On Wednesday, 9 September, Mr Barrett issued an 'edict' that George was to find lodgings for the whole family 'either at Dover, Reigate, Tunbridge, . . Papa did "not mind which," he said, & "you may settle it among you" [. . .] we are to go therefore & not delay'. It was past midnight as she wrote; she was 'embarrassed to the utmost degree, as to the best path to take. If we are taken away on monday . . what then? [. . .] It seems quite too soon & too sudden for us to set out on our Italian adventure now—& perhaps even we could not compass—'. There she paused. But the last words of her letter were to be crucial: 'I will do as you wish—understand' (9 Sept. 1846, pp. 1057–8).

   Browning had written and sealed a letter to Elizabeth Barrett early on Thursday morning, and then gone to town before the post came, leaving his letter at home (it is not clear why he did not take it to the post). 'What a glorious dream,—thro' nearly two years—

without a single interval of blankness,—much less, bitter waking! [. . .] my perfect angel you have been!' So the letter ends. When Browning came home, he found Elizabeth Barrett's letter waiting for him; his eye leaped to the last sentence, and he broke the seal of his own letter and added a postscript which has the terse authority of an order scribbled by a general on the field of battle:

'I will do as you wish—understand'—then I understand you are in earnest. If you *do* go on Monday, our marriage will be impossible for another year—the misery! You see what we have gained by waiting. We must be *married directly* and go to Italy—I will go for a licence today and we can be married on Saturday. I will call to-morrow at 3 and arrange everything with you.

(10 Sept. 1846, p. 1059.)

So he did; so they were. In a letter which he sent later that afternoon (both of them arrived the same day at Wimpole Street), he was a little calmer and more deliberate, but just as determined: 'Your words, first & last, have been that you "would not fail me"—you will not— [. . .] *Now your* part must begin—It may as well begin and end, both, *now* as at any other time' (10 Sept. 1846, p. 1060).

'Dearest, I write one word, & have one will which is yours', Elizabeth Barrett wrote on Thursday night. 'At the same time, do not be precipitate—we shall not be taken away on monday, no, nor for several days afterward. George has simply gone to look for houses' (10 Sept. 1846, p. 1061). But it was she herself who had expressed the fear that they might be moving on Monday. A hint, perhaps, that Elizabeth Barrett, without realizing what she was doing, had 'bounced' Browning into taking action? Browning, at any rate, responded by 'bouncing' her. 'I will act by your decision,' she repeated, '& I wish you to decide.' After this letter, Browning recorded two successive meetings, with no letters intervening. The first was his visit on the afternoon of Friday, 11 September, at which he and Elizabeth Barrett finalized their plans. The second was the marriage itself:

Sat. Sepr 12, 1846.
$\frac{1}{4}$ 11 – 11 $\frac{1}{4}$ a.m. (91.)

He underlined the '91' three times—without doubt 'triumphantly',

as Elvan Kintner says. (Kintner also points out that the marriage
was actually the ninety-*second* meeting, since Browning's count had
gone wrong after number sixty-five.) It was the first time that he
and Elizabeth Barrett had met outside her room in Wimpole Street.
After the ceremony came the scene which I described at the opening
of this book: Browning and Elizabeth Barrett got into separate
hackney carriages and drove off in different directions. Elizabeth
Barrett went to recuperate at Mr Boyd's house; Browning went
home to New Cross. There he wrote Elizabeth Barrett the only
letter of his in the whole correspondence which is—almost—free of
artifice and affectation, free of *pressure*; which is direct and serene in
both its praise and its self-regard:

> 1 p.m. Saturday.
>
> You will only expect a few words—what will those be?
> When the heart is full it may run over, but the real fulness stays within—
> You asked me yesterday 'if I should repent'? Yes—my own Ba,—I could
> wish all the past were to do over again, that in it I might somewhat more,—
> never so little more,—conform in the outward homage to the inward feel-
> ing: what I have professed . . (for I have performed nothing—) seems to fall
> short of what my first love required even—and when I think of *this*
> moment's love . . I could repent, as I say.
> Words can never tell you, however,—form them, transform them
> anyway,—how perfectly dear you are to me—perfectly dear to my heart
> and soul.
> I look back, and in every one point, every word and gesture, every letter,
> every *silence*—you have been entirely perfect to me—I would not change
> one word, one look—
> My hope and aim are to preserve this love, not to fall from it—for which
> I trust to God who procured it for me, and doubtlessly can preserve it.
> Enough now, my dearest, dearest, own Ba! You have given me the high-
> est completest proof of love that ever one human being gave another. I am
> all gratitude—and all pride (under the proper feeling which ascribes pride to
> the right source—) all pride that my life has been so crowned by you.
>   God bless you prays your very own
>
>   R.
> I will write to-morrow of course. Take every care of *my life* which is in
> that dearest little hand; try an be composed, my beloved.
> Remember to thank Wilson for me.
>
>   (12 Sept. 1846, pp. 1062-3.)

This letter is a consummate expression of the rhetoric of Browning's
love for Elizabeth Barrett—its gestures of deference and self-

reproach, its powerful use of language to scorn the use of language—but it is the one occasion on which, within the limits of the rhetoric, Browning comes close to what, in 'One Word More', he says is the aim of every artist who 'lives and loves': 'to find his love a language / Fit and fair and simple and sufficient' (ll. 59–62). He was never to surpass it, until the letter he sent to his sister Sarianna, nearly fifteen years later, in which he described the death of Elizabeth Barrett Browning in his arms.

5 Flight

While Browning was writing, Elizabeth Barrett was doing. 'Oh, SUCH *a day*!' she wrote later on that afternoon—reassuring her husband, however, that she was not 'slain downright'. She had taken some of Mr Boyd's Cyprus wine, and 'had some bread & butter for dinner, to keep me from looking too pale'; when her sisters arrived, they went to Hampstead Heath in the carriage, and Elizabeth Barrett 'talked & looked' as normally as she could. (She was not to know that Arabel had, in fact, guessed her secret.) 'How necessity makes heroes—or heroines at least!' she reflected. 'For I did not sleep all last night, & when I first went out with Wilson to get to the flystand in Marylebone Street, I staggered so, that we both were afraid for the fear's sake,—but we called at a chemist's for sal volatile & were thus enabled to go on.' Elizabeth Barrett, too, had her characteristic touches in this first letter written after the wedding: 'Ask your mother to forgive me, Robert', she wrote, 'If *I* had not been there, *she* would have been there, perhaps'; and she concluded with a familiar prayer: 'if either of us two is to suffer injury and sorrow for what happened there to-day—I pray that it may all fall upon *me*!' (12 Sept. 1846, pp. 1063–4.)

Now, however, they had other things to think about besides the rhetoric of their relationship. There were new worries—that the register of the church might be examined by 'penny-a-liners' seeking out scandal for the newspapers, for example—and there were urgent practical arrangements to be made, if their joint determination to leave England as soon as they were married was to be put into effect. Some of these arrangements concerned details of social decorum, which Browning and Elizabeth Barrett took seriously, in spite of the incongruous context. The advertisement which they were to leave behind them: how should Elizabeth Barrett be described—should Mr Barrett's connection with Jamaica be mentioned?—and above all, should there be a date, which would reveal the clandestine nature of the marriage? (The advertisement, in *The Times* of 21 September, has no date, and describes Elizabeth Barrett as 'eldest daughter of Edward Moulton Barrett, Esq., of Wimpole Street'.) There were cards to be printed and sent to relatives and friends; there were letters, too, which Elizabeth Barrett, weak with nervous exhaustion, found herself unable to write. Besides all this, there was packing—what to take? books, clothes, a portable writing desk?—and how to get Elizabeth Barrett's and Wilson's luggage out of Wimpole Street, since they could not carry it themselves without being observed? (It was sent by cab to Vauxhall Station on the night before the departure.) Then again, Elizabeth Barrett could not actually leave the house until the late morning or afternoon, because Arabel slept in her room and would have to be told of an early morning departure. Elizabeth Barrett was adamant that no member of her family should have either to lie to her father, or suffer for telling the truth. Browning, too, had his scruples: he would not call at Wimpole Street and ask to see his wife under her maiden name. 'Browning's respectability', wrote Chesterton, 'was an older and more primeval thing than the oldest and most primeval passions of other men' (Chesterton, 79).

Last of all, the actual time of the journey. The departure of the Barrett household to Little Bookham (near Leatherhead in Surrey) was fixed for Monday, 21 September. Browning and Elizabeth Barrett considered, but dismissed as impractical, the possibility of her leaving from there; they decided, therefore, to go at the end of the preceding week, the week which followed their wedding. Friday? Saturday? Sunday? Browning, with various railway and shipping timetables to consult, and various cross-Channel routes to choose from, got into the most awful muddle, which it would exasperate the reader, as it has exasperated the author of this book, to follow. He sent three notes on Thursday, 17 September, changing his mind each time, and ending up with a mistake which Elizabeth Barrett noticed, though by now so dizzy with fatigue that she could not remember half the addresses to which cards were to be sent. At last the arrangement was made: she and Wilson would meet Browning between half-past three to four in the afternoon of Saturday, 19 September, at Hodgson's bookshop in Great Marylebone Street. They would travel in a cab to Vauxhall, collect their luggage (sent there in advance), and board the Southampton train, which left at five and arrived at eight. The night boat for Le Havre left Southampton at a quarter past eight.

Elizabeth Barrett wrote to Browning on the night of Friday, 18 September: the last letter, the five-hundred-and-seventy-third of the extant collection. In it, she summed up her sense of the past and her trust in the future; and she made clear to Browning both how firmly that trust was founded, and, at the same time, how near the relationship had come to foundering. But her spirit, 'fairly roused', had the last word:

At from half past three, to four, then—four will not, I suppose, be too late—I will not write more—*I cannot*—. By tomorrow at this time, I shall have *you* only, to love me—my beloved!—

You *only*!—As if one said *God only*—And we shall have *Him* beside, I pray of Him—[. . .]

Is this my last letter to you, ever dearest?—Oh—if I loved you less . . a little, little less . .

Why I should tell you that our marriage was invalid, or ought to be—& that you should by no means come for me tomorrow. It is dreadful . . dreadful . . to have to give pain here by a voluntary act—for the first time in my life—[. . .]

Do you pray for me tonight, Robert? Pray for me, & love me, that I may have courage, feeling both—

Your own Ba—

The boxes are *safely sent*. Wilson has been perfect to me—And *I* . . calling her 'timid,' & afraid of her timidity!—I begin to think that none are so bold as the timid, when they are fairly roused.

(18 Sept. 1846, pp. 1086–7.)[1]

The departure took place as planned. On the morning of Sunday, 20 September, Robert and Elizabeth Barrett Browning, their maid Elizabeth Wilson, and their dog Flush, stepped ashore from the Southampton boat at Le Havre. They left behind them a very angry man.

---

[1] The comma after 'three' in 'half past three, to four' is not in Kintner, who also omits to italicize 'only' in '*God only*'; the dash after 'late' in 'be too late—' is emended from a full stop in Kintner.

PART TWO

7

The Poetry of Love

1

You think . . for I must get to *you* . . that I 'unconsciously exaggerate what you are to me'—now you don't know what *that* is, nor can I very well tell you, because the language with which I talk to myself of these matters is spiritual Attic, and 'loves contractions,' as grammarians say; but I read it myself, and well know what it means . . that's why I told you I was self-conscious,—I meant that I never yet mistook my own feelings, one for another—there! Of what use is talking?

(11 Mar. 1845, pp. 38–9.)

This passage comes from Browning's seventh letter to Elizabeth Barrett—seventh, let us remember, out of the 288 he was to write to her during the twenty months of their courtship. In a great many of these letters he reiterates the point he makes here about feeling, and language, and the language of feeling. 'Of what use is talking?' he asks—again and again. You sometimes have the impression that he talks of nothing save the uselessness of speech. Before I come back to this particular passage, I want to stress the repetitiveness, the copiousness and redundant variation with which Browning deploys this single rhetorical device. Here, then, are four passages, occurring among many others in letters covering a period of three months. The first is from a letter of 9 November 1845:

there is nothing in you that does not draw out all of me: you possess me, dearest . . and there is no help for the expressing it all, no voice nor hand, but these of mine which shrink and turn away from the attempt: so you must go on, patiently, knowing me, more and more, and your entire power on me, and I will console myself, to the full extent, with your knowledge,—

penetration, intuition . . *somehow* I must believe you can get to what is here, in me, without the pretence of my telling or writing it—

(p. 261.)

From a letter written a month later:

But it all hangs together; speaking of you—, to you—, writing to you—all is helpless and sorrowful work by the side of what is in my soul to say and to write—

(7 Dec. 1845, p. 307.)

From a letter of 14 January 1846:

When I am away from you—a crowd of things press on me for utterance . . 'I will say them, not write them,' I think:—when I see you—all to be said seems insignificant, irrelevant,—'they can be written, at all events'—I think *that* too. So, feeling so much, I say so little!—

(p. 387.)

And last—briefest, simplest, and most direct of all—the opening sentence of a letter written three days before the preceding one: 'I have no words for you, my dearest,—I shall never have—' (11 Jan. 1846, p. 378.)

'I have no words for you'; 'Of what use is talking?' But Browning palpably had many words for Elizabeth Barrett, and an obvious use for them. What, then, is he on about? Why does he harp throughout the correspondence on the same string, his inadequacy of expression, the 'helpless and sorrowful work' of communicating his feelings? Is he—dread word—sincere? Or is the whole thing a pose, a way of saying something in the act of pretending not to be able to say it? If so, it is a way trodden to death by the time we reach letter 279, written when Browning had returned home on the day of their wedding, and we read, yet again, the familiar lament: 'I could wish all the past were to do over again, that in it I might somewhat more,—never so little more,—conform in the outward homage to the inward feeling' (12 Sept. 1846, p. 1062). We may excuse Browning from considering our sensibilities in the matter. But what about Elizabeth Barrett? If Browning's tongue-tied pose served a deliberate rhetorical purpose, you would expect him to anticipate the danger of monotony. Elizabeth Barrett was a heroic correspondent, a generous and a tolerant lover; but would not even she surfeit on an epistolary diet of perpetual self-abasement?

As a matter of fact, there are very few occasions on which Elizabeth Barrett directly responds to Browning's comments about his inability to say what he feels. When she does respond, she can be quite sharp. 'I have your letter', she wrote to him on one occasion, ' . . you who cannot write! [. . .] After all it seems to me that you can write for yourself pretty well—rather too well I used to think from the beginning' (29 May 1846, p. 740). But it would be misleading to suggest that this enjoyable riposte is typical. Mostly, the overt pressure of Browning's concern meets, in her, a blankness, a saving indifference, possibly even a shrewd perception that, in so far as ends mattered more than means, Browning's anxieties about the language of feeling were beside the point.

To us, however, as readers now both of his letters and of his poems, Browning's odd insistence on his expressive weaknesses and failures is of profound importance. It illuminates not just his writing, but his creativity, the mind of his art. The lover and the writer share a common preoccupation with language and feeling: you might say a common passion. The source of both love and writing is, for Browning, the same, an act of the mind, an appropriation of imaginative space from which to speak; and expression, whether of the man's love or the artist's ideas (the distinction, as we shall see, is often blurred) is the desired justification of that initial act, the fulfilment of intentions and the proof of value. It is also inherently inadequate to the task—self-corrupted and self-destroying. And yet, in the very agony which expression inflicts upon feeling, feeling is vindicated and expression redeemed.

In the passage with which I began, Browning was responding to the concluding paragraph of Elizabeth Barrett's most recent letter. She had written:

How kind you are!—how kindly & gently you speak to me!—Some things you say are very touching, & some, surprising—& although I am aware that you unconsciously exaggerate what I can be to you, yet it is delightful to be broad awake & think of you as my friend.

(5 Mar. 1845, pp. 35–6.)

In his reply, Browning changes the form in which he quotes what he takes to be the key phrase of this passage. He writes: 'You think [. . .] that I "unconsciously exaggerate what you *are* to me" ', whereas Elizabeth Barrett had actually written 'what I *can be* to you'. This is a significant shift of focus. Elizabeth Barrett was giving him a reminder, which the syntax softens into a compliment, that

her age and personal circumstances precluded certain kinds of relation between them. The phrase 'you unconsciously exaggerate what
I can be to you' is centred on the 'I', not the 'you': that is, it is not
about Browning's consciousness, but Elizabeth Barrett's—her sense
of her own inadequacy, her anxiety, her vulnerability. But Browning's form of words makes it seem as though Elizabeth Barrett were
saying, 'You don't know the nature of your own feelings'. He mis-
reads her, in other words: and misreading, like murder, always has a
motive.

Consider Browning's account of the way he thinks. 'The
language with which I talk to myself of these matters is spiritual
Attic, and "loves contractions," as grammarians say; but I read it
myself, and well know what it means'. 'Spiritual Attic' is a complex
formula. It packs in the idea of wit, from the French 'spirituel', since
wit is an economy of association, and 'loves contractions' (not just
brevity, but *contracts* or *connections*); 'Attic wit' was a catch-phrase
for 'refined, delicate, poignant wit', according to *OED*, which cites
Pope's *Epilogue to the Satires*: 'While Roman Spirit charms, and
Attic Wit'. The discourse is 'spiritual', also, in that it takes place
within, and refers to, the mind or spirit, and, unlike a voice, has no
material being; and it is 'Attic', again, because the Attic style was
the 'pure' style of classical Greek, and therefore the model of choice
expression. Browning apparently makes a considerable claim for the
value of the 'language with which I talk to myself of these matters';
but notice how 'talk to myself' becomes 'read it myself', inner
speech becomes inner text, the expressive wit of the primary
language turns to the difficult grammar of the secondary language;
reflexive utterance becomes an object of reflective interpretation.
What can be spoken in one kind of 'Attic', or 'pure' language, must
be read in another; the 'contractions' which mark the presence of
feeling—its birth-pangs—also signal a cutting-short or constriction
of feeling. 'I know my own mind', Browning is saying to Elizabeth
Barrett; 'I know *what* I think because I know *how* I think, I have
access to my own meaning'.

But what is the value of a meaning which, being known, cannot
be communicated to anyone else? The value is in proportion to the
difficulty of expression; Browning's inability to say what he feels
proves the truth of his feeling in a way that words themselves could
never do. Facility would be a sign of shallowness; obscurity denotes
the presence of something worth struggling (and failing) to articu-

late. Language, in Browning's idea of creativity, is not a process of achievement of, or approximation to, 'meaning', but a process of inevitable and necessary failure—necessary, that is, if the meaning is to justify itself. 'Now I kiss you,' he wrote to Elizabeth Barrett on one occasion, 'and will begin a new thinking of you,—and end, and begin, going round and round in my circle of discovery,—' (8 Feb. 1846, p. 443). But this 'circle of discovery' may in fact be dis-covering or revealing nothing, because of its very perfection. The circle is the symbol of infinity, but also of zero, a nothingness which encompasses everything in a form of terminal closure. For, as the speaker in stanza xvii of 'Old Pictures in Florence' puts it, 'What's come to perfection, perishes'; and he goes on:

> Thyself shalt afford the example, Giotto!
>   Thy one work, not to decrease or diminish,
> Done at a stroke, was just (was it not?) 'O!'
>   Thy great Campanile is still to finish.

Browning inverts the meaning traditionally ascribed to Vasari's famous anecdote about how the painter, asked to demonstrate his skill to a papal envoy, drew a perfect circle with one sweep of his brush. Such perfection, for Browning, is self-contained, and therefore without value; whereas Giotto's aspiring Campanile 'is still to finish', that is, endures as a meaningful design because it is prospective and imperfect.

The topic of love is the topic of art: this is the 'motive' for Browning's misreading of that phrase of Elizabeth Barrett's about his 'unconscious exaggeration'. It is in terms of Browning's poetics that the language of his love-letters to Elizabeth Barrett, and by extension 'the language in which he talks to himself of these matters', requires to be read.

2

Browning's poetics centre on the *process of composition* as he experienced it. Briefly, the composition of poetry takes place in two stages: *conception* (the instant of primary vision in which the poem is perceived whole and perfect) and *execution* (in which the timeless moment of conception is broken up into the sequential articulations of language). 'I *know* that I don't make out my conception by my language,' Browning wrote to Ruskin, 'all poetry being a putting of the infinite within the finite'.[1] The opposition between these two terms finds expression in a wide variety of ways both in Browning's writing about poetry, and in his poems themselves. It occurs straightforwardly in the description of the troubadour Sordello's failure to write up to the level of his imagination:

> Because perceptions whole, like that he sought
> To clothe, reject so pure a work of thought
> As language: thought may take perception's place
> But hardly co-exist in any case,
> Being its mere presentment—of the whole
> By parts, the simultaneous and the sole
> By the successive and the many.
>
> (*Sordello*, ii. 589–95.)

Language is a 'work of thought' because it takes place in time; 'perception' is timeless (or gives the illusion of being so). Thought and language are 'the successive and the many', since thoughts succeed each other in the mind, and language is a succession of elements; whereas perception is 'the simultaneous and the sole', occupying the 'moment, one and infinite' ('By the Fireside', l. 181) which Browning celebrates throughout his work. Completeness and singularity are necessary and reciprocal features of the imagination and its conceptions: the tag 'whole and sole', with its internal rhyme like a signal of the conjunction of ideas, is a favourite of Browning's. The pun on 'sole' reminds us of another property of perception, its immateriality. In the penultimate chapter of Samuel Johnson's *Rasselas*, entitled 'Imlac Discourses on the Nature of the Soul', the philosopher deduces the immortality of the soul from its immateriality, since what is immaterial is also indivisible: 'nor can we conceive how that which has no parts [. . .] can be naturally corrupted or impaired'. Rasselas objects that he finds it difficult 'to conceive of any thing without extension; what is extended must have parts, and you allow, that whatever has parts may be destroyed'.

'Consider your own conceptions,' replied Imlac, 'and the difficulty will be less. You will find substance without extension. An ideal form is no less real than material bulk; yet an ideal form has no extension. [. . .] As is the

---

[1] This letter is reprinted in W. G. Collingwood, *Life and Work of John Ruskin* (London, 1893), vol. i, pp. 193–202.

effect, such is the cause: as thought, such is the power that thinks; a power impassive and indiscerptible.'

Browning thinks of the creative imagination as such a power, and its 'perceptions whole' as 'ideal forms'. Thought is the 'mere present-ment' of these forms, a secondary process; it is material, bound up with time, and therefore subject to corruption. There can be no equi-valence between perception and thought; there can only be an alter-nation, a power-struggle between them, in which 'thought may take perception's place'. In taking perception's place, thought, and its instrument language, destroy the nature of what they appropriate. 'Words!' Browning exclaimed on one particularly breast-beating occasion, ' . . it was written I should hate and never use them to any purpose' (17 Sept. 1845, p. 204). But the very phrase he uses to express his fated and fatal disability has an ironic catch: 'it was *writ-ten*'. Unless language takes perception's place, perception could not, itself, take place at all, in terms of human communication. The dilemma for the creative artist is simple and apparently insoluble: his medium and his message are completely at odds. Of course, the dilemma is only posed in this way within the text: what happens to the poet Sordello is not what happens to the poet Browning, author of *Sordello*. The idea that perception cannot be communicated in language is, itself, communicated in language, which thus becomes the origin of the process in which it is supposed to be secondary: the very terms 'perception', 'vision', 'imagination' and so on, are gener-ated and sustained by an energy which is supposedly dedicated to their dissolution. Sordello is used (literally, consumed, wasted) by his language; but Browning is pre-eminently a language-user.

This differentiation between what is said in the text, and what the text says, operates with equal force in Browning's love-letters, as we shall see. But before coming to that, I want to look at another pas-sage in which the terms of conception and execution are suggest-ively paired. From 1841 to 1846, Browning published his poems and plays in a series of cheap paperbacked pamphlets entitled *Bells and Pomegranates*. The title had been the subject of much specula-tion, and Elizabeth Barrett, shamelessly taking advantage of her pri-vileged position, had as early as October 1845 pressed Browning to explain what he meant by it. Here is his reply:

The Rabbis make Bells & Pomegranates symbolical of Pleasure and Profit, the Gay & the Grave, the Poetry & the Prose, Singing and Sermonizing—

such a mixture of effects as in the original hour (that is quarter of an hour) of confidence & creation, I meant the whole should prove at last [. . .]

(18 Oct. 1845, p. 241.)

At Elizabeth Barrett's insistence, Browning grudgingly included a version of this explanation in the last number of the series, which appeared in April 1846.[2] Here, the principle appears as 'an endeavour towards something like an alternation, or mixture, of music with discoursing, sound with sense, poetry with thought'; to which Browning added 'another fancy' of 'Faith and good works', with learned allusions to Giotto and Raphael, and Vasari's commentary on the latter (helpfully given in the original Italian). But the mystification is not impenetrable. These paired terms, both in the letter to Elizabeth Barrett and the 'official' note, correspond to those of 'perception' and 'thought' which make up the process of composition. Perception is musical, carefree, and intuitive; thought is serious, discursive, and self-conscious. The pleasure of singing is set against the profit (that is, benefit) of sermonizing. The 'first fine careless rapture' of the 'wise thrush' in 'Home-Thoughts, from Abroad' (l. 16) is a model of perception, the *seizure* of experience in a moment of transfiguring awareness; Rabbi Ben Ezra, on the other hand, with his call to 'Grow old along with me', is the type of the 'sermonizing' artist who has abandoned the notion of divine insight in favour of an approximate and humane search for enlightenment. *Bells and Pomegranates* itself, as a work, exemplifies the fatal process by which the 'gay' turns into the 'grave': Browning speaks of the 'original hour (that is, quarter of an hour) of confidence & creation' in which he conceived the idea of the series; he strongly implies that this act of *faith* had not resulted in any justificatory *good works*.

That last phrase reminds us of the connection between Browning's poetics and his Nonconformist upbringing. Faith, which in Calvinist doctrine is the sole means of salvation, translates in the idiom of art as intention, or what one Browning character calls 'the bright moment of promising';[3] and the 'assurance' of salvation

---

[2] This last number contained two plays, *Luria* and *A Soul's Tragedy*. DeVane (*Handbook*, 89) quotes the explanatory note in full, but incorrectly states that its position between the two works was intended to exclude *A Soul's Tragedy* from the series. Elizabeth Barrett thought so (13 Apr. 1846, p. 619), but Browning explicitly denied it (14 Apr. 1846, p. 623).

[3] The speaker is no Calvinist, but, by a pleasing irony, a Papal Legate—Ogniben in *A Soul's Tragedy*. (He does not mean it, either.)

which is the mark of the elect appears as the pride with which the visionary poet sets out on his doomed enterprise—'confidence & creation', since 'confidence' implies both having faith in oneself and entrusting one's faith to someone or something else.

It is time, now, to make a distinction between Browning's poetics as he applies them to himself and to other poets. A double standard operates here, which involves Browning in a crucial inconsistency. On the one hand, his idea of his own poetry remains that of an inadequate or impoverished discourse. He writes to Elizabeth Barrett, early on in the correspondence: 'what I have printed gives *no* knowledge of me [. . .] I have never begun, even, what I hope I was born to begin and end,—"R.B. a poem." ' (11 Feb. 1845, p. 17.) The formula ' "R.B. a poem." ' fuses the identity of the poet with that of his text, each denoting the other; the signature is in initials, so that the text is 'signed' (identified, given meaning, and finished all at once) with the *beginnings* of a name—one of those 'contractions' which we were looking at earlier. (As for the 'hope' which Browning entertains of being 'born' to accomplish this work, we shall see its deployment, with supercharged ambivalence, in Browning's anticipations of his life and work in Elizabeth Barrett's company.)

If, as I have argued, the foundation of this sense of failure, which makes Browning in the same letter describe his work to date as 'sadly imperfect demonstrations of even mere ability', lies in a *necessary* relation between conception and execution, or between imagination and language—necessary, that is, in terms of Browning's poetics—then it would be logical to expect the same conditions to apply to other writers. If language is inadequate to experience, then no adequate poem can come into being. But Browning's work contains a gallery of figures, real and imaginary, who *are* fully in command of their medium. There is the 'consummate orb' of Dante's poetry (*Sordello*, i. 350), and the 'spheric poetical faculty of Shelley' with 'its own self-sufficing central light' (*Essay on Shelley*, in *Poems*, vol. i. p. 1006); both of these are associated with circles, the 'orb' or 'sphere' functioning, in their cases, without the overt irony which attached to Giotto's empty 'O'. On the contrary, Dante and Shelley are associated with plenitude, with the fulfilment of vision: Shelley in *Pauline* figures famously as the 'sun-treader', not a fallen rival of Apollo like Icarus or Phaethon, but a victor over him, who treads on the sun like a conqueror, in an image drawn directly, I think, from the successive tramplings and treadings-out of light in Shelley's *The Triumph of Life*. But of these figures of creative supremacy in Browning, undoubtedly the most important and the most revealing is the living figure of Elizabeth Barrett herself.

3

'You speak out, *you*,—I only make men & women speak—give you truth broken into prismatic hues, and fear the pure white light, even if it is in me' (13 Jan. 1845, p. 7). So runs the best-known of Browning's comments to Elizabeth Barrett about their respective status as poets, which occurs in his second letter to her. It is hard, when we reflect that the origins of the title of Browning's most admired collection, *Men and Women*, lie here, to take seriously that phrase 'I only make men & women speak', particularly when we set Browning's dramatic speakers against Elizabeth Barrett's 'speaking out' in some of the weaker parts of her work. It is hard, but it is necessary. Only if we acknowledge and take as the premiss of our argument Browning's decisive evaluation of the two kinds of poet represented by himself and Elizabeth Barrett will we be in a position to trace the windings of his language of feeling. In setting up the contrast between her creativity and his own, Browning was not making a mistake, since his motive in doing so sprang neither from a disinterested desire for truth, nor from a generous impulse of affection; it was self-centred, and accurate in exactly the terms that it needed to be, those of his own self-consciousness.

The question of what Browning found to admire in Elizabeth Barrett's poetry can, I think, be answered in a word: nothing. It was not poetry that he read, it was personality: 'E.B.B., a poem'. Her poetry was perfectly blank to him, and this blankness was, to adapt the phrase which Browning later applied to Shelley, 'the very radiance and aroma of [her] personality, projected from it but not separated' (*Essay on Shelley*, in *Poems*, Penguin vol. i. p. 1002). She was inscribed in her poems, and this inscription also constituted an effacement, a deconstruction of language by language, so that that which language normally concealed and displaced—the presence and fullness of the creative force itself—was miraculously restored. 'You speak out, *you*'—the emphasis is Browning's own, and we can match it in a number of other passages, particularly from the early letters. One of them I quoted at the beginning of this chapter: 'You think . . for I must get to *you* . . that I "unconsciously exaggerate what you are to me" '. 'I must get to *you*'—that, really, is the key-note of Browning's enterprise in the courtship. In a late letter, he wrote: 'I love *you*, dearest, with a love that seems to separate you from your very qualities . . the essential from its accidents' (27 Aug. 1846, p. 1010). And the note is struck from the very start. Here, again, are the opening sentences of Browning's first letter:

I love your verses with all my heart, dear Miss Barrett,—and this is no off-hand complimentary letter that I shall write,—whatever else, no prompt matter-of-course recognition of your genius, and there a graceful and natural end of the thing: since the day last week when I first read your poems, I quite laugh to remember how I have been turning and turning again in my mind what I should be able to tell you of their effect upon me—for in the first flush of delight I thought I would this once get out of my habit of purely passive enjoyment, when I do really enjoy, and thoroughly justify my admiration—perhaps even, as a loyal fellow-craftsman should, try and find fault and do you some little good to be proud of hereafter!—but nothing comes of it all—so into me has it gone, and part of me has it become, this great living poetry of yours, not a flower of which but took root and grew—oh how different that is from lying to be dried and pressed flat, and prized highly and put in a book with a proper account at top and bottom, and shut up and put away . . and the book called a 'Flora,' besides! After all I need not give up the thought of doing that, too, in time; because even now, talking with whoever is worthy, I can give a reason for my faith in one and another excellence, the fresh strange music, the affluent language, the exquisite pathos and true new brave thought—but in this addressing myself to you—your own self, and for the first time, my feeling rises altogether. I do, as I say, love these books with all my heart—and I love you too: do you know I was once not very far from seeing—really seeing you?

(10 Jan. 1845, p. 3.)

Browning interprets Elizabeth Barrett's poetry in terms of his own creativity. In fact, he has apparently experienced it like the composition of one of his own poems, the 'first flush of delight' (corresponding to the primary act of 'perception')[4] giving rise to the

[4] For the link between blushing and perception/conception, see Christopher Ricks, *Keats and Embarrassment* (Oxford, 1976), ch. vii. Ricks quotes 'The Eve of St. Agnes', st. xvi: 'Sudden a thought came like a full-blown rose, / Flushing his brow'; compare Browning's 'A Death in the Desert', l. 59: 'Stung by the splendour of a sudden thought'. There is a particularly rich use of the figure in the concluding lines of *Red Cotton Night-Cap Country*.

impulse to 'thoroughly justify [his] admiration' or to 'try and find fault' (both of these are seen as positive acts of expression); but, as in the composition of poetry, 'nothing comes of it all'. At this point, however, there is an unexpected development. The fact that Browning fails to find fault with Elizabeth Barrett's poetry combines with the fact that he cannot praise it adequately; her poetry is beyond praise or blame, it is perfect: 'nothing' does, truly, 'come of it all', since her writing signifies both all and nothing. The syntax makes an intensely ironic causal connection between Browning's failure to express his feelings and the strength of those feelings themselves. 'Nothing comes of it all—*so* into me has it gone, and part of me has it become, this great living poetry of yours'. Suppose, then, that something *had* come of it all? The clear implication is that the whole experience would have been spoiled. Only by not being able to articulate his admiration of Elizabeth Barrett's poetry can Browning really grasp the ground of that admiration. This paradox is further enforced by the metaphor of the living and dead flowers which follows. Browning's anticipation of being able at some stage to compile exactly the kind of literary-critical 'Flora' he despises is the exact counterpart of his hope that one day he will write 'R.B.—a poem'. It will not come about: Elizabeth Barrett's creative divinity puts her out of reach. Browning appears to give vent to his admiration in his praise of 'one and another excellence', but this praise is controlled by a characteristic indirection, projected in a dialogue between himself and 'whoever is worthy', not communicating his feeling directly to its object. 'You—your own self' demands a corresponding completeness of response: 'my feeling rises altogether'. Feeling overrides expression and suppresses any partial revelation, leaving the primary act of perception, or love. 'I do, as I say, love these books with all my heart—and I love you too': love posits an unimaginable reciprocity of appropriation, in which the lover fulfils his own identity in the process of being 'taken over' by what he loves.

Browning speaks of 'addressing myself to you—your own self', and then of 'seeing—really seeing you'. These repetitions stress the notion of an authentic self—the 'ideal form' which Elizabeth Barrett's physical self embodies is the same as that which her poetry expresses. Elizabeth Barrett is a type of what Browning, in the *Essay on Shelley*, was later to call the 'subjective poet', whose writing is 'less a work than an effluence':

Therefore, in our approach to the poetry, we necessarily approach the personality of the poet; in apprehending it we apprehend him, and certainly we cannot love it without loving him. Both for love's and for understanding's sake we desire to know him, and as readers of his poetry must be readers of his biography also.

(*Essay on Shelley*, *Poems*, vol. i. p. 1002.)

Notice how 'approach' becomes 'apprehend'; in the same way, Browning's 'addressing [him]self' to Elizabeth Barrett opens a campaign in which 'seeing—really seeing' her is at issue, in the sense both of physical sight and of intellectual and imaginative grasp. In this process, Elizabeth Barrett's poetry is of supreme importance to Browning, and simultaneously of no importance. In one letter, for example (16 Nov. 1845, pp. 270–3), he first imagines discovering that she is not, after all, *the* Elizabeth Barrett, the one who wrote the poems, claiming that it would make no difference to him; and then, later in the same letter, after reading her sonnet 'Past and Future', 'which affects me more than any poem I ever read', he turns on himself and says, 'How can I put your poetry away from you, even in these ineffectual attempts to concentrate myself upon, and better apply myself to what remains [. . .] for is not that sonnet to be loved as a true utterance of yours?'

   In thus becoming a double reader, of Elizabeth Barrett's poetry and of her 'biography', Browning is also engaging in a double process of interpretation. His feeling for her is conditioned by his understanding of her, and so is his expression of that feeling. This *under*standing is, literally, the adoption of a secondary position towards her, as the source, the pure origin of his own creativity: in 'addressing [him]self' to her, he is addressing his own inner self, the imagination which creates but cannot communicate. It is a rhetorical *prise de position*, a 'taking place': Browning's authority to speak derives from an abdication. Here, for example, is a passage from a letter which comes immediately after the retailing of an (apparently) trivial anecdote:

Now I get to you, my Ba! How strange! It does so happen that I took the pen and laid out the paper with, I really think, a completer, deeper yearning of love to *you* than usual even—I seemed to have a thousand things that I *could* say *now*—and on touching the paper . . see—I start off with a foolish story and still foolisher comment as if there were no Ba close at my head all the time, straight before my eyes too! So it is with me—I give the *expressing* part up at once! It must be understood, inferred,—(*proved*, never!) <Yet,

yet I do appear to myself> All nonsense, so I will stay—and try to be wise
to-morrow—*now*, I have no note to guide me and half put into my mouth
what I ought to say.

(3 Apr. 1846, p. 584.)

'Now I get to you, my Ba!' The opening phrase is both true and
false, since what Browning is describing is the process of *not* getting
to her, and yet this failure becomes the vehicle of his feeling. It is
also both triumphant and self-accusing: it is an exclamation of
delight at addressing her directly, and an exclamation of dismay at
doing it so late in the letter. The story which follows is a little fable
of Browning's poetics: the 'completer, deeper yearning of love to
you than usual even' represents the conception or originating energy
of feeling, corresponding to the perfection of the '*you*', the real self;
this conception, in turn, contains a potential for instantaneous and
perfect expression ('a thousand things that I *could* say *now*'), which
is bathetically rendered down into the 'foolish story and still foolisher comment'. And this happens 'on touching the paper', that is,
as soon as the immaterial mind incarnates itself in writing.
Accordingly, Browning 'give[s] the *expressing* part up', abdicates
from the attempt to 'prove' the strength of his feeling; Elizabeth
Barrett must 'infer' it from its very absence. The 'foolish story' is
actually a negative indication of that which it has displaced. The
more foolish it is, the stronger the feeling 'understood' behind it.
And then, in an inspired gesture, Browning sums up the argument
by means of that intensely expressive fragment which he leaves
embedded in the text of his letter. 'Yet, yet I do appear to myself':
Browning summons the ghost of himself; self-cancellation becomes
the very medium of self-realization.[5]

---

[5] Compare a passage from a late poem, 'Parleying with Christopher Smart', in
which Browning describes what happened to Smart in his madness, during which he
composed, for the only time in his life, authentic visionary poetry: 'straight you used
the power wherewith / Sense, penetrating as through rind to pith / Each object, thoroughly revealed might view / And comprehend the old things thus made new, / So
that while eye saw, soul to tongue could trust / Thing which struck word out, and
once more adjust / Real vision to right language' (ll. 145–51). Notice how the phrase
'thing which struck word out' combines the senses of production and deletion. Compare also the way in which Aristophanes cuts short his song 'Thamuris marching' at
the point at which Thamuris is about to claim equality with the Muses (*Aristophanes'
Apology*, ll. 5264–5). The exclamation 'All nonsense' with which Browning follows
his self-cancellation recurs in a suggestive context in the letter to Ruskin quoted
above (see p. 178): 'People make foolish fables about Orpheus enchanting stocks and
stones, poets standing up and being worshipped,—all nonsense and impossible
dreaming'.

Browning's emphasis on the word '*now*' relates, of course, to the 'good minute' in which 'true utterance' is possible, but which, being timeless, cannot articulate itself—for him—in 'real' time. And so, from the very start of the correspondence, he *looks forward* to his relationship with Elizabeth Barrett, in terms both of the poetry he and she are to write, and the love they are to give and receive. In his second letter, he writes that he 'will joyfully wait for the delight of your friendship' (13 Jan. 1845, p. 7); a year later the prospect has widened:

I look forward to a real life's work for us both: *I* shall do all,—under your eyes and with your hand in mine,—all I was intended to do: may but *you* as surely go perfecting—by continuing—the work begun so wonderfully—

(RB, 6 Feb. 1846, p. 439.)

The difference between the '*I*' and the '*you*' is the difference between the secondary and the primary, between dependence— 'under your eyes and with your hand in mine'—and self-sufficiency. It is also the difference between a projected and an achieved fulfilment. In looking forward to doing 'all [he] was intended to do', Browning implies that his work remains at the level of intention; whereas Elizabeth Barrett has only to *continue* the 'work begun so wonderfully'. Browning's advance in his relationship with Elizabeth Barrett—from correspondent to visitor, from friend to lover—is, on the one hand, a process of accumulation, each stage being subsumed by the next; on the other hand, it is a process of deferment, in which fulfilment perpetually recedes from the dis-illusioning 'now' to an imagined 'real life' in the future, as it does in the following passage:

And now, my heart's love, I am waiting to hear from you,—my heart is *full* of you. When I try to remember what I said yesterday, *that* thought, of what fills my heart—only *that* makes me bear with the memory . . I know that even such imperfect, poorest of words *must* have come *from* thence if not bearing up to you all that is there—and I know you are ever above me to receive, and help, and forgive, and *wait* for the one day which I will never say to myself cannot come, when I shall speak what I feel—more of it—or *some* of it—for now nothing is spoken.

(RB, 12 Dec. 1845, p. 317.)

The passage, framed by two occurrences of the word 'now', mimes Browning's secondariness to Elizabeth Barrett: 'now [. . .] I am waiting to hear from you [. . .] now nothing is spoken'. But at the heart of the passage it is Elizabeth Barrett who waits, with divine patience, 'for the one day which I will never say to myself cannot come,' as Browning puts it, invoking the curse in the act of abjuring it. And immediately the curse begins to operate, impoverishing the imagined fulfilment: 'I shall speak what I feel—more of it—or *some* of it—for now nothing is spoken'—and we circle back to zero.

The god-like position which Browning allots to Elizabeth Barrett in the scheme of their relationship—'ever above me to receive, and help, and forgive'—is especially significant when this passage is set alongside others which treat of their life together as poets. On one of the several occasions when he was trying to calm Elizabeth Barrett's anxiety that she would do him harm by allowing him to devote himself to her, he wrote:

I desire in this life (with very little fluctuation for a man & too weak a one) to live and just write out certain things which are in me, and so save my soul. [. . .] I should best do this if I lived quietly with myself and with you.

(RB, 18 Sept. 1845, p. 206.)

And again, much later in the courtship:

I do lift up my heart in an aspiration to lead the life that seems accorded by your side, under your eyes,—< . . . . >I cannot write on this, dear Ba,—to say, I will live and work as I ought, seems too presumptuous. Understand all, and help me with your dearest hand, my own love!—

(10 Aug. 1846, p. 950.)

Once again, a deletion in the manuscript (illegible in this case) indicates the status of 'aspiration' as against achievement, as far as Browning himself was concerned. But Elizabeth Barrett's 'dearest hand' was different. In one letter, Browning anticipates that they will, from their Italian retreat, ' "let sail winged words, freighted with truth from the throne of God" ' (30 June 1846, p. 826). He is quoting Shelley's 'Ode to Naples': instantly he flinches from the parallel. 'Ah, presumption all of it! Then, you shall fill the words with their freight, and I will look on and love you'. It is Elizabeth Barrett, not Browning, who is akin to Shelley, who is the divine messenger. But there is something worth noting about the grammar of the last sentence. Strictly speaking, 'shall' and 'will' ought to be in the reverse positions—that is, if you expect the verbs to be simply predictive. As it stands they can both be read as imperatives: 'You *shall* fill the words with their freight, and I *will* look on and love you'. Browning's 'presumption' survives his disavowal.

It would be difficult to exaggerate the persistence with which Browning harped on this one aspect of deferred fulfilment. 'I feel I *must* live with you,' he writes on one occasion, '—if but for a year, a month—to express the love which words cannot express, nor these letters, nor aught else' (12 Apr. 1846, p. 617). And later on in the same letter: 'it does seem to me, that the love I have gained is as nothing to the love I trust to gain. I want the love at our lifes' [*sic*] end, the love after trial, the love of *my* love, when mine shall have had time and occasion to prove itself!' (p. 618.) The word 'prove' keeps coming up in this context: it is a matter of course for Browning to write, 'I shall not attempt to speak and prove my feelings' (12 Oct. 1845, p. 228). The word is a favourite of Browning in his poetry, too, where it almost always has the same sense as here of a demonstration of the truth or reality of a proposition or appearance. Such demonstrations are only authentic for Browning if they remain at the visionary level. If they are imagined as actual, they are usually treated ironically. The poet-narrator of *Red Cotton Night-Cap Country*, for example, has his tongue firmly in his cheek when he describes his poem as a 'Conception proved by birth,—no other change!' (l. 4238.) He knows the crucial significance of the 'change' from 'conception' to 'birth'. Still Browning himself is not averse to trying:

my whole heart does, *does* so yearn, love, to do something to prove its devotion for you; and, now and then, amuses itself with foolish imaginings of real substantial services to which it should be found equal if fortune so granted,—

(1 Mar. 1846, p. 506.)

These 'real substantial services' are, of their very nature, impossible to perform: they are 'ideal forms' which, if embodied in action, would be, philosophically speaking, 'substantial' no longer. The 'foolish imaginings' to which Browning refers here are like conceptions of poems whose pretensions to 'true utterance' are punctured before they even take place. The word 'foolish' is sharp-edged in Browning's work. It denotes the shame of failure, as in the 'foolish story and still foolisher comment' in the letter from which I quoted before; but this shame, like the reflex of blushing, is intimately associated with creation. *Pauline*, for example, Browning's first

published poem, was intended as the first of a whole series of productions, not just poems but plays, operas, political speeches; it was
a miserable flop, and Browning was haunted by the shame of it to
the end of his life: he said of it, 'Only this crab remains of the
shapely Tree of Life in this Fool's Paradise of mine.'[6] And he wrote,
again, to Elizabeth Barrett: 'oh, my best, dearest Ba,—it is all right
that I cannot speak here,—if I *could*, by some miracle, speak, it
would be foolish' (29 May 1846, p. 739).

Expression, in the sense in which we are considering it here, is by
no means confined to language—or rather, 'language' is not confined to words: in relation to feeling, Browning devalues actions,
gestures, and even, in one exceptional passage, feelings themselves,
those which have been superseded:

At the beginning, I used to say (most truly) that words were all inadequate
to express my feelings,—now, those very feelings seem, as I see them from
this present moment,—just as inadequate in their time to represent what I
am conscious of now. I *do* feel more, widelier, strangelier . . how can I tell
you? You must believe,—my only, only beloved! I daresay I have said this
before, because it has struck me repeatedly,—and, judging by past experience, I shall need to say it again—and often again.

(1 May 1846, p. 668.)

He had indeed 'said this before', and he did 'say it again—and often
again'; as I remarked at the beginning of this chapter, it sometimes
seems that he never said anything else. But the motive was strong.
Courtship, which is, after all, an elaborate ritual of deferral, brought
Browning out in a rash of deference. Desire is necessarily secondary
to its object, but it is also a great opportunity for the realization of
identity, an opportunity to 'feel more, widelier, strangelier':
Browning's language of feeling both grasps this opportunity and
problematizes it, in terms of the difficult relation between intention
and performance, between the source of feeling and its voice or text.

[6] From a holograph note in a copy of *Pauline* now in the Forster-Dyce collection
of the Victoria and Albert Museum; reprinted in *Poems*, vol. i. p. 1021.

8

Letters and Meetings

1

See how I go on and on to you,—I who, whenever now and then pulled, by the head and hair, into letter-writing, get sorrowfully on for a line or two [. . .] and then come down 'flop' upon the sweet haven of page one, line last, as serene as the sleep of the virtuous!

(RB, 13 Jan. 1845, p. 7.)

But this is too much indeed—past all bearing, I suspect. Well—but if I ever write to you again, . . I mean, if you wish it,—it may be in the other extreme of shortness. So do not take me for a born heroine of Richardson, or think that I sin always to this length!

(EBB, 3 Feb. 1845, pp. 15–16.)

From the first, Browning and Elizabeth Barrett were self-conscious about the form of their letters. The subject continued to interest them long after they had lost any inhibitions about writing to each other at inordinate length. The two passages I have just quoted come from Browning's second letter, and Elizabeth Barrett's third. Right at the other end of the courtship, in June 1846, we find Elizabeth Barrett joking about what had caused her real anxiety in the beginning: 'The stars threaten you with a long letter today, it seems, for I stretch out my hand & take blindly the largest sheet' (8 June 1846, p. 766); and Browning replied, '*Is* your letter "long," my own Ba? I seem to get to the end, each time I read it, just as sorrowfully soon as usual—so much for thankfulness!' (9 June 1846, p. 769.) Nor was length the only aspect of letter-writing that preoccupied them. Far from it. As the courtship proceeded, the letters that carried it forward acquired, in the eyes of both, a concrete identity of their own. We hear of them being counted, of Elizabeth Barrett ceremonially arranging them into bundles of twenty tied with ribbon, of Browning kissing them before he opens and reads them, or proposing to 'institute solemn days whereon such letters are to be read years hence' (13 Aug. 1846, p. 959). Elizabeth Barrett devoted one of the *Sonnets from the Portuguese* to them:

> My letters! all dead paper, . . mute & white!
> And yet they seem alive and quivering
> Against my tremulous hands which loose the string
> And let them drop down on my knee tonight.
>
> (Sonnet XXIX, ll. 1–4.)

Along with this sense of the substantial identity of the letters goes the feeling that they are an extension of the identity of the writers: in the same sonnet, Elizabeth Barrett says of one of Browning's letters, 'This said "*I am thine*"—and so, its ink has paled / With lying at my heart that beat too fast' (ll. 11–12). It is in this area that we shall find both Browning and Elizabeth Barrett making some of their most fascinating and revealing comments.

My purpose in this chapter is, first, to bring forward some of the passages in the correspondence which bear upon letters and letter-writing, and to say what, in my belief, they tell us about Browning and Elizabeth Barrett, individually and in their relation to each other; second, to comment on the interplay between letters and meetings which became one of the most striking features of the courtship in its mature phase.

Elizabeth Barrett may have denied being a 'born heroine of Richardson', but she was certainly a letter-writer on a heroic scale. Browning repeatedly told her how much he hated writing letters, except to her, and he was as good as his word, or lack of words, if we consider the comparatively meagre harvest of his seventy-seven years, as against the abundance of her fifty-five. In writing as he did to her, he was going against his natural bent, while she was following hers; the pressure on him, therefore, was greater, and emerges in a greater complexity and intensity of response to the activity of letter-writing.

Browning was a compulsive, or rather an explosive talker—brilliant or intolerable, depending on whether you considered yourself a privileged listener or a gagged victim. (In dramatic monologue, listeners are natural victims: think of the envoy in 'My Last

Duchess', or Lucrezia in 'Andrea del Sarto', or, most famous of all, Gigadibs the literary man, bored through his skull by Bishop Blougram.) It is a mistake, moreover, to think that Browning's career as a conversationalist got under way only on his return to England after Elizabeth Barrett's death. He complains in his opening letters to Elizabeth Barrett that he is sick of society, and the sickness sprang from surfeit. The need for solitude and the love of company are not incompatible, especially in writers, and Browning had them both in full measure. In one sense, then, he did not need to write letters, since he expended their one-sided energy in the art of dramatic monologue—both in conversation and verse.

For Elizabeth Barrett, of course, things were very different. It was a difference of which she was keenly aware. 'I write more letters than you do,' she wrote to Browning; '. . . I write in fact almost as you pay visits' (1 May 1845, p. 52). Letters were the medium of her social existence: she carried on whole friendships by correspondence with people such as Richard Horne whom she never met, and indeed deliberately avoided meeting. She singled Browning out, however, declaring in the same letter from which I have just quoted: 'I never could think of "making conversation" in a letter to *you*— never.' She had been alarmed by what she understood as a hint, in Browning's last letter, that he suspected her of doing just that—of prattling to him—whereas, she emphasized, 'I was not dealing round from one pack of cards to you & to others.' It remains true, nevertheless, that she was making a distinction which Browning had no occasion to make with his own letters. Elizabeth Barrett's letters to him are recognizably hers; place them among her correspondence as a whole, and they stand out by virtue of greater intensity and strength of mind, but they are still part of the family; Browning's letters, on the other hand, are unlike any others he wrote, and are comparable only to his poems.[1]

In fact Elizabeth Barrett had given Browning some cause for his anxiety not to be placed on a level with Richard Horne or Harriet Martineau. 'If you hate writing to me as I hate writing to nearly everybody,' he angled in his third letter, 'I pray you never write'

---

[1] There are a few exceptions to this rule, of course, among them the letters which Browning wrote giving the news of Elizabeth Barrett's death to his family and closest friends; but where we might expect comparison, as in the letters of 1864–5 to Julia Wedgwood, whom Browning came close to marrying, we find a *poise* which is uncharacteristic of the courtship letters.

(27 Jan. 1845, p. 12). Elizabeth Barrett duly rose. 'Why how could I hate to write to you, dear Mr. Browning? Could you believe in such a thing?' (3 Feb. 1845, p. 12.) But the gap between these letters is over a week, and it is plain from the way she continued that Elizabeth Barrett did not at first see the full impropriety of making Browning a member of her epistolary salon, 'this talking upon paper being as good a social pleasure as another, when our means are somewhat straightened'. In the passage which follows, it is hard to say whether the dungeon image or the allusion to Mary Russell Mitford would have made Browning more uneasy:

As for me, I have done most of my talking by post of late years—as people shut up in dungeons, take up with scrawling mottos on the walls. Not that I write to many in the way of regular correspondence [. . .] but that there are a few who will write & be written to by me without a sense of injury. Dear Miss Mitford, for instance [. . .] has filled a large drawer in this room with delightful letters, heart-warm & soul-warm, . . driftings of nature (if sunshine cd drift like snow)—& which, if they shd ever fall the way of all writing, into print, wd assume the folio shape as a matter of course [. . .]

One of Miss Mitford's sunny snowflakes, wafted to a friend of hers in 1847, describes Browning as 'a girl drest in boy's clothes', with 'long ringlets & no neckcloth', whose poetry was 'one heap of obscurity confusion & weakness' (quoted in Kintner, p. 1096). Pausing only to remark that Elizabeth Barrett had a miscarriage in March of this same year 1847, and gave birth to a child two years later, so that Browning's lack of a neckcloth cannot have signified what Miss Mitford hoped or feared, we may sense Browning's concern at the way in which Elizabeth Barrett draws on images of containment—the dungeon, the drawer, the 'folio shape' of a bound volume—to describe a process which he, on the contrary, saw in terms of release and renewal: 'meaning to begin work in deep earnest,' he had declared to her at the end of his last letter, 'BEGIN without affectation, God knows—I do not know what will help me more than hearing from you'. (Even at this early stage, he is pressing for the contact to go beyond that of mere writing, since 'hearing from you' implies a voice rather than a text.)

But Elizabeth Barrett had her own ideas how such communication was to be managed. She went on with her alarming reassurances:

I write this to you to show how I can have pleasure in letters, and never think them too long, nor too frequent, nor too illegible [. . .] And if you will only promise to treat me 'en bon camarade,' without reference to the conventionalities of 'ladies & gentlemen,' taking no thought for your sentences, (nor for mine) nor for your blots, (nor for mine), nor for your blunt speaking (nor for mine), nor for your badd speling (nor for mine), & if you agree to send me a blotted thought whenever you are in the mind for it, & with as little ceremony & less legibility than you would think it necessary to employ towards your printer . . why, *then*, I am ready to sign & seal the contract, and to rejoice in being 'articled' as your correspondent. Only *don't* let us have any constraint, any ceremony! *Don't* be civil to me when you feel rude,—nor loquacious when you incline to silence,—nor yielding in the manners when you are perverse in the mind. See how out of the world I am! Suffer me to profit by it in almost the only profitable circumstance . . & let us rest from the bowing & the courtesying, you & I, on each side. You will find me an honest man on the whole [. . .]

There was much here to give Browning pause, summed up in that last rhetorical phrase, in which Elizabeth Barrett changes sex behind the epistolary screen. And although he was as willing as she to defy conventions of false sentiment and artificial propriety, he did not subscribe to the 'contract' which she offered him in their place. Eventually, everything which she stipulated came to pass—she and Browning wrote to each other without 'constraint' or 'ceremony' if ever two people did—but the condition of this freedom turned out to be not masculine camaraderie but passion; and passion devised ceremonies and constraints of its own.

It was two months after this letter that Elizabeth Barrett acknowledged, by her vigorous disclaimers about 'making conversation' in her letters to him, Browning's right to special treatment as a correspondent. What of Browning himself? He had no such awkwardness at the start: in response to her 'contract', he wrote:

now, what you say of the 'bowing,' and convention that is to be, and *tant de façons* that are not to be, helps me once and for ever—for have I not a right to say simply that, for reasons I know, for other reasons I don't exactly know, but might if I chose to think a little, and for still other reasons, which, most likely, all the choosing and thinking in the world would not make me know, I had rather hear from you than see anybody else [. . .]

(11 Feb. 1845, p. 17.)[2]

---

[2] By the 'convention that is to be', Browning means the 'contract' of plain speaking; but the word comes oddly close to Elizabeth Barrett's 'conventionalities', which the plain speakers are to shun.

In contrast to Elizabeth Barrett's proposal of friendship, which appeals to enlightened consciousness, Browning's declaration calls into play a level of the mind which is wholly inaccessible to consciousness, and which, by implication, is the most powerful source of feeling. Along with this contrast goes another, to do with the value which Browning placed on letters as a means of communication. Two long opening paragraphs in his ninth letter announce a theme to be pursued throughout the correspondence:

I heard of you, dear Miss Barrett, between a Polka and a Cellarius the other evening, of Mr. Kenyon—how this wind must hurt you! And yesterday I had occasion to go your way—pass, that is, Wimpole Street, the end of it,—and, do you know, I did not seem to have leave from you to go down it yet, much less count number after number till I came to yours,—much least than less, look up when I did come there. So I went on to a viperine she-friend of mine who, I think, rather loves me she does so hate me, and we talked over the chances of certain other friends who were to be balloted for at the 'Athenaeum' last night,—one of whom, it seems, was in a fright about it—'to such little purpose' said my friend—'for he is so inoffensive—now, if one were to style *you* that!'—'Or you'—I said—and so we hugged ourselves in our grimness like tiger-cats. Then there is a deal in the papers to-day about Maynooth, and a meeting presided over by Lord Mayor Gibbs, and the Reverend Mr. Somebody's speech—And Mrs. Norton has gone and book-made at a great rate about the Prince of Wales, pleasantly putting off till his time all that used of old to be put off till his mother's time—altogether, I should dearly like to hear from you, but not till the wind goes, and the sun comes—because I shall see Mr. Kenyon next week and get him to tell me some more. [. . .]

    Monday—Last night when I could do nothing else I began to write to you, such writing as you have seen—strange! The proper time & season for good sound sensible & profitable forms of speech—when ought it to have occurred, and how did I evade it in these letters of mine? For people begin with a graceful skittish levity, lest you should be struck all of a heap with what is to come, and *that* is sure to be the stuff and staple of the man, full of wisdom and sorrow,—and then again comes the fringe of reeds and pink little stones on the other side, that you may put foot on land, and draw breath, and think what a deep pond you have swum across. But *you* are the real deep wonder of a creature,—and I sail these paper-boats on you rather impudently.

                                        (15 Apr. 1845, pp. 45–6.)[3]

---

[3] The word 'it' in 'to go down it yet' is emended from 'in' in Kintner.

This letter is the first in the correspondence to break rank; that is, Browning sent it without having had a reply to his preceding letter of 31 March. It was now a fortnight later, and the letter sends a clear signal of anxiety about being neglected. Browning has heard *of* Elizabeth Barrett (in the interval between two dances), but he would 'dearly like to hear *from*' her (again the phrase 'hear from' prefers voice to text); all he has to look forward to is meeting Mr Kenyon 'next week' and getting some more second-hand information. Her apparent disregard of him translates itself into a prohibition to express his feelings, even in dumb-show and without her knowledge—a prohibition which he imposes on himself and then attributes to her in the neat phrase 'I did not seem to have leave from you'. He is kept at a distance in such a way that he cannot perform the stereotyped actions of a lover gazing up at his mistress's window. So what happens instead? 'So I went on to a viperine she-friend of mine who, I think, rather loves me she does so hate me': Elizabeth Barrett's neglect has driven Browning into the vipers' nest of London literary gossip, which is all to do with *voices* (since voices are also votes, as *Coriolanus* reminds us); discussion of the ballot for the Athenaeum displaces Browning's real anxiety about being admitted into the much more privileged club of Elizabeth Barrett's visitors. The report of the discussion relishes its nastiness –'Toads in a poisoned tank, / Or wild cats in a red-hot iron cage' ('Childe Roland to the Dark Tower Came', ll. 131–2)—'we hugged ourselves in our grimness like tiger-cats'. Instead of mooning in sentimental silence outside Elizabeth Barrett's window, there he is committing unnatural verbal acts in the interior of another woman's house.

But the story makes a further and more subtle point, leading into the next paragraph, which is the important one for our purpose here. The frivolity of gossip and the newspapers affects not only real life, but the life of Browning's letter. 'Last night when I could do nothing else I began to write to you, such writing as you have seen—strange!' In a sense, then, we have three letters in the sequence: the first which Elizabeth Barrett ignored, the second which Browning wrote when he 'could do nothing else', and now this third, which comments on the preceding. It does so by characterizing it as precisely that kind of 'talking upon paper' which Elizabeth Barrett had thought 'as good a social pleasure as another, when our means are somewhat straightened'. But Browning's means are not 'straightened'; he goes out dancing and visiting, he takes an interest in current affairs and the latest publications: and the result is, that his real 'means' of expression are stifled, and he can only repeat on paper what he has been practising in person, a 'graceful skittish levity'. He sees himself as an epistolary man-about-town, a stranger to 'good sound sensible & profitable forms of speech'; the particular kind of relation which he seeks with Elizabeth Barrett cannot be accommodated in speech which purports to substitute itself for presence, for the missed opportunity of direct communication with 'the real deep wonder of a creature'. Notice how the metaphor of the 'deep pond' begins by representing the *letter* which Browning ought to have sent, and then becomes an image of Elizabeth Barrett *herself*, on whom Browning sails the 'paper boats' of his inadequate self-expression. They are analogous in their inaccessibility: just as he cannot say the 'stuff and staple' of himself, 'full of wisdom and sorrow', so he cannot do more than float on the surface of her existence, when his desire is to dive into its depths. The image of himself which Browning presents is that of someone who does have something to say; only in his letter this something appears, as it were, as an absence: there are the two banks of the pond, but the pond itself is missing. In tracing his identity, Browning has erased it, and yet this erasure has left its own trace; like an empty wine bottle, his letter advertises fullness.

'Remember that I write letters to nobody but you,' Browning wrote disarmingly, 'and that I want method and much more' (30 Apr. 1845, p. 50). But this self-presentation is itself rhetorical, and so it is in the passages which I have just been analysing. They are not the whole of the letter which contains them, but gestures of that letter, part of its display; or to put it another way, the idea that letters are a poor substitute for human presence (the idea which the letter puts forward) is not the idea which it has of itself (the idea which it embodies). By means of this subterfuge, Browning reaches Elizabeth Barrett as effectively as if he really had stood under her window and serenaded her with his silence.

2

Browning's attitude to letter-writing related only to his own letters. Elizabeth Barrett's were different. He made the same distinction between them as he did with their poetry. Her faculty of expression was adequate to her feelings; his was not. Her writing, therefore, contained and conveyed the plenitude of herself; in referring to her letters, he uses imagery which emphasizes their material value, their tangibility: he compares them in one place to 'gold pieces' (21 Nov. 1845, p. 284), and in another he writes: 'Dearest words, dearest letters—as I add each to my heap, I say,—I *do* say—"I was *poor*, it now seems, a minute ago, when I had not *this*' " (12 Mar. 1846, p. 534). His letters, on the other hand, were a pattern of signs which had displaced the content of what they signified. 'I know,' he told her, 'there have been many, very many unutterable vows & promises made,—that is, THOUGHT down upon—the white slip at the top of my notes,—such as of this note,—and not trusted to the pen,—that always comes in for the shame,—but given up, and replaced by the poor forms to which a pen is equal' (27 Oct. 1845, p. 250). It is by writing that he draws attention to the blankness where his true, 'unutterable' feelings lie inscribed; the 'shame' of writing, like the colour of a blush, indicates the purity of the heart.

In Browning's view, Elizabeth Barrett, as the reader of these letters, was ideally placed to supplement their deficiency, just as Browning had expected the early readers of his poems to do. In the preface to the first edition of *Paracelsus* (1835), he wrote: 'a work like mine depends [. . .] on the intelligence and sympathy of the reader for its success—indeed were my scenes stars it must be his co-operating fancy which, supplying all chasms, shall connect the scattered lights into one constellation—a Lyre or a Crown.' In the same way, he wrote to Elizabeth Barrett that his letters were 'merest attempts at getting to talk with you thro' the distance . . yet always with the consolation of feeling that you will know all, interpret all & forgive it and put it right' (15 Mar. 1846, pp. 538–9). Or again, in a letter which I shall be looking at in more detail further on, he describes 'the feeling with which I write to you, not knowing that it is writing,—with *you*, face and mouth and hair and eyes opposite me, touching me, knowing that all *is* as I say, and helping out the imperfect phrases from your own intuition' (19 Feb. 1846, p. 474). 'In all I say to you, write to you, I know very well that I trust to your understanding me almost beyond the warrant of any human capacity', one letter begins; and it ends, 'God bless you, my best, dearest friend—think what I would speak' (31 July 1845, pp. 138–9). The same injunction occurs in the opening of yet another letter, in which Browning represents his physical frustration with the medium of writing: 'I must not go on tearing these poor sheets one after the other,—the proper phrases *will not* come,—so let them stay, while you care for my best interests in their best, only way, and say for me what I would say if I could— dearest,—say it, as I feel it!' (18 Oct. 1845, p. 240.) After this outburst, Browning drew a neat line across the page, and continued, as it were, in a normal tone of voice: 'I am thankful to hear of the continued improvement of your brother [. . .]'

How did Elizabeth Barrett react to this image of herself? On one or two occasions at least, she felt that Browning had protested too much, and she showed a sparkle of malice. 'Not more now, dearest,' he finished one letter, 'for time is pressing—but you will answer this,—the love that is not here,—not the idle words' (16 Mar. 1846, p. 540), to which she replied, 'Ah—how you speak,—with that pretension, too, to dumbness!' (16 Mar. 1846, p. 540.) In raptures over one of her letters, Browning exclaimed, 'they were *too* delicious to bear, the things you say to me! Why will you not say rather what I feel,—for you can perhaps, being what you are,—and let me subscribe it! It is a real pain to me to feel as I feel, and speak no more than I speak—' (29 May 1846, p. 739). Elizabeth Barrett began her reply with the playful but shrewd remark which I quoted in the preceding chapter: 'I have your letter . . you who cannot write! [. . .] After all it seems to me that you can write for yourself pretty well— rather too well I used to think from the beginning' (29 May 1846, p. 740). What follows has an even sharper edge:

But if you persist in the proposition about my doing if for you, leaving room for your signature . . . shall it be this way?—
Show me how to get rid of you.

(signed) *R.B.*

Like many good jokes, this one has a foundation of anxiety: Elizabeth Barrett's persistent worry that she was a hindrance to Browning both as a person and as a poet, that he would be better off without her whether he admitted it or not, and that it might be her duty to sacrifice herself in his best interests. It is the reverse of Browning's conviction that she completed and justified his identity. By putting down these particular words, Elizabeth Barrett was warding off the possibility of their being true, but she was also ironically agreeing with Browning that she knew what was best for him, and could express it better than himself. All he had to do was sign in the blank space, and he would be a nominal man indeed, a name without substance. But he did not sign.

In setting up Elizabeth Barrett as an ideal reader, Browning was requiring her to understand not what he wrote, but the feeling with which he had written it. This feeling irradiates the text, but is not located in any part of it, even (or especially) those parts which are specifically concerned with the expression of feelings. Conventionally, a letter-writer starts with a process (of making signs) and ends up with a signed object, the letter itself, which is sealed from interpretation; the reader reverses the sequence, starting with the object, breaking the seal and beginning a process of reading the signs. Because Browning believed that his signs were degenerate versions of his ideas, he naturally discounted any such reader's activity as futile. Instead, he wanted his ideal reader to re-generate his meaning; to animate his dead letters with their original spirit. But Elizabeth Barrett clung obstinately to her benighted opinion that Browning's letters were valuable in themselves, both as they affected her personally—'they are sun, air, & human voices, at the very lowest calculation', she wrote (30 Mar. 1846, p. 574), and again, 'the daily letter which is my daily bread' (12 May 1846, p. 700)—and as they were, in her judgement, true expressions of his identity. This identity was capable, in her imagination, of swallowing the poor figment of a postman who conveyed it. Asking him to send her a lock of his hair, she wrote: 'send it to me [. . .] by that Lewisham post [. . .] which reaches me at eight in the evening when all the world is at dinner & my solitude most certain. Everything is so still then, that I have heard the footsteps of a letter of yours ten doors off' (24 Nov. 1845, p. 292). She also had a strong line of imagery of her own. 'But after all, how have I answered your letter?—& how *are* such letters to be answered? Do we answer the sun when he shines?' (10 Nov. 1845, p. 264.) And she could be just as emphatic in a direct sense: once, when he had recommended one of Landor's *Imaginary Conversations* to her, she wrote back; 'I will read what you tell me in Landor . . but no words of inspired lips or pen . . no poet's word, of the divinest, . . ever went to my heart as yours in these letters!' (22 June 1846, p. 808.) (In fact, as we shall see in a later section, he appeared to her at first more real in his letters than in his visits.) Her association of his letters with his presence was simpler and more humanly poignant than Browning's equivalent concept of hers:

Only do you still think of this, dearest beloved—, that I sit here in the dark but for *you*, & that the light you bring me (from *my* fault!—from the nature of *my* darkness!) is not a settled light as when you open the shutters in the morning, but a light made by candles which burn some of them longer & some shorter, & some brighter & briefer, at once [. . .] & that there is an intermission for a moment now & then between the dropping of the old light into the socket & the lighting of the new—Every letter of yours is a new light which burns so many hours . . & *then!*

(21 Dec. 1845, p. 339.)

We are a long way here from the light-hearted image of Browning as the sun-god; the sombre tone of this passage, its greater seriousness and conviction, is signalled by its opening injunction 'do you still think of this', a grammatical form which Elizabeth Barrett generally adopts when she is especially in earnest. Again the sense of being shut in, which is so pervasive in Elizabeth Barrett's letters; here she sits in the dark, the shutters are closed: windows are a recurrent image in her work of the ambivalence of freedom, and the dark here is life to her, a fallen 'nature' which she attributes to a 'fault', an original sin; and in this condition, Browning's letters are as provisional as the illuminations of grace, for which the candle, of course, is a traditional symbol. But by their very provisionality, they insist on their living energy, 'brighter & briefer, at once'. There is no doubt in Elizabeth Barrett's mind that when Browning's letters are there, *he* is there. Passages like these sometimes make me wonder how Browning could deny in himself the power to communicate his presence which Elizabeth Barrett so needed to find there; but perhaps it never mattered to her whether he denied it or not; or perhaps she understood the denial for what it was, part of a larger argument, rhetorical in the generous sense of the word.

Throughout the correspondence, at any rate, both she and Browning are conscious of the way that letters embody their writers; but Browning's consciousness is the more edged. 'When your letter came,' she wrote to him after their quarrel over the morality of duelling, 'I kissed it by a sort of instinct [. . .] because the writing did not look angry . . not vexed writing. Then I read . . "First of all, kiss". . . . So it seemed like magic' (8 Apr. 1846, p. 607.) She did not quote the whole of the opening phrase of Browning's letter, which runs, 'First of all kiss *me*, dearest' (8 Apr. 1846, p. 601; my italics), since she was blurring the distinction between kissing his letter and kissing him. In the same way, Browning wrote to her that a letter of hers was 'one of her very kisses incorporated & made manifest' (31 Aug. 1846, p. 1025). But whereas Elizabeth Barrett would never have objected to Browning's image, Browning objected strongly to hers. 'But nobody in the world writes like you . . not so *vitally*—and I have a right, if you please, to praise my letters,' she wrote to him (15 Feb. 1846, p. 470). But Browning did not please:

One thing vexed me in your letter—I will tell you, the praise of *my* letters: now, one merit they have—in language mystical—that of having *no* merit. If I caught myself trying to write finely, graphically &c &c, nay, if I found myself conscious of having in my own opinion, so written—all would be over! yes, over! I should be respecting you inordinately, paying a proper tribute to your genius, summoning the necessary collectedness,—plenty of all that!—But the feeling with which I write to you, not knowing that it is writing,—with *you*, face and mouth and hair and eyes opposite me, touching me, knowing that all *is* as I say, and helping out the imperfect phrases from your own intuition—*that* would be gone—and *what* in its place?

(19 Feb. 1846, p. 474.)

Browning is quite right, of course, to draw attention to one of the features of 'ordinary' letters which writers such as Richardson, Rousseau, and Laclos had exploited in the masterpieces of the epistolary novel—namely, their inherent self-consciousness, their incorrigible rhetoricizing of experience. And unlike other first-person forms, letters insist on their status as written texts. Dramatic monologists, for example, do not know that they are in a dramatic monologue: the Duke in 'My Last Duchess' does not realize that his words are, as it were, being taken down and used in evidence. He knows that he is speaking, but not that what he speaks is a poem; how could he, when such knowledge would destroy the premiss on which his consciousness is being imagined in the first place? But the writer of a letter, whether this letter is presented as a poem or not, must be conscious of producing a written text, and must therefore be implicated in the strategies of representation and interpretation which that text calls into play. Yet here we have Browning denying exactly this implication, claiming in fact that he writes to Elizabeth Barrett *not knowing that it is writing*. Taken literally, the claim is disingenuous; but it acts as a kind of hyperbole to distance Browning's use of the medium of letters as far as possible from his use of any other form of writing. He tries to secure his letters from the contagion of consciousness, of rhetoric, even though he has to resort to rhetorical manœuvres in order to do so. To write *graphically* is the great sin: graphic description, or graphic sentiment, would endow the shapes of the written words themselves with power, a power of realization: the source of this power, from which the words would be stealing, and which they would leave impoverished, could only be the reality of that which they were supposed to represent. But Browning is not interested in representations of Elizabeth Barrett, he is not addressing himself to an image of her (as a writer of genius to whom he owes 'tribute'), but to her *presence*—'*you*, face and mouth and hair and eyes opposite me, touching me'—and this presence is summoned in imagination as a deliberate counterpoise to the distancing effect of writing, the fact that to write a letter presumes the absence of the person being written to. Not so, says Browning; on the contrary, the letters I write prove, by their unconsciousness of themselves as writing, that the object of their address is present.

We need not dwell on the paradox of this position being itself articulated in a letter; we may assume that the paradox was evident to Browning himself, and that nevertheless he adopted the position because it expressed a fundamental division between himself and Elizabeth Barrett which he felt compelled to keep in view. Along with dispraise of his own letters went praise of hers; and here, too, the same preoccupation emerges:

Now to these letters! I do solemnly, unaffectedly wonder how you can put so much pure felicity into an envelope so as that I shall get it as from the fount head. This to-day, those yesterday—there is, I see, and know, thus much goodness in line after line, goodness to be scientifically appreciated, *proved there*—but over and above, is it in the writing, the dots and traces, the seal, the paper,—here does the subtle charm lie beyond all rational accounting for? The other day I stumbled on a quotation from J. Baptista Porta—wherein he avers that any musical instrument made out of wood possessed of medicinal properties retains, being put to use, such virtues undiminished,—and that, for instance, a sick man to whom you should pipe on a pipe of elder-tree would so receive all the advantage derivable from a decoction of its berries. From whence, by a parity of reasoning, I may discover, I think, that the very ink and paper were . . ah, what were they? curious thinking won't do for me and the wise head which is mine, so I will lie and rest in my ignorance of content and understand that without any magic at all you simply wish to make one person—,which of your free goodness proves to be your R.B.,—to make me supremely happy, and that you have your wish—you *do* bless me!

(21 Feb. 1846, p. 484.)

The imagery and phrasing—'pure felicity [. . .] as from the fount head', 'goodness to be scientifically appreciated, *proved there*', 'you simply wish [. . .] and [. . .] you have your wish'—display both Elizabeth Barrett's divine authority and the material authenticity of her revelation. She communicates with godlike directness from the 'fount head' of her feeling, and requires no rhetorical subterfuge to dissociate her feelings from her words, since the two are consubstantial; and, although what she communicates is 'pure felicity', an essence which can be demonstrated in the laboratory of interpretation, there is nevertheless a 'subtle charm beyond all rational accounting for'; the soul cannot be found in a line-by-line dissection of the body of the letter. But the passage not only *contains* Browning's opinion of the superiority of Elizabeth Barrett's faculty of expression, it *enacts* it by means of a little exemplary drama. Just as Elizabeth Barrett is the mistress of direct communication, so Browning is master of the inferior art of indirection and analogy; off he goes then, with his extended metaphor of 'Baptista Porta' and his medicinal musical instruments. Browning is quoting from Giovanni Battista della Porta's *Magiae Naturalis*, a sixteenth-century treatise which he most probably found in his father's library, and the allusion links this whole topic to Browning's lifelong fascination with the occult as an image of art. The alchemist, the magician, the spiritualist—these are devious figures, like the kind of poet Browning felt himself to be, for whom the ritual conjuring of language was a substitute for vision. How appropriate, then, that the analogy should break down; that Browning should fail to convey what he intends, and should rebuke himself for his attempt to do so. Moreover, this attempt was concerned precisely with analysing the nature of the divinity he adores—a divinity who defies such 'rational accounting for', whose ways remain unsearchable, and whose 'free goodness' confers its blessing: in short, Elizabeth Barrett emerges from this stream of words surprisingly transformed into a Protestant-flavoured Almighty God. In *Paracelsus*—a poem whose hero is one of della Porta's alchemical confraternity—the poet Aprile exclaims, 'God is the perfect poet, / Who in his person acts his own creations.' 'You simply wish', says Browning to Elizabeth Barrett, 'and [. . .] you have your wish—you *do* bless me!' In comparison, the 'pipe of elder-tree'—the tree of the old Law, perhaps—is an outworn channel of healing.

In disparaging his own letter-writing, and praising Elizabeth Barrett's, Browning was consciously favouring speech over writing, not just in the sense of preferring meetings to letters, once meetings became possible, but in the sense of what the letters themselves were like. He played with the idea that the very material of which they were made might lose its connection with writing: 'I would not wait for paper,' he wrote on one occasion, 'and you must forgive half-sheets instead of a whole celestial quire to my love and praise' (11 Mar. 1846, p. 531). The pun on quire/choir, which is an *aural* pun, not a visual one, attempts to convert the medium itself from script to sound, one being associated with doing things by halves, the other with wholeness and fulfilment. For Browning, this remained a 'fancy'; he began another letter: 'I feel at home, this blue early morning,'—seven o'clock, to be precise, as he noted in his heading—'now that I sit down to write (or, *speak*, as I try & fancy) to you' (21 Aug. 1845, pp. 164–5). It was a fancy he took to its extreme in the case of Elizabeth Barrett's letters. On a different kind of grey morning, in December, when the post had brought no letter from her, he wrote: 'A letter from you would light up this sad day: shall I fancy how, if a letter lay *there* where I look,—rain might fall and winds blow while I listened to you, long after the *words* had been laid to heart?' (19 Dec. 1845, p. 328.) Here the written word would convey speech so successfully that the words themselves would disappear, leaving voice in the abstract to represent pure presence.

It was in the contrast with 'real' speech, of course, the speech of their meetings, that Browning felt the inferiority of letters most keenly. But this feeling was part of a larger response to the interplay of letters and meetings, and to the nature of the meetings themselves. A sense of the limit of the topic of letters is expressed for us in one of Browning's own letters, an evening one to match the letter he wrote in the 'blue early morning'—and in fact they belong to the same month. The letter opens:

> This sweet Autumn evening, Friday, comes all golden into the room and makes me write to you—not think of you—yet what shall I write?
> It must be for another time, . . after Monday, when I am to see you
> [. . .]

                                                          (29 Aug. 1845, p. 175.)

3

Let us go back to Browning's reproach to Elizabeth Barrett for her praise of his letters, and look at her reply to the charge. She denied that she 'meant to praise them in the way you seem to think . . by calling them "graphic," "philosophic" . . why, did I ever use such words?' (She is quite right—she never had used them.) And she went on:

I agree with you that if I could play critic upon your letters, it would be an end!—but no, no . . I did not, for a moment. In what I said I went back to my first impressions—& they were *vital* letters, I said—which was the resumé of my thoughts upon the early ones you sent me . . because I felt your letters to be *you* from the very first [. . .]

(19 Feb. 1846, p. 477.)

From Browning's point of view, worse and worse! Far from endorsing his distinction between 'graphic' letters and ones which have 'no merit' (except as signs of the writer's inability to communicate), she contrasts 'graphic' letters with 'vital' ones, which actually bring his presence to her. Anxious about his health, she wrote to him: 'Beloved, when you write, *let* it be, if you choose, ever so few lines. Do not suffer me (for my own sake) to tire you—because two lines or three bring YOU to me . . remember . . just as a longer letter would' (16 Mar. 1846, p. 541). And in an earlier letter she had made this point even more emphatically by describing the effect made on her by his early visits, when she was more used to reading than seeing him:

You never guessed perhaps . . what I look back to at this moment in the physiology of our intercourse . . . the curious double feeling I had about you . . you personally, & you as the writer of these letters, . . & the crisis of the feeling, when I was positively vexed and jealous of myself for not succeeding better in making a unity of the two. I could not!—And more-over I could not help but that the writer of the letters seemed nearer to me, long . . long . . & in spite of the postmark . . than did the personal visitor who confounded me, & left me constantly under such an impression of its being all dream-work on his side, that I have stamped my feet on this floor with impatience to think of having to wait so many hours before the 'can-did' closing letter cd come with its confession of an illusion. [. . .] But in the letters it was different—the dear letters took me on the side of my own ideal life where I was able to stand a little upright & look round—I could

read such letters for ever & answer them after a fashion . . that, I felt from
the beginning. But *you*—!

(4 Jan. 1846, p. 358.)

Nearly half a century before Henry James offered his ironic homage
to Browning's double identity, in his story 'The Private Life', we
find Elizabeth Barrett in the same predicament of interpretation,
but without the saving resource of fiction. Her imagination is
strongly at work, though, even in such minor details as her having
stamped her feet on the floor ('in spite of the postmark'), and in
effect she tells Browning a story of her own about 'first impressions'
(as she calls them in the letter I quoted just before), about the
different ways in which he made his mark in letters and visits. The
ground of this difference is a division in herself—'I was positively
vexed & jealous of myself'—a division, that is between self-loving
and self-hating sides of her personality. On the one hand there was
'my own ideal life where I was able to stand a little upright & look
round', and on the other hand there was her 'real' physical life in
which, at any rate in the early visits of which she is speaking here,
she lay on a sofa and *received* Browning in an attitude of helpless
passivity. She could understand Browning loving her through the
medium of writing, but not through the medium of flesh; as she had
written to him just before his first visit, her poetry was the 'flower'
of her identity, '& so it has all my colours; the rest of me is nothing
but a root, fit for the ground & the dark' (15 May 1846, p. 65). For
Browning to associate her 'ideal' and her physical selves must be
'dream-work'; and she believed, on the evidence of the different
impression he made in his letters and visits, that he would wake up
and write her a ' "candid" closing letter'. The link between *candour*
and *closure* is alive to the pain of how other people's openness to
you is so often a way of their closing you down, and that to open a
'closing letter' would be to slam shut a whole echoing series of open
doors made up of the letters of the past.

  In his reply to this letter, Browning attributed what he called 'that
discrepancy you see, that nearness in the letters, that early farness in
the visits' to inhibition on his part in speaking his mind, for fear of
overstepping the mark; and he drew a distinction between letters
and meetings based on the different kinds of discourse which they
implied:

there is safer going in letters than in visits, do you not see? In the letter, one may go to the utmost limit of one's supposed tether without danger—there is the distance so palpably between the most audacious step *there*, and the next . . which is no where, seeing it is not in the letter: quite otherwise in personal intercourse, where any indication of turning to a certain path, even, might possibly be checked not for its own fault but lest, the path once reached and proceeded in, some other forbidden turning might come into sight, we will say: in the letter, all ended *there*, just there . . and you may think of that, and forgive; at all events, may avoid speaking irrevocable words—and when, as to me, those words are intensely *true, doom-words*—think, dearest!

(6 Jan. 1846, p. 364.)

Notice that Browning has introduced into the discussion a premiss which does not appear to have been in Elizabeth Barrett's mind when she made the original comparison, namely, that there is a 'forbidden' area of discussion between them, whose boundaries were set by her, and that any trespass on his part might result in banishment from the whole preserve of her friendship. He is thinking, of course, of the abortive declaration of love which he made after their first meeting; then, indeed, she had threatened to break with him completely if he made any further reference to the topic.[4] At the time he made this declaration, Browning had not been aware of any forbidden territory in his relations with Elizabeth Barrett; the barbed wire sprang up behind him as he dashed into the pasture. What saved him was precisely the fact that his declaration had been made *in a letter*. He was able to convert his *action* into a *gesture*, to strike an attitude where he had intended to secure a prize; from then on, within the confines of rhetoric, he found himself free; in 'personal intercourse', bound.

In explaining all this to Elizabeth Barrett, Browning virtually admits to her that he had deliberately played safe during his early visits; that he had, in other words, been conscious of the 'supposed tether' in a way which did not apply to his letters. (Could not apply, indeed, by his own account, since he declared that he was not conscious of 'writing' them at all.) Artificial behaviour was impossible in the letters, then; but it seems it was mandatory in the visits. Does Browning mean that his letters were, even for a time, more authentic—because more honest—spokesmen of his feelings than his

---

[4] 'Now, if there shd be one word of answer attempted to this,—or of reference; *I must not . . I* WILL *not see you again*' (EBB, 23 May 1845, p. 72). For a discussion of this episode in the courtship, see Part One, pp. 78–84.

visits? And if so, where would that leave the boasted superiority of living speech over dead text?

Our problem is made worse by the fact that, on occasion, Browning contradicted his own account of his letter-writing and revealed the same tactical sense in his letters as in his behaviour during the meetings. 'God bless you' he writes at the end of one letter; 'do not be otherwise than kind to this letter which it costs me pains, great pains to avoid writing better, as truthfuller—this you get is not the first begun' (?18 July 1845, p. 129). He is referring to the 'supposed tether' again, only this time the epistolary form proves no advantage; and on another occasion, he explains his not having written to her by the fact that he *had* written her a letter 'which was too good & true to send, & met, five minutes after, its natural fate accordingly', and he had not been able to send his 'real letter' (that is, the bad and false one!) in time to catch the post (24 June 1845, p. 103). It is the 'natural fate' of true speech to be suppressed, and for falsehood to take its place and represent it; the foundation of Browning's creativity is the sense that language itself is such a falsehood, that representation is inadequate to experience, and yet that representation is all we have.[5]

In this light, the superiority of speech over writing, which Browning constantly affirms in the correspondence, is relative to a value which transcends them both. Undoubtedly, letters are secondary to meetings: 'Do see me when you can,' he wrote before he had yet visited her, 'and let me not be only writing myself / Yours / R.B.' (13 May 1845, p. 63); and much later: 'All you can, you compensate me for the absence—that such letters, instead of being themselves the supremest reward and last of gains, should be—compensation, at the best!' (6 July 1846, p. 849.) But this last remark, with its reference to compensation for *absence*, makes it clear what it was that Browning preferred to letter-writing. It was not speech itself. Looking at what Browning says about speaking to Elizabeth Barrett, we find the same devaluation of speech as a means

---

[5] See the opening of his letter of 15 Mar. 1846 (p. 538): 'How will the love my heart is full of for you, let me be silent? Insufficient speech is better than no speech, in one regard—the speaker had *tried* words, and if they fail, hereafter he needs not reflect that he did not even try—so with me now, that loving you, Ba, with all my heart and soul,—all my senses being lost in one wide wondering gratitude and veneration, I press close to you to say so, in this imperfect way, my dear dearest beloved!' See the preceding chapter for a fuller discussion of this subject.

of communication which we have seen applied to writing. Speech is good *compared to writing*; in itself it is just as frustrating, just as ineffective, because it is being compared in turn to something better. 'There is a lesson from all this writing and mistaking and correcting and being corrected', he wrote on one occasion; 'and what, but that a word goes safely only from lip to lip, dearest?' (27 Feb. 1846, p. 501.) Not from lip to ear, but from lip to lip—the kiss which stops speech, as it does in many of Browning's poems. The highest value is not speech, but presence.

For Elizabeth Barrett, such presence was not part of a hierarchy, but a unity; meetings, letters, and gifts were aspects of the same human transaction. 'Your beautiful flowers!—none the less beautiful for waiting for water yesterday. As fresh as ever, they were; & while I was putting them into the water, I thought that your visit went on all the time' (17 Oct. 1845, p. 239). She marvelled that his flowers, unlike others, lived in the close atmosphere of her room: 'To be sure they know that I care for them & that I stand up by the table myself to change their water & cut their stalks freshly at inter-vals—*that* may make a difference perhaps. Only the great reason must be that they are yours, & that you teach them to bear with me patiently' (30 Dec. 1845, p. 348). And again: 'You always, you know (*do* you know?), leave your presence with me in the flowers,—and, as the lilies unfold, of course I see more & more of you in each apocalypse' (21 June 1846, p. 803). For Browning there could be no such mystical confounding of impressions. On the contrary, his whole feeling for Elizabeth Barrett expressed itself in the juxtaposition of sharply differentiated elements. Some of the most passionate utterances in his letters concern themselves with just this work of differentiation. The following passage begins inno-cuously enough, with Browning confirming that a planned meeting can take place, since another engagement has been fixed for a differ-ent day:

It is as I expected—Rachel plays on Wednesday in Phèdre, and our friend writes to say he has secured places. May nothing overcast the perfect three hours on Tuesday,—those dear, dear spaces of dear brightness: why cannot a life be made up of these . . with the proper interposition of work, to jus-tify God's goodness so far as poor mortality and its endeavours can,—a week of Tuesdays—then a month—a year—a life! I most long to see you again,—always by far the most I long,—the *next day*—the very day after I have seen you—when it is freshest in my mind what I did *not* say while I

might have said it,—nor ask while I might have been answered—nor learn
while you would have taught me—<feel when the vibrations settle and
the> no, it is indescribable. Did I call yesterday 'unsatisfactory'? Would I
had it back now! Or better, I will wish you here where I write, with the
trees to see and the birds to hear thro' the open window—I see you on this
old chair against the purple back . . or shall you lie on the sofa?—Ba, how I
love you, my own perfect, unapproachable mistress.

(12 July 1846, pp. 869–70.)

This passage, as with so many in Browning's letters, has a kind of
dramatic development which is as much part of its meaning as the
content of the individual phrases. The development consists in an
alternation of realistic and fantastic movements. First, Browning
anticipates seeing Elizabeth Barrett for 'the perfect three hours on
Tuesday'; then comes his vain wish that 'a life be made up of these';
then his reflection on the frustration of it not being so; and last, his
surmounting of this obstacle in a fantasy of realization. What does
this sequence mean? To begin with, notice the transformation
which the idea of meeting Elizabeth Barrett undergoes according to
whether Browning is looking forward or back. The meeting in prospect is 'the perfect three hours'; the meeting of 'yesterday' is 'unsatisfactory'. How could this transformation be avoided? Browning
imagines one solution: running the meetings together, so that the
element of anticipation vanishes, leaving only an undifferentiated
present, a sequence without succession: 'a week of Tuesdays—then
a month—a year—a life!' But this answer is inadequate, because it
depends on an appeal to the material conditions of life. The futility
of wishing for things to be different—'why cannot a life be made up
of these'—is exposed by the acknowledged futility of the wish to
reverse the course of time—'Did I call yesterday "unsatisfactory"?
Would I had it back now!' But the person who utters that last
phrase has already given up the idea of having yesterday back; he is
making a conventional gesture, and making it in order to emphasize
the sudden swerve of imagination which he is about to perform. 'Or
better, I will wish you here where I write': the 'will' is imperative,
and translates the presence of Elizabeth Barrett from the hell of lost
opportunity—represented by an act of closure in the text itself, the
truncated and deleted phrase with its despairing comment—into a
paradisal garden which is possessed (by the senses and the imagination) 'thro' the *open* window'. By being 'here where I write', Elizabeth Barrett heals the pain of writing by abolishing the distance

which writing normally presupposes. Writing is blissful when it is redundant.

The whole passage moves from the seemingly trivial report of the first sentence to the direct exclamation of the last; from the 'secured places' of worldly meetings to the bliss of imagination; from the actress whose appearance on stage is governed by conventions of displacement and distance, to the 'perfect, unapproachable mistress'. She is perfect *because* 'unapproachable' ('unsurpassably excellent' and 'impossible to reach'); by being inaccessible *in time* (each step towards her would push her back), she is 'my own' in the non-time of Browning's vision.

By the time he wrote this letter, Browning had already had a difference of opinion with Elizabeth Barrett about the legitimacy of such visions, a difference which they never quite resolved, but tacitly let pass. This exchange, which gave rise to perhaps the oddest and most powerful of Browning's reflections on the relative value of letters and meetings (real and imaginary) began when Elizabeth Barrett, noticing a gap in Browning's letters, teased him: 'Is it not the truth now that you hate writing to me?' (21 Mar. 1846, p. 550.) This was on a Saturday; Browning would have received the letter in the evening, and on Sunday he wrote: 'Oh, my Ba—how you shall hear of this to-morrow—that is all: *I* hate writing? See when presently I *only* write to you daily, hourly if you let me?' (pp. 550–1.) On Monday afternoon they met (she would have had his Sunday letter had he posted it early on Monday morning), and she must have maintained her point, whether in jest or earnest we do not know, for on Tuesday Browning opened his letter with the following reasoned case:

My own dearest, if you *do*—(for I confess to nothing of the kind)—but if you *should* detect an unwillingness to write at certain times, what would that prove,—I mean, what that one need shrink from avowing?—If I never had you before me except when writing letters to you—then! . . Why, we do not even *talk* much now! [. . .] Oh, how coldly I should write,—how the bleak-looking paper would seem unpropitious to carry my feeling—if all had to begin and try to find words *this* way!

Now, this morning I have been out—to town & back—and for all the walking my head aches—and I have the conviction that presently when I resign myself to think of you wholly, with only the pretext,—the make-believe of occupation, in the shape of some book to turn over the leaves of,—I shall see you and soon be well,—so soon! You must know, there is a chair (one of the kind called gondóla-chairs by upholsterers—with an emphasized o)—which occupies the precise place, stands just in the same relation to *this* chair I sit on now, that yours stands in and occupies—to the left of the fire: and, how often, how *always* I turn in the dusk and *see* the dearest real Ba with me—

How entirely kind to take that trouble, give those sittings for me!

(24 Mar. 1846, pp. 554–5.)

As though Elizabeth Barrett sat in the 'gondola-chair' by design! But in fact this last exclamation refers not to imaginary 'sittings' in the 'gondola-chair', but real 'sittings' for a sketch which she had intended to give to him, but which turned out 'short of an adequate likeness'. How well it fits both contexts, though! since the whole passage attributes identity to an image, and gives that image a higher status than 'reality'; Browning calls the 'likeness' of Elizabeth Barrett in his imagination 'the dearest real Ba', with whom he can communicate more effectively than he could with her physical counterpart in Wimpole Street. 'If I never had you before me except when writing to you—then!' Then, Browning implies, he would be culpable for not writing as often as possible, since to have her 'before him' is the greatest good. But he cannot mean having her before him literally, in the flesh, since he goes on to make her real and her figurative 'presence' of equivalent value: 'I shall see you and soon be well' refers not to a real meeting, but to the fantasy in which he is about to plunge.

Why, we may now ask, should Browning need a 'pretext' in order to invoke this fantasy-presence of Elizabeth Barrett? And why does he use the phrase 'resign myself to think of you wholly'? Because such resignation is a letting go (of writing) which simultaneously 're-signs' the self which that writing could not represent, re-inscribes it in its original value. To do this, a 'pre-text' is necessary, something which is there to be displaced by having her 'before him'; and so 'the shape of some book' precedes, with its 'make-believe of occupation', the presence which 'occupies the precise place'. He *turns* to this presence, away from his book whose print fades from view in the dusk, a dusk which creates vision in the act of obliterating sight: 'I turn in the dusk and *see*'. It is only a chair, and yet it contains 'the dearest real Ba'; in its absence (its 'emphasized o'), her presence is magically realized.

Humanly sensible as ever, and with a keen perception of the comedy latent in Browning's imaginative rhetoric, Elizabeth Barrett replied to this letter with a plea to be considered in herself and not her likeness, however magical:

[. . .] I beg you to stand convinced of one thing, . . that whenever the 'certain time' comes for you to 'hate writing to me' [. . .] *I shall not like it at all*—not for all the explanations . . & the sights in gondola chairs, which the person seen is none the better for!—The εἴδωλου sits by the fire—the real Ba is cold at heart through wanting her letter.

(24 Mar. 1846, p. 556. The Greek word *eidolon* means 'image'.)

Her own strength of feeling surprised her—'I began by half a jest & end by half-gravity'—and she repeated the point only a few lines further on:

I confess to being more than half jealous of the εἴδωλου in the gondola chair, who isn't the real Ba after all, & yet is set up there to do away with the necessity 'at certain times' of writing to her. Which is worse than Flush. For Flush, though he began by shivering with rage & barking & howling & gnashing his teeth at the brown dog in the glass, has learnt by experience what that image means, . . and now contemplates it, serene in natural philosophy.

It is human beings who are meant to learn 'by experience'; here, however, the 'natural philosophy' of empiricism serves Flush, the dog, better than Elizabeth Barrett, the woman; she cannot contemplate with equanimity her image in the 'glass' of Browning's mind, and accept it for 'what it means'. It must be said that her task is the more difficult. For whereas Flush has to cope only with his own reflection, and discovers that it 'means' (and does) nothing, Elizabeth Barrett is dealing with an image of herself for which (despite her 'sittings') she was not responsible; and she acknowledges the power of this image to 'do away with' an actual pleasure of hers.[6] To this Browning could make no effective reply: 'I *do* hate *hate* having to write, not kiss my answer on your dearest mouth [. . .] to-morrow I will try', he wrote; but he added, 'Ba by the fire will not be cold at heart [. . .] and I will talk to *her* & more than talk'

---

[6] Years later, Browning picked up Elizabeth Barrett's term *eidolon* in a letter to Julia Wedgwood: 'Then, what a strange fancy is that of Euripides on which he has founded his whole play of *Helena*—"that it was not really Helen, only an apparition of her, that fled to Troy, and caused all the fighting—the true Helen living sadly and saintly in Egypt [. . .] her husband finds her again, wringing her hands at the world's misconception of her character through the doings of the *eidolon*. Q[uer]y: does this mean, a good poem suffering from the world's misconception of it?' (*RB & JW*, 79). See also Browning's poem 'Ixion' in the collection *Jocoseria*.

(25 Mar. 1846, p. 559). He persisted in stealing from her to pay her image; perhaps, by a final ironic twist, it is only in writing, in the despised text of the letter, that he can reconcile theft with gift.

9

Other People

1 Mr Buckingham's Voyage

And . . will you tell me? . . How can a man spend four or five successive months on the sea, most cheaply . . at the least pecuniary expense, I mean? Because Miss Mitford's friend Mr. Buckingham is ordered by his medical adviser to complete his cure by these means; & he is not rich. Could he go with sufficient comfort by a merchant's vessel to the Mediterranean . . & might he drift about among the Greek islands?

(EBB, 16 Mar. 1846, pp. 541–2.)

This passage comes at the end of a letter, as a postscript in fact, and begins an exchange devoted to poor Mr Buckingham which is of some interest for what it tells us, not about that obscure and impecunious gentleman, but about the two people who discussed—or failed to discuss—his affairs: Let us follow the development a stage further. Browning's reply was prompt enough. In his next letter, he wrote:

It would be easy for Mr. Buckingham to find a Merchant-ship bound for some Mediterranean port, and after a week or two in harbour, to another and perhaps a third—Naples, Palermo, Syra, Constantinople, & so on. The expense would be very trifling—but the want of comfort *enormous* for an Invalid—the one advantage is the solitariness of the *one* passenger among all those rough new creatures—*I* like it much, and soon get deep into their friendship, but another has other ways of viewing matters—No one article provided by the ship in the way of provisions can *anybody* touch. Mr. B. must lay in his own stock,—and the horrors of dirt and men's ministry are portentous,—yet by a little arrangement beforehand much might be done. Still, I only know my own powers of endurance, and counsel nobody to gain my experience—on the other hand, were all to do again, I had rather have seen Venice *so*—with the five or six weeks' absolute rest of the mind[']s eyes, than any other imaginable way,—except Balloon-travelling.

(17 Mar. 1846, p. 543.)

Mr Buckingham is one of dozens of people who figure casually in the correspondence between Browning and Elizabeth Barrett—casually in the sense that they were not of central interest to either of the writers (unlike, for example, Mr Kenyon or Mrs Jameson), nor of any real importance in the development of the courtship. In such a protracted drama, we take it for granted that a multitude of spear-carriers will pass over the stage, and so they do. Some have identities familiar to us from other sources: Fanny Trollope, for example, or Lord Chesterfield (in both his eighteenth and nine-teenth-century incarnations); others have eluded even Elvan Kintner's industry: a Mrs Bracebridge, with whom Elizabeth Bar-rett was to have gone to see Samuel Rogers's famous collection of painting and sculpture, is not identified for us, though Elizabeth Barrett was told that she was 'an artist & lives or lived on *Mount Hymettus*!' (17 June 1846, p. 796); a Miss Emma Fisher is similarly untraced (despite being mentioned in the *English Review* as one of England's 'living poets'). Sometimes a famous and an obscure figure are unwittingly yoked, as in Elizabeth Barrett's mockery of provin-cialism and pretentious sentimentality in her American admirers, including Edgar Allan Poe:

Today I had a book sent to me from America by the poetess Mrs. Osgood. Did you ever hear of a poetess Mrs. Osgood? . . and her note was of the very most affectionate, & her book is of the most gorgeous, all purple & gold–and she tells me . . oh, she tells me . . that I ought to go to New York, only 'to see Mr. Poe's wild eyes flash through tears' when he reads my verses. It is overcoming to think of, even . . isn't it?

(6 May 1846, p. 683.)[1]

Perhaps it would have been worth going to New York to see that! At least both Browning and Elizabeth Barrett had heard of Poe. Browning did not reply to Elizabeth Barrett's question as to whether he had heard of 'the poetess Mrs. Osgood', but it is a safe

---

[1] Frances Sargent Osgood (1811–50), a friend to whom Poe addressed several poems. Her *Cries of New York* was published in 1846 (Kintner, p. 684 n. 2). Poe had dedicated *The Raven and Other Poems* to Elizabeth Barrett in 1845.

bet that he had not. So it is with numbers of figures in the correspondence: not only are they historically indistinct, but they were indistinct to the correspondents themselves. Mr Buckingham is a prime example. Why, then, should we be interested in his fleeting and inconsequential appearances?

Partly because they are precisely that—appearances. Mr Buckingham is a figure of speech (or rather, of writing) whose importance as a rhetorical property quite outweighs that of his 'real' identity. This identity is, in any case, inaccessible to us, and any attempts to recover it through references in the letters is doomed to failure. On the other hand, certain *rhetorical* qualities may be ascribed to him, not as matters of historical fact, but as components of the transaction (between Browning and Elizabeth Barrett) in which he figures.

Looking back at the first reference to Mr Buckingham in Elizabeth Barrett's letter of 16 March 1846, what do we learn of him from this passage? Among other things, that he is not well; that he is not rich; and that his name begins with B. He is advised to leave the country, and Elizabeth Barrett suggests that he might 'drift about among the Greek Islands'.

Here are some other passages from the same letter:

Dearest, you are dearest always! Talk of Sirens, . . there must be some masculine ones [. . .] to justify this voice I hear. [. . .] You are better you say, which makes me happy of course. And you will not make the 'better' worse again by doing wrong things . . *that* is my petition. [. . .]

But where, pray, did I say . . & when, . . that 'everything would end well'? [. . .] I did not really say so I think. And 'well' is how you understand it. If you jump out of the window you succeed in getting to the ground, somehow, dead or alive . . but whether *that* means 'ending well,' depends on your way of considering matters.

(16 Mar. 1846, pp. 540–1.)

The reference to the Sirens ties in, of course, with the prospect of Mr Buckingham 'drift[ing] about among the Greek islands', but it also alludes to one of the key complexes of imagery in the correspondence. In November 1845, after the publication of *Dramatic Romances and Lyrics*, Walter Savage Landor wrote a sonnet addressed to Browning whose concluding lines pick up a reference to the Sirens in 'The Englishman in Italy', one of the poems in *Dramatic Romances and Lyrics*:

> warmer climes
> Bring brighter plumage, stronger wing; the breeze
> Of Alpine heights thou playest with, borne on
> Beyond Sorrento and Amalfi, where
> The Siren waits thee, singing song for song.

We are not concerned here with analysing the transformations which this image underwent in the hands of Browning and Elizabeth Barrett, simply with recording its association with the theme of *departure* which comes up in connection with Mr Buckingham.

The second passage from the letter, dealing with Browning's health, allows us to make a less oblique link between him and Mr Buckingham. Throughout the courtship, Browning's health is almost as much of an issue as Elizabeth Barrett's, and this is only one of her many anxious remarks and injunctions on the topic. Moreover, there had been earlier in the correspondence some mention of Browning's plans for going abroad, and Elizabeth Barrett had urged him to do so for the sake of his health.[2]

The third passage, on the other hand, the one about jumping out of the window, links Mr Buckingham imaginatively to Elizabeth Barrett herself, in its imagery of escape and healing. In this phase of the courtship, the decision that Browning and Elizabeth Barrett were to marry and leave England had, in principle, been taken. However, Elizabeth Barrett continually and unflinchingly insisted, as she insists here, on the uncertainty of the outcome. She believed that elopement might be the death of her, but that this death might be better than the life she was living in Wimpole Street, or even comparable to life itself in its promise of release from intolerable confinement.

We should now recall that this was not the first time that Elizabeth Barrett had asked Browning's advice about sea-travel. She too, like Mr Buckingham, had been advised to leave England for the sake of her health, and there had been a time in the summer of 1845 when the project of a trip to Pisa had been seriously mooted. Then she had written to Browning: 'I am in the greatest difficulty about the steamers. Will you think a little for me & tell me what is best to

---

[2] Browning mentions that he 'may travel' in his letter of 11 Mar. 1845 (p. 39); Elizabeth Barrett's recommendation to 'try the effect of a little change of air—or even of a great change of air' comes in her letter of 23 June 1845 (pp. 101–2).

do?' (6 Sept. 1845, pp. 183–4.)[3] On several counts, then, it appears that the topic of Mr Buckingham's voyage is not as casual as it seems. Let us now look at Browning's reply. Like Elizabeth Barrett, he turns to the topic in a postscript; in fact, he draws, below his signature, one of those lines across the page which he uses to indicate a change of mood. The preceding passage consists of a passionate response to her doubt about the outcome of their adventure. The link between these two passages is apparently one of contrast: love language followed by practical advice. But the connection goes deeper than this. The first passage describes Browning's conviction that he is indissolubly bound to Elizabeth Barrett and dependent on her:

are not you my 'mistress'? Come, some good out of those old conventions, in which you lost faith after the Bower's disappearance—(it was carried by the singing angels, like the House at Loretto, to the Siren's Isle where we shall find it preserved in a beauty 'very rare and absolute')—is it not right you should be my Lady, my Queen?—and you are, and ever must be, dear Ba—

(17 Mar. 1846, p. 543.)

Browning alludes to Elizabeth Barrett's poem 'The Lost Bower', published in her 1844 collection. The allusion is packed with meaning. The speaker in the poem tells of finding and then losing an enchanted 'bower' in the forest when she was a child. This loss prefigures all the sorrow and disillusionment of her adult life; and yet, transformed by its loss into an *idea*, the 'bower' sustains the speaker's faith in eventual salvation. In other words, Elizabeth Barrett was looking forward to a 'vertical' resolution of her grief-stricken life—a journey out of life, in which that which gave life its meaning would be recovered in a transcendent mode of being. But Browning discounts this notion, as his mocking reference to the miraculous transportation of the Virgin Mary's house from Palestine to Loreto shows. Instead, he proposes a 'horizontal' solution: the 'lost bower' will not be found in heaven, but in the 'Siren's Isle' of their future earthly bliss together. Again the theme of *departure* appears, in the two modes of death and a voyage, with Browning arguing, by a characteristic obliquity, for life over death. But this

[3] Browning had personal and family connections with the merchant navy and the shipping trade, hence his knowledgability about being a passenger on a freighter. See Maynard, 96–102.

argument is not without its equally characteristic twist. After all, though Browning mocks the ignorant superstition of the Catholic faith, he is setting up an idol of his own in Elizabeth Barrett—'my Lady, my Queen'. The dangers of transporting this idol to the Earthly Paradise are tacitly present in the image of the 'singing angels' (a close echo of the ending of 'The Lost Bower'); these angels are figures of eternal bliss, and are juxtaposed with the sirens, whose song, for all its beauty, portended death. In other words, Browning's intricate reference here suggests that the two schemes of salvation—Elizabeth Barrett's, expressed in her poem and in her letter, and his own—were uncomfortably close to one another in his mind.

In this light, Browning's emphasis, in the second passage of the letter, on 'the solitariness of the *one* passenger among all those rough new creatures', is strikingly well chosen. He is putting forward a personal and social image of himself in complete contrast to the one he has just given of himself in relation to Elizabeth Barrett. Instead of absolute subjection to her, he speaks of absolute self-possession: the *consciousness* of being different (and of a superior class) is what makes the voyage in the 'Merchant-ship' delightful— Browning soon gets friendly with the crew, but does not eat their food, and a certain kind of intimacy only places in sharper focus 'the horrors of dirt and men's ministry'. At ease in this all-male company, Browning remains self-reliant: 'Mr. B. must lay in his own stock'. The voyage thus undertaken is seen as a symbolic oblivion, an 'absolute rest of the mind[']s eyes', after which Venice—a longstanding symbol for Browning of life itself in its rich diversity[4]— can appear in unjaded splendour. The simplicity of this idea, the sense of release with which it is articulated, are in profound and significant relation to the embroilment of feeling in the preceding part of the letter.

The course of Mr Buckingham's voyage did not run smooth after this initial exchange. Having (temporarily) exhausted their personal interest in the topic, Browning and Elizabeth Barrett apparently found it hard to keep Mr Buckingham's affairs in the forefront of their minds. They forgot to discuss him on at least two occasions:

---

[4] See, for example, *Sordello*, iii. 723–5: 'Venice seems a type / Of Life—'twixt blue and blue extends, a stripe, / As Life, the somewhat, hangs 'twixt naught and naught'.

'Why, we do not even *talk* much now!' Browning wrote after one meeting, remarking on the development of their intimacy; 'witness Mr. Buckingham & his voyage that ought to have been discussed!' (24 Mar. 1846, p. 555.) Nevertheless they had not lost sight of him, and two weeks later there was a burst of static from Browning:

My sea-friend's opinion is altogether unfavourable to the notion of an invalid's trusting himself alone in a merchant vessel—he says—'it will certainly be the gentleman's death'—So very small a degree of comfort can be secured amid all the inevitable horrors of dirt, roughness, &c The expenses are trifling in any case, on that very account. Any number of the 'Shipping *Gazette*' (I think) will give a list of all vessels about to sail, with choice of ports—or on the walls of the Exchange one may see their names placarded, with reference to the Agent—or he will, himself, (my friend) do his utmost with a shipowner, (Chas. Walton) we both know, and save some expense, perhaps. I made him remark the difference between my carelessness for accomodations and an invalid's proper attention beforehand—but he persisted in saying nothing can be done, nothing effectual.

(6 Apr. 1846, p. 594.)

This is one of two references to Mr Buckingham's voyage, in successive letters, which are juxtaposed with allusions to Browning's play *A Soul's Tragedy*. The play was about to be published in the eighth and last number of the series *Bells and Pomegranates* and, along with his letter of 6 April, Browning sent Elizabeth Barrett a batch of proofs. It was, he wrote, the 'last work I shall ever *send* you, if God please!' (p. 593.) Why should Mr Buckingham have occurred again to Browning in this connection? Because the plot of *A Soul's Tragedy*, once again, has *love* and *departure* at its centre. The play opens with Chiappino, the embittered liberal, awaiting the confirmation of his order of banishment from the town of Faenza, and declaring his unrequited passion for his friend's betrothed lover; and it ends with him fleeing the city (voluntarily) after his love and liberalism have both proved hollow. Of Browning's works published between *Sordello* and *The Ring and the Book*, *A Soul's Tragedy* is the most comprehensive study of failure and disillusion—in politics, art, and love. Chiappino, the 'hero', is destroyed not by Fate but by his own vanity, and his fall is accompanied not by grandeur and pathos, but by mocking laughter. In his combination of tormented self-opinion and catastrophic self-deception, he presents us with a nightmare image of Browning's own most deeply-rooted creative preoccupations. But the name was also picked up by Elizabeth Barrett and applied, not to Browning, but to Browning's erstwhile rival, the Reverend George Barrett Hunter. It was in her most recent letter that Elizabeth Barrett first drew the parallel. The three-cornered relationship envisaged by Elizabeth Barrett casts Browning and herself in the role of the happy and secure lovers, Luitolfo and Eulalia, with the outsider's role of Chiappino reserved for the unsuccessful suitor whom she had finally excluded from her intimacy. There is therefore no trace of ambivalence in Elizabeth Barrett's allusion to the play, no suggestion that she saw in Chiappino an image of Browning, as Browning himself undoubtedly did.

Once more, then, the mention of Mr Buckingham takes on a colouring from the context in which it seems so haphazardly to appear. But I am being less than exact in saying 'the mention of Mr Buckingham', since Browning persists in calling him an 'invalid', and, after his first mention of him, does not use his name; and it is perhaps just as well to remember that we have no objective reason for subscribing to this view. All we learn from Elizabeth Barrett is that Mr Buckingham has been ordered to take a sea-voyage 'to complete his cure', which need not imply, as Browning's phrasing does, that he was utterly incapacitated and that 'nothing effectual' could be done for him. That Browning should call Mr Buckingham an 'invalid' is not, however, surprising, when we consider that the figure of the ineffectual man, the failed or disillusioned idealist, is the cardinal figure of his poetry, one to which he returns again and again throughout his career: *Sordello*, *Paracelsus*, 'Pictor Ignotus', 'Cleon', 'Andrea del Sarto', and Guido in *The Ring and the Book*. To identify Mr Buckingham as an 'invalid', a Chiappino, is to articulate Browning's own ambivalence about *accomplishing* his flight with Elizabeth Barrett, which was, indeed, to 'complete his cure' (not to mention her own). Browning was professionally and personally committed to fulfilment, to salvation, but he expressed this commitment through the negative images of inadequacy and failure. Hence his see-saw opinion as to the advisability of Mr Buckingham setting out on his redemptive voyage.

2 Famous Names

We expect the letters of two public figures to give us an insight into the public world which they inhabit, and at first glance the letters of

Robert Browning and Elizabeth Barrett more than satisfy this expectation. Literary London in the 1840s (to take the obvious example) which Browning frequented in person and Elizabeth Barrett by proxy in her correspondence, is abundantly present:

Yes, I went to Chelsea and found dear Carlyle alone—his wife is in the country where he will join her as soon as his book's last sheet returns corrected and fit for press—which will be at the month's end about—He was all kindness and talked like his own self while he made me tea—and, afterward, brought chairs into the little yard, rather than garden, and smoked his pipe with apparent relish; at night he would walk as far as Vauxhall Road bridge on my way home.
(RB, 8 Aug. 1845, p. 147; the book referred to is *Oliver Cromwell's Letters and Speeches*.)

The anecdotal touch is potent here, and gives the modern reader a sense of reality, of authentic taste and texture. Of course the description is subjective in its point of view, but there is an implied objectivity in the narrative frame itself. That Browning liked Carlyle and saw the generous and humane side of him might be a matter of his personal prejudice, but that he sat in a real 'yard' with a real person is a matter of historical fact, and therefore of (objective) historical interest to us. Such passages are common, drawing in Tennyson, Dickens, and Landor as well as Carlyle. Other, lesser figures make regular appearances: H. F. Chorley, editor of the *Athenaeum*; R. H. Horne, author of the 'farthing epic' *Orion* and the controversial *New Spirit of the Age*; Mary Russell Mitford, dramatist and journalist and author of the minor classic *Our Village*; Harriet Martineau, whose interests ranged from mesmerism to political economy; Anna Jameson, writer on literature and art history; the publisher Edward Moxon, the critic John Forster, the novelist and playwright Bulwer-Lytton, literary lawyers such as Thomas Talfourd and B. W. Procter ('Barry Cornwall'), and many more. The correspondence is a crowded salon as often as it is a private parlour.

Besides the references to literary figures whom Browning and Elizabeth Barrett met or corresponded with, there are dozens of references to the wider contexts of modern literary life and literary history. Here, for example, is Elizabeth Barrett on the subject of a snide review of George Sand in the *Athenaeum*:

Why mention her at all . . why name in any fashion any of these French writers, for the reception of whom the English mind is certainly not

prepared, unless they are to be named worthily, recognised righteously?
[. . .] Why not say boldly 'These writers have high faculty, & imagination
such as none of our romance-writers can pretend to—but they have besides
a devil—& we do not recommend them as fit reading for English families!'
Now wouldn't it answer every purpose? Or silence would!—silence, at
least. But this digging & nagging at great reputations, . . it is to me quite
insufferable: & not compensated for by the motive, which is a truckling to
conventions rather than to morals. As if earnestness of aim was not [. . .] a
characteristic of George Sand! Really it is pitiful.

                                                    (26 Apr. 1846, p. 653.)

Again, what matters here, as much as the substance of the opinion
itself, is the sense of range in Elizabeth Barrett's mind—the fact that
she read contemporary French literature, that she thought about its
critical reception in England—and the consequent sense in us, as
readers, of being given access to a whole dimension of nineteenth-
century intellectual history. It is as though the passage—there are
dozens like it on topics of art, politics, religion—were a medium
through which we can see 'the period' in one of its most concrete
manifestations. In turn, such manifestations are seen to impinge on
the writer, who is open to receive their impression and therefore
appears to us less abstract, more humanly knowable and 'real'. Biography, autobiography, and autobiographical documents such as
letters and diaries, have traditionally been assigned this function of
conveying to posterity the sense of 'how it was'. We value them for
that reason, and we therefore tend to look in them for what we
value.

   The letters of Robert Browning and Elizabeth Barrett are rich in
this quality, but there is another way of reading their patterns of
reference. Suppose that what applies to Mr Buckingham applies to
everyone else: that the 'reality' towards which so many passages
gesture—the reality of Carlyle, of the reception of George Sand's
work in England—has a rhetorical as well as an objective function?
The very specificity of the latter might prevent us from seeing the
former. But if we change our angle of vision, then obsessive self-
image replaces the objective representation of people and events;
what looks, at first, like a view from the windows of Wimpole Street
or New Cross over a wide landscape of contemporary thought and
action, over social or political or artistic topics, turns out to be
simultaneously a view inward. The field of allusion doubles as a
labyrinth of the mind.

Let us take Browning's first reference to Carlyle in the corre-spondence.

Only last night, I had to write, on the part of Mr. Carlyle, to a certain ungainly foolish gentleman who keeps back from him, with all the fussy impotence of stupidity (not bad feeling, alas; for *that* we could deal with) a certain MS. letter of Cromwell's which completes the collection now going to press—and this long-ears had to be 'dear Sir'd' and 'obedient servanted' till I *said* (to use a mild word) 'commend me to the sincerities of this kind of thing'!

(11 Feb. 1845, p. 17.)

Reasons for Browning to mention Carlyle's name early in the corre-spondence (this is his fourth letter) are not far to seek. To begin with, straightforwardly enough, Browning knew Carlyle well and saw him often in this period; Carlyle was one of the few writers as clever as himself with whom Browning felt at ease (his relations with Dickens and Tennyson, for example, were always more prob-lematic). Then again, it would do him no harm with Elizabeth Bar-rett to indicate his connection with the great man; further on in the letter he makes it clear that the connection is friendly as well as sec-retarial by apostrophizing him as 'dear, noble Carlyle'. Finally, the whole anecdote gives Elizabeth Barrett an insight into Browning's social and intellectual 'set'; it is one of a number of signals exchanged in the early period of the correspondence by which the two explore the range and degree of their compatibility. Such sig-nals are traded in every new social encounter, particularly where a sexual development is possible. Conventionally, then, we have here a story which tells us something about Carlyle himself, and about Browning's collaboration with him, and, more speculatively, about Browning's courtship of Elizabeth Barrett in terms of the image of himself which he wanted her to have.

None of these reasons takes account of the context of the allusion, except the general one of its occurrence early on in the cor-respondence. The precise location does not really matter: it might come anywhere in the opening sequence. There is, however, another interpretation, which does take account of this local con-text, and which suggests that Browning makes use of Carlyle in a less straightforward way than as a name he thought it appropriate to drop.

In her early letters, Elizabeth Barrett was somewhat coy about her own facility as a letter-writer, and she made several jokes about Browning getting bored with her for going on too long, or for being too prying about his own affairs, and the like. Browning did not, at first, reply directly to these remarks. He did, however, write in the letter preceding the one we are considering: 'After all, you know nothing, next to nothing of me, and that stops me. Spring is to come, however!' (27 Jan. 1845, p. 12.) To this, Elizabeth Barrett replied:

Is it true, as you say, that I 'know so "little" ' of you? And is it true, as others say, that the productions of an artist do not partake of his real nature [. . .] It is *not* true, to my mind—& therefore it is not true that I know little of you, except in as far as it is true (which I believe) that your greatest works are to come.

                                                        (3 Feb. 1845, p. 14.)

'That stops me. Spring is to come': Browning's remark focuses on the inadequacy of writing and his hope that meeting Elizabeth Barrett in the spring (the time she herself had designated) would enable his identity to 'spring' to her knowledge. But Elizabeth Barrett categorically denies the premiss: for her, writing is an adequate medium of knowledge. Her phrasing could even be read as an implicit retraction of her earlier promise to see him face to face, since she is here looking forward not to knowing him better personally, but by means of his future 'works'. It was to this that Browning responded in the opening of his next letter.

Dear Miss Barrett,
    People would hardly ever tell falsehoods about a matter, if they had been let tell truth in the beginning—for it is hard to prophane one's very self, and nobody who has, for instance, used certain words and ways to a mother or a father *could* . . even if by the devil's help he *would* . . reproduce or mimic them with any effect to anybody else that was to be won over; and so, if 'I love you' were always outspoken when it might be, there would, I suppose, be little fear of its desecration at any after time: but lo! only last night, I had to write, on the part of Mr. Carlyle, to a certain ungainly foolish gentleman [. . .]

Here, then, is the local context of the Carlyle reference. And, after reporting his exclamation ' "commend me to the sincerities of this kind of thing"!', Browning goes on:

When I spoke of you knowing little of me, one of the senses in which I meant so was this . . that I would not well vowel-point my common-place letters and syllables with a masoretic *other* sound and sense, make my 'dear' something intenser than 'dears' in ordinary, and 'yours ever' a thought more significant than the run of its like; and all this came of your talking of 'tiring me,' 'being too curious,' &c. &c. which I should never have heard of had the plain truth looked out of my letter with its unmistakeable eyes [. . .]

(11 Feb. 1845, pp. 16–17.)[5]

We are now in a position to evaluate the 'other sound and sense' in Browning's allusion to Carlyle, which takes place in an exchange about letter-writing and about the 'sincerities of this kind of thing'—that is, the rhetoric of courtship. For after all Browning writing to Elizabeth Barrett and Browning writing to the 'ungainly foolish gentleman' are in the same position. Someone is 'keeping back' something they want—something necessary to the completion of their work. (We have seen already how deeply convinced Browning was, from the very beginning, of his need of Elizabeth Barrett to complete and sustain his own creativity.) The process of persuasion—the use of language to get what he wants—involves Browning in a central anxiety about writing and about his own status as a writer. Ideally, language is associated with intimacy, truth, and directness—'one's very self', the self that communicates with 'a mother or a father', where 'I love you' is 'outspoken'— forthright, clear and without ambivalence. The use of language in such relations should prevent its 'desecration at any after time'. But it is not so for Browning. He is one of those who has *not* 'been let tell truth from the beginning'. (We have here, almost incidentally, a rare glimpse into Browning's feelings about his parents and the source of his conception of language.) He has grown up accustomed to the opposed model of language—the rhetorical model, in which 'certain words and ways' can be 'reproduce[d] or mimic[ked]' in order to 'win people over'.

Browning himself had used the phrase 'I love you' in his very first letter to Elizabeth Barrett, but it was not in the least 'outspoken' there; on the contrary, it was incorporated into an elaborate rhetorical movement. For as he insisted to her: 'You speak out, *you*—I only make men & women speak'. And here he is, engaged in just

[5] The Hebrew of the Scriptures consists of consonants without any indication of where the vowels come; the Masoretes (students of the biblical text) added these 'vowel-points', which occasionally affected the interpretation of the word (Kintner, p. 20 n.2).

such a 'dramatic' performance, in which language mediates not feeling but desire—the desire to 'win over'. Is not Carlyle, here, the dramatic poet, making Browning speak on his behalf? The irony of this is strengthened when we remember Carlyle's own contemporary reputation for outspokenness. The prophet and truth-teller, with all his claims to be a plain speaker, is engaged in a devious manœuvre in order to get into his hands a letter which will 'complete the collection'—a collection of the letters of yet another such figure, Cromwell, the forthright soldier.

Browning therefore presents himself to Elizabeth Barrett as a 'speaker' in a dramatic performance scripted by Carlyle. But he himself has scripted Carlyle's appearance in his letter, so the rhetoric doubles back on itself: Browning is using Carlyle to get what he wants, just as Carlyle is using Browning to get what *he* wants. The complexity of the process is part of its point: Browning is articulating the distance which he feels separates him from Elizabeth Barrett, the distance between 'the plain truth [. . .] with its unmistakeable eyes' and 'the sincerities of this kind of thing'—the kind of letter which needs to be accounted for in terms of rhetorical strategies (including the strategy of abnegating rhetoric, which Browning elaborately pursues).

Let us now look at Elizabeth Barrett's first mention of George Sand. In a letter of July 1845, she refers to

> that wonderful woman George Sand; who has something monstruous in combination with her genius [. . .] but whom, in her good & evil together, I regard with infinitely more admiration than all other women of genius who are or have been. Such a colossal nature in every way—with all that breadth & scope of faculty which women want—magnanimous, & loving the truth & loving the people [. . .] so eloquent, & yet earnest as if she were dumb—so full of a living sense of beauty, & of noble blind instincts towards an ideal purity—& so proving a right even in her wrong.
>
> (2–3 July 1845, pp. 113–14.)

As with Browning's mention of Carlyle, there are solid circumstantial reasons for Elizabeth Barrett to bring up George Sand's name in epistolary conversation. Sand's notoriety was at its height in the 1840s, and the English reviews were filled with what Browning himself called 'spiteful and quite uncalled for' allusions to her private life (27 Apr. 1846, p. 658). The apparent unconcern with which Elizabeth Barrett mentions her familiarity with Sand's work is not, therefore, without significance. In the long (and continuing) course of her self-education, Elizabeth Barrett had acquired a good grounding in 'classical' French literature (roughly, from Ronsard to Rousseau); but she had only recently begun to read modern French writers. She wrote of her new interest to Mary Russell Mitford in November 1842:

Keep my secret—but I have been reading lately a good deal of the new French literature. Not that I would let it loose in this house for the world, no, nor in any other—but I was curious beyond the patience of my Eve-ship [. . .] And besides I live out of the world altogether, and am lonely enough and old enough and sad enough and experienced enough in every sort of good and bad reading, not to be hurt personally by a French super-fluity of bad. [. . .] Now tell me, what you think? That it is very naughty of me to read naughty books—or that you have done the same?

(*EBB to MRM*, 144–5.)

This letter initiates a fascinating discussion of the 'naughty books' which Elizabeth Barrett was reading—including Victor Hugo's *Nôtre Dame* and Balzac's *Le Père Goriot*, and, of course, several works by George Sand, among them *Leila*, 'a serpent book both for language-colour and soul-slime and one which I could not read through for its vileness myself' (*EBB to MRM*, 156). Leaving aside the question of Elizabeth Barrett's judgement of these books, how-ever, what concerns us here is her tentativeness in announcing her taste for them even to so close and long-standing a friend as Miss Mitford. It brings home to us the cultural climate of Wimpole Street and all that it represented, but it also tells us something about the terms in which Elizabeth Barrett construed her own position in that environment. Notice how the 'it' of 'let it loose' might refer either to the literature or the secret of her reading it. 'Not that I would let it loose in this house *for the world* [. . .] And besides I live *out of the world* altogether'. By seeing herself as an isolated intellectual, whose life 'in this house' is unaffected by the politics of the family (she is neither wife nor mother, and her status as daughter is quali-fied by her age and invalidism), Elizabeth Barrett allows herself a privilege she would feel it right to deny to others—the privilege of her 'Eve-ship' having to do with 'serpent-books'.

Elizabeth Barrett would naturally have a strong interest in con-veying to Robert Browning her dispensation from the constraints of certain social and moral conventions. Just as Browning's mention of

Carlyle's name would indicate to her that he was in touch with literary and intellectual ideas which she was likely to respect and
admire, so her mention of George Sand's name to him would rein-
force his sense of her as independent-minded, unprejudiced, and
well informed. She might be sheltered from the abrasive contacts of
London society, but the shelter was not a cloister. On intellectual
ground they met as equals.

But then, Browning would already have read the two sonnets
which, in her 1844 collection, Elizabeth Barrett had addressed to
George Sand; he would have known all about her admiration and
the earnest moral reservations with which it was qualified.[6] The
context of the allusion, on the other hand, tells us something new
and different about the motive and implications of its appearance. It
comes in the following passage:

Talking of poetry, I had a newspaper 'in help of social & political progress'
sent to me yesterday from America—addressed to—just my name . .
poetess, London! Think of the simplicity of those wild Americans in 'calculating' that 'people in general' here in England knew what a poetess is!
[. . .]
    And talking of poetesses, I had a note yesterday (again) which quite
touched me . . from Mr. Hemans—Charles . . the son of Felicia [. . .] His
mother's memory is surrounded to him, he says, 'with almost a divine
lustre'—& 'as it cannot be to those who knew the writer alone & not the
woman'. Do you not like to hear such things said? and is it not better than
your tradition about Shelley's son? [. . .] Not that, in naming Shelley, I
meant for a moment to make a comparison—there is not equal ground for
it. [. . .] And if you promised never to tell Mrs. Jameson . . nor Miss Martineau . . I would confide to you perhaps my secret profession of faith—
which is . . which is . . that let us say & do what we please & can . . there *is*
a natural inferiority of mind in women—of the intellect . . not by any
means, of the moral nature—& that the history of Art & of genius testifies
to this fact openly. Oh—I would not say so to Mrs. Jameson for the world!
[. . .]
    [. . .] I shd not dare, . . *ever* . . I think . . to tell her that I believe
women . . all of us in a mass . . to have minds of quicker movement, but
less power & depth . . & that we are under your feet, because we can't

---

[6] Elizabeth Barrett's two sonnets were called 'To George Sand: a Desire' and 'To
George Sand: a Recognition'. The first ('Thou large-brained woman and large-
hearted man') wishes that Sand's genius could be 'sanctified from blame' and fit for
'child and maiden'; the second ('True genius, but true woman!') claims that Sand's
masculine strength does not conceal the femaleness of her spirit.

stand upon our own—Not that we sHd either be quite under your feet!—So you are not to be too proud, if you please—& there is certainly some amount of wrong—: but it never will be righted in the manner & to the extent contemplated by certain of our own prophetesses . . not ought to be, I hold in intimate persuasion. One woman indeed now alive . . & only *that* one down all the ages of the world . . seems to me to justify for a moment an opposite opinion—that wonderful woman George Sand [. . .]

(2–3 July 1845, pp. 112–13.)[7]

Elizabeth Barrett's train of thought connects two tributes to woman writers—one to herself from the 'wild Americans' and the other to Felicia Hemans from her son—with a third, her own tribute to George Sand. But intervening between the second and the third tribute is the idea that 'there *is* a natural inferiority of mind in women'. She implicitly devalues her own status and that of all other women writers (including Mrs Jameson and Miss Martineau, who here figure ignobly as self-righteous bullies); George Sand is merely the exception who proves the rule. Sand is fitted to play this part by that 'something monstrous in combination with her genius': she is outlandish (literally and metaphorically foreign), and therefore cannot be said to embody the aspirations or capacities of her gender. Never mind that in the second of her 1844 sonnets Elizabeth Barrett had claimed that Sand's attempt to disguise or transcend her femaleness was vain, and that 'while before / The world thou burnest in a poet-fire, / We see thy woman-heart beat evermore / Through the large flame'. Elizabeth Barrett was quite capable of believing both that George Sand was a woman despite herself (countering the threat of her crossing of the gender divide) and that she was not, representatively speaking, a woman at all.

It is this last point which suggests the motive for her reference to Sand in this particular letter. It is a self-reflecting reference—as

---

[7] Felicia Hemans (1793–1835), a minor poet now remembered for a handful of anthology pieces such as 'Casabianca' ('The boy stood on the burning deck') and 'The Landing of the Pilgrim Fathers'; Elizabeth Barrett's poem in her memory, 'Felicia Hemans', appeared in *The Seraphim, and Other Poems* (1838). 'Her youngest son, Charles (1817–76) was an antiquary and the founder (1846) of Rome's first English-language newspaper' (Kintner, p. 114 n.1). The 'tradition about Shelley's son' (Percy Florence) must have been delivered verbally, and is a little puzzling; he was not noted for disrespect to his father's memory. Anna Jameson (1794–1860), essayist and art historian, became friendly with both Browning and Elizabeth Barrett in the period of the courtship (without realizing that they were lovers); she came to their assistance in Paris after their elopement and accompanied them to Pisa.

much so as Browning's reference to Carlyle had been. The local context alone proves it; but the point is strengthened when we widen the context to include topics raised previously in the letters.

Elizabeth Barrett's opening gambit, 'Talking of poetry', sprang from her comment on a passage from Browning's most recent letter, in which he spoke of bringing with him on his next visit 'the rest of the "Duchess"—four or five hundred lines' (that is, sections X–XVII of 'The Flight of the Duchess', sections I–IX of which had already appeared in a magazine), adding the comment, ' "heu, herba mala crescit" ' ('alas, the evil weed flourishes'). At the end of his letter, he related an (apparently unconnected) anecdote:

I gathered at Rome, close to the fountain of Egeria, a handful of *fennel*-seeds from the most indisputable plant of fennel I ever chanced upon—and, lo, they are come up . . hemlock, or something akin! Wherein does hemlock resemble fennel? How could I mistake? No wonder that a stone's cast off from that Egeria[']s fountain is the Temple of the God Ridiculus.

(1 July 1845, pp. 110–11.)

The nymph Egeria was the counsellor (one might say 'muse' in this context) of the ancient Roman law-giver Numa Pompilius; it is characteristic of Browning's poetics that the seeds he gathers at her shrine should come up as a poison-plant, that his god-like dignity should be lowered to the level of 'the Gòd Ridiculus'. Elizabeth Barrett saw the connection, and responded accordingly. 'I am delighted [. . .] to hear of the quantity of "mala herba",' she wrote; '& hemlock does not come up from every seed you sow, though you call it by ever such bad names' (2–3 July 1845, p. 112).

In Part One (pp. 86–94) I gave an account of how Browning persuaded Elizabeth Barrett to act as the critical judge of the poems he intended to publish in his next collection, *Dramatic Romances and Lyrics*. He did so by 'winning' the debate between them as to which of them was the superior writer, by insisting that Elizabeth Barrett, because she could transmit the 'pure white light' of truth directly in her verse, had the inherent right to judge his verse, which dealt in 'truth broken into prismatic hues' (13 Jan. 1845, p. 7). I pointed out that 'The Flight of the Duchess' was crucially placed at the head of the list of poems which Elizabeth Barrett accepted to judge, because it contained within it a series of figures (the rough old Huntsman who narrates the poem, the Duchess herself, the old gipsy woman whose visionary speech persuades her to undertake her 'flight') who embodied the terms of the 'argument' which Browning and Elizabeth Barrett had just concluded. Clearly, then, the letters which I have just been examining were written at a time when this issue was strongly present to the minds of both writers. Browning was about to bring Elizabeth Barrett the first instalment of the work upon which she, in her newly-appointed role as critic (and censor), was to pronounce. No wonder that he reiterates the *mistaken* nature of his work, in the image of fennel-seeds coming up as hemlock; no wonder that she rejects the image. And no wonder that, in so doing, she reaches for other images which convey her protest at being cast as Browning's creative superior. In one of her very first letters to him, she had remarked, 'you are "masculine" to the height—and I, as a woman, have studied some of your gestures of language & intonation wistfully, as a thing beyond me far!' (15 Jan. 1845, p. 9.) She repeated the point after reading Landor's poem to Browning on the publication of *Dramatic Romances and Lyrics*: 'he lays his finger just on your characteristics [. . .] which, when you were only a poet to me, I used to study, characteristic by characteristic, & turn myself round & round in despair of being ever able to approach, taking them to be so essentially & intensely masculine that like effects were unattainable, even in a lower degree, by any female hand' (20 Nov. 1845, p. 279). Now therefore, in her references to George Sand, she restates the case, in a disguised form (since direct objection is no longer open to her); humility towards Sand (as a greater writer than herself) is a form of humility towards Browning; casting Sand in a 'masculine' role reinforces the parallel; making Sand exceptional (unrepresentative of her sex) allows Elizabeth Barrett to formulate the syllogism that, since women (except Sand) are intellectually inferior to men, then she, Elizabeth Barrett, must be intellectually inferior to Browning.

So much, then, for the treatment of both minor and major figures in the correspondence, which turns out, in one perspective, to be a closed system of communication between the two writers; as much as, in another perspective, it opens out on to a world beyond itself. It is not surprising that, in the total absorption with each other on which they both remarked, both Browning and Elizabeth Barrett should have drawn the circle of their intimacy around almost all the people and topics that they had occasion to mention, nor that, once inside the circle, they should have 'translated' such people and topics into the language of their relationship. And with regard to

one person, and one topic, this tendency was spectacularly
increased, in proportion to the significance of the result. That topic
was male authority, what Browning, in an outburst just eight days
before his marriage, called 'the execrable policy of the world's husbands, fathers, brothers, and domineerers in general' (4 Sept. 1846,
p. 1044). The person, of course, was Mr Barrett.

10

Mr Barrett

1 Jupiter Tonans

We first hear of Elizabeth Barrett's father in the course of her fifth letter.

Some years ago [. . .] I translated or rather *undid* into English, the Prometheus of Aeschylus. To speak of this production moderately (not modestly), it is the most miserable of all miserable versions [. . .] as cold as Caucasus, & as flat as the nearest plain. [. . .] Well,—the comfort is, that the little book was unadvertised & unknown, & that most of the copies (through my entreaty of my father) are shut up in the wardrobe of his bedroom. If ever I get well I shall show my joy by making a bondfire [*sic*] of them. In the meantime, the recollection of this sin of mine has been my nightmare & daymare too, and the sin has been the 'Blot on my escutcheon.'

(27 Feb. 1845, p. 30.)

Last things first: *A Blot in the 'Scutcheon* is Browning's play, published and performed in 1843, in which an overbearing brother, a widower, discovers that his 'pure' sister has a secret lover; he kills the lover and his daughter dies of grief. ('I had no mother,' she warbles, in a passage admired by Dickens.) Why should Elizabeth Barrett associate the play with her translation? Aeschylus' *Prometheus Bound* opens with the chaining of Prometheus to the rock in the Caucasus, on the orders of another overbearing male—Zeus, or Jupiter. ('Jupiter Tonans', the thunderer, as Elizabeth Barrett calls him in another passage.) The daughter is sinful; the father covers the sin (in the *wardrobe* of his *bedroom*, a man's doubly enclosed space); the copies of the book (*Prometheus Bound*: are the copies

237

bound or unbound?), press like a guilty secret on the writer's spirit. Guilt is associated with disease; if Elizabeth Barrett gets well, she will make a purificatory sacrifice of this link with her father.

What is the nature of the sin? It springs from a translation of Aeschylus, a father-figure himself in terms of literary form. Translation is a 'crossing' or grafting of languages, which bears fruit but may be thought to be unnatural and morally indefensible (as in the Italian 'traduttore-traditore', translator-traitor). Translation is both an act of deference and a challenge to authority, a remaking which in all cases is a mis-making, but especially here (in this 'most miserable of all miserable versions') because Aeschylus is the holiest and most ancient authority conceivable, and the *Prometheus* (in contemporary critical opinion) his greatest work.

Here is another early reference to her father in Elizabeth Barrett's letters. A thunderstorm has prevented her from going out when she did not particularly want to:

You see, Jupiter Tonans was good enough to come to-day on purpose to deliver me—one evil for another!—for I confess with shame & contrition, that I never wait to enquire whether it thunders to the left or the right, to be frightened most ingloriously. Isn't it a disgrace to anyone with a pretension to poetry? Dr. Chambers, a part of whose office it is, Papa says, 'to reconcile foolish women to their follies,' used to take the side of my vanity—& discourse at length on the passive obedience of some nervous systems to electrical influences—but perhaps my faint-heartedness is besides traceable to a half-reasonable terror of a great storm in Herefordshire . . where great storms most do congregate . . (such storms!) round the Malvern Hills, those mountains of England. We lived four miles from their roots, thro' all my childhood & early youth, in a Turkish house my father built himself, crowded with minarets & domes, & crowned with metal spires & crescents, to the provocation (as people used to observe) of every lightning of heaven. Once a storm of storms happened, & we all thought the house was struck— & a tree was so really, within two hundred yards of the windows while I looked out—the bark, rent from the top to the bottom . . torn into long ribbons by the dreadful fiery hands, & dashed out into the air, over the heads of other trees, or left twisted in their branches—torn into shreds in a moment, as a flower might be, by a child!—Did you ever see a tree after it has been struck by lightning? The whole trunk of that tree was bare & peeled—& up that new whiteness of it, ran the finger-mark of the lightning in a bright beautiful rose-colour (none of your roses brighter or more beautiful!) the fever-sign of the certain death—Though the branches themselves were for the most part untouched, & spread from the peeled trunk in their

full summer foliage,—& birds singing in them three hours afterwards!
[. . .] So I get 'possessed' sometimes with the effects of these impressions
[. . .] and oh! how amusing & instructive all this is to you! When my
father came into the room to-day & found me hiding my eyes from the
lightning, he was quite angry & called 'it disgraceful to anybody who had
ever learnt the alphabet'—to which I answered humbly that 'I knew it
was'—but if I had been inpertinent, I MIGHT have added that wisdom does
not come by the alphabet but in spite of it?

(11 July 1845, pp. 119–20.)

The structure of this passage encloses the remembered scene from
Elizabeth Barrett's childhood at Hope End between two contemporary references to her father. Both these contemporary references
show him in full patriarchal cry. In the first, he dismisses Elizabeth
Barrett's doctor, William Chambers (physician in ordinary to
Queen Victoria, which makes the remark even more pointed), as
little better than a quack who 'reconcile[s] foolish women to their
follies'. In the second, unceremoniously entering his thirty-nine-
year-old daughter's room (she calls it 'the room', not 'my room'),
he turns the scornful light of scientific materialism on Elizabeth
Barrett's fear of thunder. Women are either 'foolish' and a prey to
charlatans, or primitive and a prey to superstition. His anger is
righteous; Elizabeth Barrett apparently defers to it, citing his first
pronouncement without comment, and responding 'humbly' to the
second—her mental reservation is conditional and hesitant, concluding with a question mark which is not grammatically required.
But the story in the middle of the passage tells us something different about the way Elizabeth Barrett views her father's assumption
of authority.

Once again, guilt ('shame & contrition'; 'a disgrace') is central to
Elizabeth Barrett's account of paternal power. Her father, Jupiter
Tonans below, builds a house which, by its location 'where great
storms most do congregate', and by its infidel construction ('a Turkish house [. . .] crowded with minarets & domes') deliberately
challenges Jupiter Tonans above. She is both sheltered and
oppressed by his tyranny, and from the windows of the house she
witnesses a terrifying scene of symbolic retribution, which impli-
cates her both as the punisher and as the object of punishment. The
tree is an image of male potency with which she identifies, but from
which she also recoils. (You must not shelter beneath a tree in a
storm; the shelter is itself a conductor for lightning, like the house.)

The 'dreadful fiery hands' are the hands of the male deity, but 'torn into shreds in a moment' suggests older myths of castration and dismemberment, myths in which powerful men (Orpheus, Pentheus) are torn apart by women. In the hands of the storm, the mighty tree is like a flower in the hands of a child. Storm and child are associated by Romantic primitivism: the child is natural, wild, and subversive. The child's 'wisdom' (in Wordsworth, in Blake) subverts adult structures, adult reason; the child, like the savage, has not yet learnt the alphabet, and is therefore subject to (and representative of) irrational and arbitrary forces. On the other hand, to build your house in the form of a challenge to divine power, to govern your children as a tyrant, is equally arbitrary, equally irrational; the extremes meet, and Mr Barrett, who sees himself as enlightened and rational, with his Voltairean scorn for quackery and superstition, turns out to be just as unbalanced and intemperate in the exercise of his power as the storm which his daughter fears.

The retribution which Elizabeth Barrett so graphically describes seems to affect only the trunk of the tree: 'the branches themselves were for the most part untouched [. . .] & birds singing in them three hours afterwards!' Another traditional tree image, of the trunk as father and the branches as children; the children survive, in creative life and pleasure, the devastation of their paternal stock. But the appearance of survival is deceptive: the whole tree is doomed, 'the fever-sign of the certain death' is on it. This hectic sign, the 'finger-mark of the lightning in a bright beautiful rose-colour', is compared by Elizabeth Barrett with the roses which Browning brings with him on his visits, roses from his suburban garden in New Cross (not noted for its mighty storms), roses from the joyful and hopeful present; they are '[not] brighter or more beautiful' than the death-sign from the past at Hope End.[1]

This letter gave Browning his first opportunity to comment on Mr Barrett's character and opinions. His direct response was a respectful disagreement. 'Your father must pardon me for holding most firmly with Dr. Chambers—his theory is quite borne out by my own experience,' he wrote, adding that he had seen 'a man it were foolish call a coward, a great fellow too, all but die away in a

---

[1] This is not the only storm in the correspondence with which Mr Barrett is associated: see Part One, pp. 161–2.

thunderstorm, though he had quite science enough to explain why there was no immediate danger at all' (13 July 1845, p. 121). So much for the manly scorn of 'foolish women'. Browning's indirect response, *via* praise of Elizabeth Barrett's descriptive powers ('What a grand sight your tree was—*is*, for I see it'—ibid., p. 122), was to string together a series of accounts of storms he himself had witnessed, including two anecdotes which make fun of superstition about thunder being the voice of the deity, and ending with a set piece on the Adriatic 'bora' which, in its anecdotal energy and picturesque colour, parallels the description of the scirocco in 'The Englishman in Italy', on which Browning was working at the time. The effect is to defuse the topic, to make it the subject of creative rather than neurotic reminiscence, and to offer a sympathetic and sensible counter to Mr Barrett's hostile rationalism.

Browning was new to Mr Barrett. Six months later, Elizabeth Barrett gave a graphic account of the violent and melodramatic confrontation which had taken place a few years before, when her father had discovered that her sister Henrietta had a suitor—even though he was only a prospective one, since Henrietta 'had forbidden the subject to be referred to until that consent [of her father's] was obtained'. She 'never offended as I have offended,' Elizabeth Barrett commented;

Yet how she was made to suffer—Oh, the dreadful scenes!—and only because she had seemed to feel a little. [. . .] I hear how her knees were made to ring upon the floor, now!—she was carried out of the room in strong hysterics, & I, who rose up to follow her, though I was quite well at that time & suffered only by sympathy, fell flat down upon my face in a fainting-fit. Arabel thought I was dead.

(15 June 1846, p. 394.)

This time, Browning's reaction had very different implications, though it took a similarly oblique form. 'On the saddest part of all,' he wrote, referring to Mr Barrett's conduct, '—silence. You understand, and I can understand thro' you.' In the passage that follows, he does not, indeed, refer directly to Mr Barrett; but the association is unmistakable:

Do you know, that I never *used* to dream unless indisposed, and rarely then [. . .] and *those* nightmare dreams have invariably been of *one* sort—I stand by (powerless to interpose by a word even) and see the infliction of tyranny on the unresisting—man or beast (generally the last)—and I wake just in time not to die: let no one try this kind of experiment on me or mine!

(18 Jan. 1846, p. 339.)

Of course, there had been developments in the relationship between Browning and Elizabeth Barrett which account in part for Browning's greater freedom and intimacy of tone; but there had been developments, too, in the image which Browning had of Mr Barrett. Now, the curious thing is, that what Elizabeth Barrett has described was not exactly 'the infliction of tyranny on the *unresisting*', but on the *cowardly*. Henrietta had been bullied into submission, but Elizabeth Barrett had scant sympathy for her plight. 'In fact she had no true attachment, as I observed to Arabel at the time: a child never submitted more meekly to a revoked holiday' (15 Jan. 1846, p. 394). And her own attitude was different again: it was cowardice of a kind, but not of Henrietta's kind: it did not compromise her strength of feeling, but her capacity physically and mentally to endure such a confrontation. She made this point to Browning three months before their marriage:

I would rather be kicked with a foot [. . .] than be overcome by a loud voice speaking cruel words. I would not yield before such words—I would not give you up if they were said . . but [. . .] I could not help *dropping*, dying before them—

(12 June 1846, p. 779.)

There is a discrepancy, then, between Browning's understanding of Mr Barrett's relation to his children, and the relation which Elizabeth Barrett actually described; but this discrepancy is not entirely Browning's fault. His attitude to Mr Barrett had been conditioned by a whole series of references which made it easy for him to reduce the complexities of the situation at Wimpole Street to the terms of his private nightmare.

2 Peculiar wrongness

DON'T think too hardly of poor Papa—You have his wrong side . . his side of peculiar wrongness . . to you just now. When you have walked round him you will have other thoughts of him.

(29 Sept. 1845, p. 218.)

So Elizabeth Barrett assured Browning, in the aftermath of the 'Pisa affair'—her father's refusal to countenance her going abroad (for the sake of her health) in the winter of 1845–6 (see chapter three above). But Browning never did get to 'walk round'. To be fair to him, he never had the chance. He and Mr Barrett never met; apart from one charged hour in August 1846 (see note 1), they were never even in the same house. After his marriage his father-in-law was if anything more hostile than before. Browning's knowledge of Mr Barrett was entirely derived from other people, and mainly, of course, from Elizabeth Barrett herself.

References to Mr Barrett in the early part of the correspondence are thin on the ground, and it would be wrong to assume that he loomed at all large for either of the writers in the beginning of their friendship. Browning may have been briefed by his friend John Kenyon, who had been frequenting Wimpole Street for a number of years, on Mr Barrett's domestic peculiarities, but of course he could not be the first to mention them to Elizabeth Barrett; and she herself, until the 'Pisa affair' broke in the middle of August 1845, refers to her father in only a handful of letters. The tone of these references, however, is consistent: it gives us a picture of a relationship based unequivocally on the exercise of power. The first concerns those books locked in Mr Barrett's bedroom; the second relates an anecdote of her father giving her a test of nerves when she was a child by setting her on the chimney-piece and telling her to stand up straight until she felt the walls 'growing alive behind me & extending two stony hands to push me down' (6 June 1845, pp. 85–6); the third is the passage about the storm which we have just been considering; the fourth is the prelude to the 'Pisa affair', in which Elizabeth Barrett, having heard a rumour (!) that her father is thinking of sending her abroad for the winter, remarks that 'in every case, I suppose, *I* should not be much consulted' (16–17 July 1845, p. 127); the fifth concerns her father's occasional exasperation with her invalidism (see p. 96 above).

In the Dedication of her 1844 *Poems*, Elizabeth Barrett had addressed her father as 'you, who have shared with me in things bitter and sweet, softening or enhancing them, every day', and had spoken of her feeling for him as the tenderest and holiest affection of her life. It is hard to believe that only a few months later she would set out deliberately to give Browning an unfavourable idea of her father. What makes these scattered allusions so suggestive, therefore, is in fact their very casualness, the way they simply crop up in the course of a correspondence which Elizabeth Barrett had

not yet decided to admit as a courtship. They form part of the texture of her thoughts about her father—those thoughts which
occurred to her when writing to Browning, or to other people once
the correspondence had started. There is, for example, a marked
change of tone in references to Mr Barrett after Browning's advent
in the most intimate 'other' correspondence which Elizabeth Barrett
conducted—her correspondence with Mary Russell Mitford. Ten
years previously, when the friendship started, the fact that she was a
woman, and older than Elizabeth Barrett, meant that she could be
shared with Mr Barrett; the first reference to him speaks of Elizabeth Barrett's desire to introduce him to Miss Mitford, there are frequent expressions of 'Papa's' best wishes and regards, and Mr
Barrett read some of Miss Mitford's letters (though not the ones in
which she and Elizabeth Barrett discussed the scandalous works of
Balzac and George Sand). In conjunction with this more relaxed
atmosphere, there are passages concerning Elizabeth Barrett's feelings for her father ('dearest Papa in his abundant kindness') which
would be out of place in her letters to Browning. When Miss Mitford's father died, Elizabeth Barrett wrote:

My beloved friend, when Papa came to me last night and prayed with me
his usual prayer, it was not prayed in forgetfulness of you. I did not say to
him, 'Let us pray for her': he did it out of his own mind and quite from his
heart as you would have known if you had heard—and I kissed him twice
instead of once afterwards, because it touched me.

                                                          (*EBB to MRM*, 152.)

It is not that Elizabeth Barrett never criticizes her father to Miss
Mitford. But compare the following two passages. The first comes
from a letter of June 1843.

Think of my dear naughty Papa's never asking him [R. H. Horne] to dinner! He called on Mr. Horne by his own impulse . . and through a kind
wish, quite unprompted by me, of acknowledging kindnesses done to me—
but you see the never asking him to dinner makes the calling worse than
nugatory. I am very vexed at it! [. . .] And unfortunately we never any of
us can 'reason high' with him, as Adam did with the angel Gabriel, in relation to anything done or undone—he is master as he ought to be!

                                                          (*EBB to MRM*, 183–4.)

The tone of this is light and good-humoured—the exasperation of
someone who suffers from the eccentricity, as opposed to the
malice, of authority—and criticism is balanced by concession: 'he is

master as he ought to be!' The second passage gives a different impression. It comes from a letter of July 1845, when Browning was already a visitor at Wimpole Street, but before the 'Pisa affair', and before Elizabeth Barrett had accepted Browning as a lover rather than a close friend. Hostilities with her father had not yet commenced; but already the tone is sharper. Some of Elizabeth Barrett's brothers and sisters had spent the day on a picnic at 'White-Knights', Miss Mitford's country cottage, and had thoroughly enjoyed themselves: 'Everybody came home in a sort of "tipsy jollity",' Elizabeth Barrett reported (*EBB to MRM*, 250). The snag was that the outing had to be concealed from Mr Barrett (it is not clear why), and Elizabeth Barrett was worried that Miss Mitford would disapprove of 'an *escapade* which with your true and just notions of the filial and its duties, must have struck you [. . .] as something so blameable and wrong altogether'. Miss Mitford was lenient, however, and even spoke of Mr Barrett as being too strict with his children. To this Elizabeth Barrett responded:

Yes—there is an excess of strictness. Too much is found objectionable. And the result is that everything that *can* be done in an aside, *is* done, without too much consideration perhaps of the right and wrong [. . .] dear Papa's wishes would be consulted more tenderly, if his commands were less straight and absolute. We are all dealt with alike, you know—and *I* do not pretend to more virtue than my peers. Nevertheless I could not, I think, have let that pleasure pay for the pain . . the anxiety and fear . . of the day at White-Knights, . . as they did: and as it was, I was in a complete terror the whole hours of their absence, I do admit to you, . . and in agony, when our grand Signor's step sounded on the stair just ten minutes before Arabel appeared in my room.

(*EBB to MRM*, 252.)

'Dear Papa' is vestigial in this context; Elizabeth Barrett's true feeling comes out as a curious blend of intimacy and estrangement, the feeling of a victim for a tormentor: first in the wholly personal and emphatic phrases with which she describes her state of mind—'anxiety and fear', 'a complete terror', 'an agony'—and then in the last puncturing epithet, 'our grand Signor', in which she judges her father from the impersonal distance of satire. There is nothing comparable to this in any previous letter to Miss Mitford; the influence of her relationship with Browning is making itself unconsciously felt.

Why should Elizabeth Barrett have changed her mind about her father even before he gave her overt cause? Another passage from her 1844 *Dedication* suggests a reason. After asking her father to accept 'the inscription of these volumes, the exponents of a few years of existence which has been sustained and comforted by you as well as given' Elizabeth Barrett goes on: 'Somewhat more faint-hearted than I used to be, it is my fancy thus to seem to return to a visible personal dependence on you, as if indeed I were a child again'. The dying fall is only tenuously qualified by the reminder that such regression is fanciful and illusory: 'it is my *fancy* thus to *seem to* return . . . ' Browning's presence strengthened this saving measure of common sense: he enabled Elizabeth Barrett to see her father not as *the* man in her life, but as *a* man. In that light, dependence on Mr Barrett looked less like a comfort than a threat.

3   Papa's Flowers

On Tuesday, 4 August 1846, Browning cut short his (eighty-fourth) visit to Wimpole Street, when he and Elizabeth Barrett were alarmed by the unexpected return of members of the family. In the evening Elizabeth Barrett wrote:

Dearest, it was wise of you, perhaps, to go today [. . .] My aunt, who had just had time to hear of your being in the house, found my door open, & you were noticed by a passing jest . . too passing to meet ears in authority—

(4 Aug. 1846, p. 930.)

A little over a year earlier, Elizabeth Barrett had referred to her father as 'our grand Signor'; but 'ears in authority' is an advance even on that phrase, where a trace of humour lingered. It is unequivocally hostile and distant on Elizabeth Barrett's part, because of the grotesque metonymy. Those 'ears in authority' flicker momentarily into surreal visual life. Not that Elizabeth Barrett had a monopoly on such denaturing imagery. Only the day before, Browning had raised the possibility of Mr Barrett's 'suspicious sudden return', followed by 'a scene in your presence' and himself being barred from Wimpole Street. Not, of course, that he was frightened of Mr Barrett:

Do, *re*consider, Ba,—had I better stay away to-morrow? You cannot mis-understand me,—I ONLY think of you—any man's anger to me is Flush's

barking, without the respectability of motive,—but, once the door is shut
on me, if he took to biting *you*!

(3 Aug. 1846, p. 928.)

'Once the door is shut on me' means, in terms of the metaphor's
vehicle, 'once I have left the room', but in terms of its tenor, 'once I
am shut out from Wimpole Street (by Mr Barrett's orders)'; so the
last 'he' neatly merges the identities of Flush and Mr Barrett—
except that the latter is 'without the respectability of motive'.
Flush's motive for biting Browning (as he had done the previous
month) was, Browning magnanimously conceded, 'his jealous
supervision' of Elizabeth Barrett and 'his slowness to know
another, having once known you' (10 July 1846, p. 867); but what
was 'respectable' in the dog was not so in the parent.

Later in the month, after a particularly trying visit to Wimpole
Street which had been interrupted by Mr Kenyon and in which
Elizabeth Barrett had spoken of the 'horrible position' she was in
('To hear the voice of my father & meet his eye makes me shrink
back'—30 Aug. 1846, p. 1021), Browning reached perhaps the
height of his fury at Mr Barrett's real or assumed power over his
daughter. Elizabeth Barrett figures first as a black slave (Browning
was, of course, aware of the Barrett family's interest in sugar-plantations in the West Indies) and then as Prometheus—a juxtaposition
of contemporary and mythological, archetypal and actual examples
of 'the infliction of tyranny on the unresisting' which sums up
Browning's state of mind and the apocalyptic terms in which he had
come to see the issue: 'It is delectable work, this having to do with
relatives and "freemen who have a right to beat their own negroes,"
and father Zeus with his paternal epistles, and peggings to the rock'
(30 Aug. 1846, pp. 1024–5).

These images demonstrate the lengths to which Browning and
Elizabeth Barrett went in their joint characterization of Mr Barrett
as an emblem of authority—abstract or animal as the case may be.
The reason why they did so seems plain enough. Elizabeth Barrett
needed to displace the father she had loved and revered, who had
preoccupied her (in emotional terms) for so many years, in order to
make room for Browning. She was quite clear about the process; in
a late letter, she wrote of Mr Barrett:

he might have been king & father over me *to* the end, if he had thought it
worth while to love me openly enough—yet, even *so*, he should not have let

you come too near. And you could not (so) have come too near—for he
would have had my confidence from the beginning, & no opportunity
would have been permitted to you of proving your affection for me, and I
should have thought always what I thought at first.

(16 July 1846, p. 882.)

Browning, of course, had to take this 'opportunity', part of which
consisted in collaborating with Elizabeth Barrett in her psychological separation from her father. Moreover, towards the end of the
courtship, the maintenance of Mr Barrett in his role of unrespect-
able watchdog or 'father Zeus' became vital to Browning's chances
of persuading Elizabeth Barrett to take the actual step of elopement.
Any sign of Mr Barrett weakening, and Elizabeth Barrett's own
resolve might crumble. Elizabeth Barrett herself realized this: she
could 'almost thank God', she wrote, 'that Papa keeps so far from
me . . that he has given up coming in the evening [. . .] If he were
affectionate, & made me, or *let* me, feel myself necessary to him, . .
how should I bear (even with my reason on my side) to prepare to
give him pain—?' (3 Apr. 1845, p. 581.) 'Ah, well!' she sighed at
the end of the paragraph. 'In any case, I should have ended probably, in giving up all for you'. Browning must have trembled when
he read such qualified assurances.

Displacement of Mr Barrett took the most trivial forms. In a letter of 21 May 1846 (p. 718), Browning wrote that he had just read
Dickens's *Pictures from Italy*: he gave his opinion of the book ('He
seems to have expended his power on the least interesting places,—
and then gone on hurriedly, seeing or describing less and less, till at
last the mere names of places do duty for pictures of them'), and
offered to lend it to Elizabeth Barrett 'when everybody here has
done with it'. She replied the same day: 'Dearest, when your letter
came I was cutting open the leaves of Dickens' "Letters from Italy"
which Papa had brought in—so I am glad to have your thoughts of
the book to begin with' (p. 719). The mistake ('Letters' instead of
'Pictures') indicates the direction of Elizabeth Barrett's thought;
Browning's letter affects both her opinion of Dickens and of her
father's gift, it reminds her of his intellectual and emotional priority.
She is *glad* to be so reminded.

A more poignant example comes from a letter of Elizabeth
Barrett's earlier in the month:

Papa brought me some flowers yesterday when he came home . . & they went a little to my heart as I took them. I put them into glasses near yours, & they look faded this morning nevertheless, while your roses [. . .] are luxuriant in beauty as if they had just finished steeping themselves in garden-dew.

(15 May 1846, p. 702.)

Poor Mr Barrett! Bought flowers from a stall in the City are unlikely to have been as fresh to begin with as the ones Browning had brought from his garden in New Cross that same day. But what matters is not the 'unfairness' of the competition, which is in any case absurd, but the fact that Elizabeth Barrett consciously set it up and reflected on it as a serious event. She went on:

I look gravely from one set of flowers to the other—I cannot draw a glad omen—I wish he had not given me these. Dearest, there seems little kindness in teazing you with such thoughts . . but they come & I write them: and let them come ever so sadly, I do not for a moment doubt . . hesitate. One may falter, where one does not fail. And for the rest, . . it is my fault, and not my sorrow rather, that we act so? It is by choice that we act so? If he had let me I should have loved him out of a heart altogether open to him—It is not my fault that he would not let me. Now it is too late—I am not his nor my own, any more—

She is over-anxious, over-insistent. 'Falter' is too close for comfort to 'fault'. The syntax itself 'falters': statements ('it is my fault', 'It is by choice') turn out to be questions—albeit rhetorical ones. All this illustrates the danger to Browning of Mr Barrett stepping out of his alloted role of paternal ogre.

This danger soon afterwards became a direct subject of discussion between Browning and Elizabeth Barrett, in the aftermath of an odd 'misreading' on Browning's part. On Tuesday, 14 July 1846, he saw Elizabeth Barrett (their seventy-eighth meeting); on the following morning Elizabeth Barrett wrote:

At dinner my aunt [Mrs Hedley] said to Papa . . 'I have not seen Ba all day—and when I went to her room, to my astonishment a gentleman was sitting there.' 'Who was *that*?' said Papa's eyes to Arabel—'Mr. Browning called here today,' she answered—'And Ba bowed her head,' continued my aunt, 'as if she meant to signify to me that I was not to come in'— 'Oh,' cried Henrietta, '*that* must have been a mistake of yours. Perhaps she meant just the contrary.' 'You should have gone in,' Papa said, 'and seen the *poet*.'

(15 July 1846, p. 875.)

You have to remember that Elizabeth Barrett is not present at this
scene, since she never dined with the family. It is her sisters, Arabel
and Henrietta, both of them in the know by this time, who, like
diplomats at the 'grand Signor's' downstairs court, represent her
interests and report back. Mrs Hedley stumbles unaware into a
domestic minefield. Mr Barrett is on the alert—' "Who was *that*?"
said Papa's eyes to Arabel'—Elizabeth Barrett creates this eloquent
and threatening moment with a writer's economy. Arabel is matter-
of-fact, but Mrs Hedley plunges on, and Henrietta has to move
quickly to smother a potentially embarrassing implication (that
Elizabeth Barrett had some reason for wanting to see Browning
alone and was excluding her aunt from the secret). 'Perhaps she
meant just the contrary,' she brightly and disingenuously suggests.
Fortunately the tyrant is in a jovial mood tonight. ' " You should
have gone in," Papa said, "and seen the *poet*." ' Later on in the day
Mr Barrett has occasion to refer to Browning again, and he does so
with the same note of genial scorn. Mrs Hedley has brought her
future son-in-law to meet Elizabeth Barrett:

My aunt [. . .] said when she introduced him: 'You are to understand this
to be a great honour—for she never lets anybody come here except Mr.
Kenyon, . . & a few other gentlemen' . . . (laughing). Said Papa—'only
ONE other gentleman, indeed. Only Mr. Browning, the poet—the man of
the pomegranates.'

(ibid., p. 876.)

Browning's response is at first sight distinctly odd: it looks as
though he has misread Mr Barrett's tone:

I think your Father's words on these two occasions, very kind,—very!
They confuse,—perhaps humble me [. . .] I dare say he is infinitely kind at
bottom—

(16 June 1846, p. 880.)

But the concession is soon withdrawn; already the phrase 'at bottom' signals a distinction between what Browning allows Mr Barrett potentially to be, and what Mr Barrett actually is. It is the hard
reality with which they have to deal, and so Browning goes on (with
a glancing reference to his own poem about false chivalry, 'The
Glove') to translate the possibility of making his peace with Mr Barrett into the terms of a picaresque fantasy which is in no danger of
coming true:

If he could know me, I think he would soon reconcile himself to all of it
[. . .] but that is impossible—and with the sincere will to please him by
any exertion or sacrifice in my power, I shall very likely never have the
opportunity of picking up a glove he might drop. In old novels, the implac-
able father is not seldom set upon by a round dozen of ruffians with
blacked faces, from behind a hedge,—and just as the odds prove too many,
suddenly a stranger (to all save the reader) leaps over an adjacent ditch, &c
'Sir, under Providence, I owe you my life!' &c &c [. . .] Absurdity! Yet I
would fain . . fain!—you understand.

(ibid., pp. 880–1.)

Browning knows that no 'exertion or sacrifice' will be required of
him: none would be of any use, as Elizabeth Barrett had told him.
Life, after all, the passage suggests, is not a novel, and the 'implac-
able father' in Wimpole Street will remain really (and safely) implac-
able. But Elizabeth Barrett winced again at the thought of her father
being 'kind':

Dearest, if *you* feel *that*, must I not feel it more deeply? Twice or three
times lately he has said to me 'my love' and even 'my puss,' his old words
before he was angry last year, . . and I quite quailed before them as if they
were so many knife-strokes. Anything but his *kindness*, I can bear now.

(16 July 1846, p. 881.)

Browning might well echo that last cry. And in fact they did not
have to cope with too much more of Mr Barrett's kindness. When,
at the end of the summer, Mr Barrett decided to move the household to the coast and have Wimpole Street cleaned and redecorated,
Elizabeth Barrett felt able to remark:

Of course I decline to give any opinion & express any preference,—as to
places, I mean. It is not for my sake that we go:—if *I* had been considered at
all, indeed, we should have been taken away earlier, . . & not certainly now,
when the cold season is at hand—And so much the better it is for me, that I
have not, obviously, been thought of.

(9 Sept. 1846, p. 1058.)

So much the better for Browning, too. 'This conduct of your
Father's is quite characteristic,' he replied (10 Sept. 1846, p. 1060).
Two days later he and Elizabeth Barrett were married.

11

Elizabeth Barrett's Return

1

'A Drama of Exile', the major poem of Elizabeth Barrett's two-volume collection of 1844, ends with the departure of Adam and Eve from Eden, while a chorus of angels comforts them with the slogan *'Exiled is not lost'*. They have lost the earthly paradise, but (*felix culpa*) they have gained something better: the prospect of salvation supersedes the experience of contentment. There is, in fact, more status, more dignity in the human predicament after the Fall: 'curing . . . exalts the wounded'. Transcendence is the crucial process here, transcendence of the human by the divine, of the material by the spiritual. You cannot come to terms with time, you cannot accommodate the facts of decay and death: the only solution is a vertical movement, of mortality into immortality, of time into eternity.

Transcendentalist philosophy assumes two levels of existence, one 'superior' to the other: the spiritual level is primary and immutable, the material level is secondary and contingent. But neither of these levels is itself the proper focus of attention. It is the relation between them that counts. Material life is both subject to spiritual life, and is its subject: that which it transforms or transcends. Material is of little value in itself, but it is of essential value to the process of which it forms part. Transcendentalism devalues the material conditions of human life in comparison with 'pure' spirituality; but it then revalues these same material conditions as the vehicle of human spiritual achievement. The chorus of angels exhorts Adam and Eve:

> Live, work on, O Earthy!
>   By the Actual's tension,
> Speed the arrow worthy
>   Of a pure ascencion!
> From the low earth round you,
>   Reach the heights above you . . .

Elizabeth Barrett is not, therefore, advocating a naïve dualism, but a system in which human life is given its orientation, its purpose and direction, by the process of transformation and transcendence. Human beings must acknowledge the corruption and inadequacy of their physical existence; but they can take comfort from that very acknowledgement, since it is the condition of their eventual salvation. The chorus of angels again:

> Exiled human creatures,
>   Let your hope grow larger!
> Larger grows the vision
>   Of the new delight.
> From this chain of Nature's
>   God is the Discharger,
> And the Actual's prison
>   Opens to your sight.

As they go into exile, Adam and Eve enter 'the Actual's prison', the experience of mortality; at the same time, they are given the prospect of release from this bondage. The prison 'opens' both to let them in, now, and to let them out, in the visionary future; and it also 'opens up' to their 'sight' (their understanding). The plain word 'sight' turns out to be metaphorical; the syntax itself displays the openness, the capacity for transformation, which Elizabeth Barrett takes to be the hope of human life.

  Such fine local effects are rare in 'A Drama of Exile', which is mostly strained and derivative. There are much better poems in the collection, particularly some of the sonnets. But the idea is strong and consistent whether the verse is good or bad. 'A Drama of Exile' strikes the keynote of the two volumes, and poem after poem repeats it. And besides its length and ambition, Elizabeth Barrett had good reason for giving 'A Drama of Exile' pride of place in a collection of poems which, she says in the Preface, she was offering to the public as 'the completest expression of [my] being to which I could attain'. Of the work itself she remarks: 'The subject of the

Drama rather fastened on me than was chosen'; for she herself was
an exile, she herself was in prison. The paradise from which she had
been expelled was her own past, the past of her childhood at Hope
End and her passionate attachment to her eldest brother, Edward
('Bro').[1] The prison was her invalidism. In writing, her prison
'opened' to her and became her material, the ground on which she
effected the psychological transformations of faith and hope.

And yet, precisely because Elizabeth Barrett had this urgent personal motive for her transcendentalist ideas, she also had a sense of
their limitations and ambiguities. One of the most explicitly autobiographical poems in the collection, a sonnet called 'The Prisoner',
is a good example:

> I count the dismal time by months and years
> Since last I felt the green sward under foot,
> And the great breath of all things summer-mute
> Met mine upon my lips. Now earth appears
> As strange to me as dreams of distant spheres
> Or thoughts of Heaven we weep at. Nature's lute
> Sounds on, behind this door so closely shut,
> A strange wild music to the prisoner's ears,
> Dilated by the distance, till the brain
> Grows dim with fancies which it feels too fine:
> While ever, with a visionary pain,
> Past the precluded senses, sweep and shine
> Streams, forests, glades, and many a golden train
> Of sunlit hills transfigured to Divine.

The movement here is characteristic, from the 'dismal time' of the
opening to the visionary landscape of the last lines. This landscape is
not supernatural, but 'transfigured to Divine'; as always, it is the
process that matters. The prison turns inside out: deprivation (the
'precluded senses') becomes the condition of revelation. But the

---

[1] See Part One, pp. 21–4, 30–3. Alethea Hayter (*Mrs Browning*, p. 27) points out
that 'the idea of the vanity of human hopes of happiness, which can only be enjoyed
in the life to come' is strongly present in Elizabeth Barrett's 1838 volume, *The Seraphim and other Poems*, and therefore 'antedates the two great sorrows of [her] life,
her brother Edward's death and her prolonged and apparently incurable illness'. Not
that Elizabeth Barrett's life before 1838 had been devoid of sorrows—the death of
her mother and the loss of her childhood home are both alluded to in 'The Deserted
Garden'—but it is true that the melancholy of the 1838 poems seems more reli-
giously than personally inspired. Elizabeth Barrett's Congregational theology gave
her sufficient intellectual grounds for her attitude; it was powerfully strengthened by
her personal experiences.

poet is not sure that this transformation is altogether desirable. It is certainly not natural. 'The brain / Grows dim with fancies which it feels too fine': the imagination feels that its own 'fancies' are 'too fine' for it; or it feels them 'too finely', too exquisitely to accord with the reality on which they should be based. Either way, there is an unease, a strain in the idea and expression, which marks some of the most thoughtful of the 1844 *Poems*. The key concept of these poems is loss, but Elizabeth Barrett is divided in her creative approach to it. Is her own suffering representative or peculiar to her? The doctrine of the Fall states that the primary and archetypal loss of Eden determines the nature of all human experience. Elizabeth Barrett's own life amply confirms this. But look at it the other way round: suppose Elizabeth Barrett endorses the doctrine of the Fall *because* it gives her life meaning and herself the means to cope with it?

This division comes out clearly in the course of the sonnet called 'Insufficiency':

> When I attain to utter forth in verse
> Some inward thought, my soul throbs audibly
> Along my pulses, yearning to be free
> And something farther, fuller, higher, rehearse,
> To the individual, true, and the universe,
> In consummation of right harmony:
> But, like a wind-exposed distorted tree,
> We are blown against for ever by the curse
> Which breathes through Nature. Oh, the world is weak!
> The effluence of each is false to all,
> And what we best conceive we fail to speak.
> Wait, soul, until thine ashen garments fall,
> And then resume thy broken strains, and seek
> Fit peroration without let or thrall.

The sonnet has three movements, of six, five, and three lines.[2] The first movement takes us to the height of the poet's ambition, the

---

[2] As often in Elizabeth Barrett's sonnets, the form of the sonnet is nominally Petrarchan, but the rhetorical structure overrides the conventional division between the octet and the sestet ('The Prisoner', quoted above, is another example). Here, the opening clause echoes Shakespeare ('When I do count the clock that tells the time', 'When I consider everything that grows', 'When to the sessions of sweet silent thought' etc.), and later poets who adopted this gambit in famous single poems, such as Milton ('When I consider how my light is spent') or Keats ('When I have fears that I may cease to be').

'consummation of right harmony'; the second counters this movement, and takes us down to flat despondency: 'what we best conceive we fail to speak'; the third rebounds from this check, and
looks forward to a transcendent future achievement. The idea is
again characteristic of Elizabeth Barrett's work at this period: the
realization of the world's fallen nature destroys the possibility of
earthly fulfilment, but opens the prospect for fulfilment in heaven;
and this realization is, itself, the material out of which the poem is
made.

But there is something odd about the poem's rhetorical method.
The first six lines, the ones which describe the poet's ambition to
'utter forth in verse / Some inward thought', are personal: 'When *I*
attain . . . *my* soul . . . *my* pulses'. 'But,' the second movement goes
on, 'like a wind-exposed distorted tree, / *We* are blown against for
ever . . . ' Suddenly the scope has widened: the breath of life is a
curse to everyone, not just the particular poet whose inspiration
fails her: 'And what *we* best conceive *we* fail to speak.' The third
movement has yet another grammatical shift: now the poet apostro-
phizes a 'soul'—but whose? If the exhortation followed from the
first six lines, the soul being exhorted would be the poet's own; but
the intervening lines allow—perhaps encourage—a wider, more
general application. The point cannot be settled—that is what makes
the poem interesting for our purpose. Elizabeth Barrett is torn
between interpreting loss, or grief, or frustration, as universal,
which would make her experience of them exemplary in human
terms, or as personal afflictions with which she must come to terms,
but which do not weigh on everyone alike.

There is, then, a personal context for Elizabeth Barrett's intellectual preoccupation, in the 1844 *Poems*, with loss and transcendence; but this combination of personal and intellectual interests
has a context of its own, that of Elizabeth Barrett's peculiar social
position. She might complain of R. H. Horne's account of her in the
New Spirit of the Age as a mystic recluse, but she herself, in her
published writings as well as in her letters, strengthened the image
of herself as incurable and inconsolable. Far from insisting, as
Browning did in the 'Advertisement' to *Dramatic Lyrics* (1842),
that her poems represented 'so many utterances of so many imaginary persons', she went out of her way to draw attention to their personal bearing. The Preface to the 1844 *Poems* speaks of them as
'variously coloured, or perhaps shadowed, by the life of which they

are the natural expression'; the Dedication to her father heaves a similarly public sigh:

When your eyes fall upon this page of dedication, and you start to see to whom it is inscribed, your first thought will be of the time far off when I was a child and wrote verses [. . .] Of all that such a recollection implies of saddest and sweetest to both of us, it would become neither of us to speak before the world; nor would it be possible for us to speak of it to one another, with voices that did not falter. Enough, that what is in my heart when I write thus, will be fully known to yours.

Such histrionic reticence was unlikely to stifle public interest in Elizabeth Barrett's 'saddest and sweetest' past. Part of her status as a writer arose, inevitably, from the mystery of her suffering and her isolation; she cultivated this mystery, not just in these prefatory passages, but in the poems themselves:

> My wine has run
> Indeed out of my cup, and there is none
> To gather up the bread of my repast
> Scattered and trampled . . .
> ('Past and Future'.)

This is plangent, but hardly specific; and the nearest we get to a real clue is in passages which refer to 'beloved voices' which 'brake off in the middle of that song / We sang together'. About her physical disability Elizabeth Barrett is no more explicit, though silence on this subject is enjoined on her by decorum as well as tactics.

Self-pity was not so much Elizabeth Barrett's vice as her resource. Her display of suffering and endurance brought her to public notice, and simultaneously shielded her from importunity; she might (and did) complain of being pestered and besieged by admirers, but the fact was that she saw whom she chose, and she chose virtually nobody. She was thirty-nine years old, no longer pretty, and neurotically unsure of her own personal worth; seclusion allowed her to displace her talent, her ambition, and her strength of intellect entirely into her work, so that she need never face the artist's perennial anxiety about living up to her own image. Her father, too, might breathe freely; his daughter's fame did not entail the risk of her leaving home, since she was partly famous for staying put. She was able to articulate her real sense of grief and frustration without alienating his affection or that of other members of the family. Solitude and invalidism gave her a professional standing which was denied to other women writers (such as Harriet Martineau or Anna Jameson) who had to compete directly with the male literary establishment. Her plight was her opportunity, and it is doing her no injustice to say that she made the most of it. Then came Robert Browning.

Browning posed a dilemma for Elizabeth Barrett. She was strongly attracted to him and wanted to see him; but seeing him would jeopardize her public persona, as he would have encountered it in Horne's *New Spirit of the Age* and in the 1844 *Poems*. Her early response was self-contradictory: she managed to give Browning the impression both that she was a victim of 'pangs of heart & bodily weakness', and that she was '*essentially better*'. Some of her statements could have come straight out of her 1844 volumes: 'between me & that time,' she said of her childhood, 'the cypresses grow thick & dark' (27 Feb. 1845, p. 31). But not everything she said about herself was marked by imprecision and deliberate mystery. In the same letter where she described herself in the familiar melodramatic way as 'a recluse, with nerves that have been all broken on the rack', she wrote:

I have lived only inwardly,—or with *sorrow*, for a strong emotion. Before this seclusion of my illness, I was secluded still [. . .] My sympathies drooped towards the ground like an untrained honeysuckle—& but for *one* . . in my own house . . but of this I cannot speak.

(20 Mar. 1845, p. 41.)

But of course she *has* spoken—the gesture of reticence is just as expressive here as it was in the 1844 Dedication ('Of all that such a recollection implies . . . it would become neither of us to speak before the world' etc). But *what* it expresses is fundamentally different. This is no vague suggestion of private griefs, but concrete information. Elizabeth Barrett lets Browning know that she has lost someone dear to her, and that this someone was not a lover, but a sibling. With hindsight, you could say that Elizabeth Barrett took the first real step towards her elopement when she gave Browning this clue, this signal; nor is it surprising that this same letter should also contain the first real indication that she could conceive of a different life, when she laments the 'disadvantages' to her poetry 'if I live on & yet do not escape from this seclusion'. The word 'escape' is unequivocally positive here; it sows the seed of a future resolution.

In due course, Elizabeth Barrett told Browning the full story of her brother Edward's death, and of her own mental breakdown (20 Aug. 1845, pp. 167–71); and some time between late May and mid-September 1845, Browning also learned that Elizabeth Barrett's illness was not, as he had at first believed, 'a spinal injury irremediable in the nature of it' (18 Sept. 1845, p. 206), but a lung complaint aggravated by nervous debility. For Browning, there was no longer any terrible or even seductive mystery about Elizabeth Barrett's condition; there was, much more satisfactorily, a *problem*—how to effect the 'escape' which, it was clear, she needed and desired. But for Elizabeth Barrett herself, things were not that simple. Acknowledging that she loved Browning and wanted to marry him and leave home meant more than a clarification or a change of mind. It meant a comprehensive revision of the intellectual and emotional system which she had developed over the past decade, which she had articulated in her writing, and which had governed her relationships with men and women. She managed it: as early as November 1845, she was clear in her own mind about the nature of the process involved. She gave a succinct account of her old way of thinking:

When grief came upon grief [. . .] I always felt that there must be cause enough . . corruption enough, needing purification . . weakness enough, needing strengthening . . *nothing* of the chastisement could come to me without cause and need.

(17 Nov. 1845, p. 275.)

And then she offered an alternative interpretation—equally providential, but with Providence acting a different part:

Could it be that heart & life were devastated to make room for you?—If so, it was well done,—dearest!—They leave the ground fallow before the wheat.

(ibid., p. 276.)

That last image, with its anticipation of earthly fertility and fulfilment, measures the distance from her old self which Elizabeth Barrett had set herself to cross, until, in the end, three weeks before her marriage, she was able to write to Browning:

Oh, to look back! It is so wonderful to me to look back on my life & my old philosophy of life, made of the necessities of sorrow & the resolution to attain to something better than a perpetual moaning & complaint,—to that

state of neutralized emotion to which I did attain—that serenity which
meant the failure of hope!

(21 Aug. 1846, p. 981.)

Here Elizabeth Barrett looks at her past self from a comparative,
and therefore liberating perspective; she sees that her 'old philosophy of life' is not absolute, but contingent; that it does not suit her
new circumstances; that the past itself might be subject to a revised
interpretation. If we look at the self-portrait of herself in Wimpole
Street which she gave to one of her regular correspondents, Mr
Westwood, in October 1843, and compare it with what she wrote
to her close friend Mrs Martin three years later and two months
after her marriage, from the security of Pisa, we can see the full
extent of the revision. To Mr Westwood she gave an account of
pious melancholy, of seclusion without discontent, of a kind of
lively resignation to her lot:

I live in London, to be sure, and except for the glory of it I might live in a
desert, so profound is my solitude and so complete my isolation from
things and persons without. I lie all day, and day after day, on the sofa, and
my windows do not even look into the street. To abuse myself with a vain
deceit of rural life I have had ivy planted in a box, and it has flourished and
spread over one window [. . .] it is my triumph when the leaves strike the
window pane, and this is not a sound like a lament. Books and thoughts and
dreams [. . .] and domestic tenderness can and ought to leave nobody
lamenting. Also God's wisdom, deeply steeped in His love, *is* as far as we
can stretch out our hands.

(*Letters of EBB*, vol. i. p. 158.)

The account of her condition which she gives to Mrs Martin is radi-
cally different—in fact, incompatible. Particularly revealing (besides
the death imagery, more of which I shall be considering further on)
is the sharp comment she makes at the outset on the debilitating
effects of that very 'domestic tenderness' which she spoke of as one
of her chief comforts in the earlier letter:

the personal feeling is nearer with most of us than the tenderest feeling for
another; and my family had been so accustomed to the idea of my living on
and on in that room, that while my heart was eating itself, their love for me
was consoled, and at last the evil grew scarcely perceptible. It was no want
of love in them, and quite natural in itself: we all get used to the thought of
a tomb; and I was buried, that was the whole. [. . .] for years together,
after what broke my heart at Torquay, I lived on the outside of my own life,
blindly and darkly from day to day, as completely dead to hope of any kind

as if I had my face against a grave [. . .] A thoroughly morbid and desolate state it was, which I look back now to with the sort of horror with which one would look to one's graveclothes, if one had been clothed in them by mistake during a trance.

> (?20 Oct. 1846, *Letters of EBB*, vol. i. p. 288.)

However 'natural in itself' may seem to us the revulsion of feeling which Elizabeth Barrett expresses here, she did not arrive at this position, or maintain herself there, without struggle and pain. The 'trance' in which she lay was of her own devising; she had not 'been clothed' in her shroud 'by mistake', but had wrapped it deliberately round her. It was against the odds that she got out at all.

2

Elizabeth Barrett's 1844 *Poems* are, on the whole, a gloomy lot. 'Irreparableness' is the title of one sonnet, which ends:

> My heart is very tired, my strength is low,
> My hands are full of blossoms plucked before,
> Held dead within them till myself shall die.

The collection admittedly included a pair of sonnets with the titles 'Patience Taught by Nature' and 'Cheerfulness Taught by Reason'; but the comfort they offered was somewhat grim. Exhorting her own 'pusillanimous Heart' to behave like a 'cheerful traveller', the speaker of 'Cheerfulness Taught by Reason' asks:

> What if the bread
> Be bitter in thine inn, and thou unshod
> To meet the flints? At least it may be said
> 'Because the way is *short*, I thank thee, God.'

Thank you for tormenting me briefly, when you might have done it at length! No wonder that when Elizabeth Barrett began to sense, however dimly, what Browning might mean to her, she felt she had some ground to make up. She wrote to him in her sixth letter:

you are not to think,—whatever I may have written or implied,—that I lean either to the philosophy or affectation which beholds the world through darkness instead of light, & speaks of it wailingly. Now, may God forbid that it shd be so with me.

> (5 Mar. 1845, p. 34.)

Why is Browning not to think this? He had plenty of evidence in Elizabeth Barrett's writing, as she herself conceded. The answer is, because Elizabeth Barrett tells him so. Her disavowal is *willed*: and it is enjoined as much on herself as on Browning. She, too, needed convincing. In fact she probably needed it more than he. Simply reversing the polarities of 'darkness' and 'light' was not, however, sufficient to create such conviction. Elizabeth Barrett did something subtler and more effective, and more in accord with her vocation; she made up a story.

In a sense, this is what she had always been doing: her state of mind in the period of the 1844 *Poems* sprang from her selective reading of the past (paradisal childhood, loss, despair, precarious recovery); and this interpretation was designed also to 'read' the future, to define and determine the way that lay ahead of her. Or you could put it the other way round, and say that in 1844 Elizabeth Barrett had little to look forward to in her physical and emotional life: she therefore wrote the history (or historical myth) of herself which would not just explain how this bleak prospect had come about, but would explain it away. Like Milton in the aftermath of the failure of the Revolution and the collapse of the Commonwealth, she needed to 'assert eternal Providence / And justify the ways of God to men', in order to justify the ways of God to herself.[3]

Elizabeth Barrett's new story incorporated many elements of the old. There was still the golden age of childhood, the loss of Hope End and her father's financial calamities, her illness, the death of 'Bro' and the 'course of bitter mental discipline & long bodily seclusion' which followed (5 Mar. 1845, p. 35). What changed was not the history, but the myth.

It is tempting to view this change as the straightforward abandonment of a religious for a secular model. Instead of seeing her past as an example of human suffering and deprivation on earth, for which she will be compensated by a transcendent fulfilment after death, Elizabeth Barrett comes to see it as a series of personal disasters for

---

[3] Milton, of course, presides over 'A Drama of Exile'; and Elizabeth Barrett also turned in this period to Aeschylus, with her re-translation of *Prometheus Bound*, which offered her a confirmatory myth of the nobility and ultimate value of suffering. But this second translation did not appear until 1850, despite the fact that it was virtually finished in early 1845; possibly Elizabeth Barrett did not want to publish any more eloquence of suffering while she was remaking her own myth.

which she is to be compensated now. Not pie in the sky, but a slice of life; not salvation, but marriage; not God, but Browning.

But Elizabeth Barrett's progress was both more difficult than that, and more consistent with her creative identity. She did not exchange despair for bliss like a set of clothes. In June 1845, for example, she wrote to Miss Mitford:

Here is the summer, and for the last fortnight or longer [. . .] I have been growing and growing just like the trees—it is miraculous, the feeling of sprouting life in me and out of me—

(*EBB to MRM*, 248.)

Nearly a month later—the weather not having deteriorated in the mean time—she wrote to Browning: 'Sometimes—it is the real truth, . . I have haste to be done with it all' (16–17 July 1845, p. 126). She was subject to this feeling almost throughout the court-ship; in some of the most troubled passages of the letters, she speaks to Browning, with remarkable candour, of her reluctance to give up the religion of death, the effort she had to make to face the prospect of a real recovery and a real relationship. Her own identity was piti-ful to her at best, hateful at worst; and she contrasted it insistently with his:

it is hard for you to understand what my mental position is after the pecu-liar experience I have suffered, & what τί ἐμοὶ καὶ σοί a sort of feeling is irrepressible from me to you, when, from the height of your brilliant happy sphere, you ask, as you did ask, for personal intercourse with me.

(21 May 1845, p. 71.)

The Greek is from Mark 5: 7, 'What have I to do with thee?'—the cry to Jesus of the man 'who had his dwelling among the tombs', or rather the cry of the devil that possesses him. That was how Eliza-beth Barrett saw herself, dwelling among tombs (the implication that Browning is a Christ-like saviour I will consider later); in another letter, she wrote:

I shudder to look back to the days when you were not for me. Was ever life so like death before? My face was so close against the tombstones, that there seemed no room even for the tears.

(3 June 1846, p. 755.)

Her best prospect was to be rid of herself. She liked, for example,

those long, long books, one can live away into . . leaving the world & above all oneself, quite at the end of the avenue of palms—quite out of sight & out

of hearing!—Oh, I have felt something like *that* so often—so often!—and
you never felt it, & never will, I hope.

(16 Aug. 1845, p. 160.)

She spoke in the same terms of her own writing, as a cherished
means of 'escape from pangs of heart & bodily weakness . . when
you throw off *yourself* . . what you feel to be *yourself*, . . into
another atmosphere & into other relations, where your life may
spread its wings out new, & gather on every separate plume a
brightness from the sun of the sun!' (3 Feb. 1845, p. 15). But this
longing did not always take the form of imaginative escape, whether
into reading or writing; it occasionally envisaged the ultimate escape
of death:

ah, you do not see my innermost nature, . . *you*!—you are happily too
high, & cannot see into it . . cannot perceive how the once elastic spring is
broken with the long weights! [. . .] Do not judge me severely, you [. . .]
who are more to me than I can be to you, even by your own statement . .
better to me than life . . or than death even, as death seemed to me before I
knew you.

(5 May 1846, p. 679.)

At times, she looks back almost with regret to the period when
death, and not life, seemed the desirable option: 'I had done *living*, I
thought, when you came & sought me out! and why? & to what
end?' (17 Sept. 1845, p. 204.) To that last question Elizabeth Barrett eventually found a satisfactory answer: 'I have come back for
you alone . . at your voice . . & because you have use for me!' (29
July 1845, p. 915.) But the strain of having to give up her settled
non-identity continued to tell on her:

You stand in between me & not merely the living who stood closest, but
between me & the closer graves, . . & I reproach myself for this sometimes
[. . .]

(12 Dec. 1845, p. 318.)

She felt that, before Browning came, her 'warmest affections [were]
on the other side of the grave' (21 Dec. 1845, p. 339), and the fact
that the grave is traditionally the place where both passion and
blood freeze gives this phrase a morbid edge. It was something more
powerful, even, than being 'tired of living . . unaffectedly tired' (13
Jan. 1846, p. 385)—a weariness, a backward-looking, against which
both she and Browning had to struggle. She found it difficult to
convey to him what it meant to her to 'come back to live a little for

you' (29 July 1846, p. 915). In the spring and summer of 1846, he exhorted her to get out of her room and take exercise, as he had done the year before; and after one such outing she wrote:

what a summer-sense in the air—& how lovely the strips of sky between the houses!—And yet I may tell you truly, that, constantly, through these vivid impressions, I am thinking & feeling that mournful and bitter would be to me this return into life, apart from you, apart from the consideration of you. How could ever I have borne it, I keep feeling constantly. But you are *there*, in the place of memory.

(24 May 1846, pp. 727–8.)

The 'place of memory' was the place of guilt and negation—negation of self even more than of others. On Browning's birthday in 1846, she wrote:

A year ago, I thought, with a sort of mournful exultation, that I was *pure of wishes*. Now, they recoil back on me in a spring-tide . . flow back, wave upon wave, . . till I should lose breath to speak them!

(7 May 1846, pp. 686–7.)

And on the eve of another anniversary in the same month, the anniversary of their first meeting, she wrote in similar terms:

Heavens!—how I had different thoughts of you & of myself & of the world & of life, last year at this hour! The spirits who look backward over the grave, cannot feel much otherwise from my feeling as I look back.

(19 May 1846, p. 713.)

Notice that in both these passages Elizabeth Barrett uses death imagery to describe her new found hope: in the first passage the 'spring-tide' of her wishes, 'wave upon wave', threatens to drown her voice (the image of drowning has a special force for her, because of her brother's death); in the second, she compares her escape from the desire for death to death itself. Dying into life is the traditional image of Christian salvation—one which Elizabeth Barrett had persistently used in her writing up to this time—[4] but the difference here is that the whole process takes place within the terms of earthly life. Spiritual salvation as a metaphor for earthly fulfilment! Transcendentalism turns inward on itself, and its energy of metaphor

---

[4] For example, Christ's promise to Adam and Eve towards the end of 'A Drama of Exile': 'As I shall be uplifted on a cross / In darkness of eclipse and anguish dread, / So shall I lift up in my pierced hands, / Not into dark, but light—not unto death, / But life,—beyond the reach of guilt and grief / The whole creation. [. . .] Your

applies in the reverse direction, from the heavenly to the mundane, from the divine to the human.

We can see this reversal at its most striking in the imagery which Elizabeth Barrett applied to her relationship with Browning as the courtship progressed. Several times she compared her former life to a desert or wilderness: and almost always these comparisons draw on their biblical precedents:

> it seems to me, to myself, that no man was ever before to any woman what you are to me—the fulness must be in proportion, you know, to the vacancy . . & only *I* know what was behind . . the long wilderness *without* the footstep, . . without the blossoming rose . . and the capacity for happiness, like a black gaping hole, before this silver flooding.
>
> (9 Jan. 1846, p. 376.)

The passage echoes two texts: 'He turneth the wilderness into a standing water, and dry ground into watersprings' (Psalms 107: 34); and 'The wilderness and the solitary place shall be glad for them [the redeemed]; and the desert shall rejoice, and blossom as the rose' (Isaiah 35: 1). The headings to the chapters where these passages occur give an idea of the associations on which Elizabeth Barrett was drawing: Psalm 107 is headed, 'The psalmist exhorts to praise God, and to observe his manifold providence'; Isaiah 35 is headed, 'Joyful flourishing of Christ's kingdom'. It was in these rhapsodic terms that Elizabeth Barrett interpreted her relationship with Browning, and through that relationship the whole of her renewed identity:

> 'As the doves fly to the windows,' so I think of you!—As the prisoners think of liberty, as the dying think of Heaven, so I think of you. When I look up straight to God . . nothing, no one, used to intercept me—now there is *you*—only you under Him!
>
> (4 Jan. 1846, p. 362.)

The doves, as I mentioned elsewhere, are from Isaiah 60: 8, the gathering in of the Gentiles; again a passage about salvation and

grave shall be as smooth as Eden's sward, / Beneath the steps of your prospective thoughts, / And, one step past it, a new Eden-gate / Shall open on a hinge of harmony / And let you through to mercy.' The 'hinge of harmony', which translates a material thing into an immaterial effect, is a good example of the 'transcendentalism' of Elizabeth Barrett's metaphors, and also of their strong affinity with biblical imagery, especially in the prophetic books. Compare, for example, Isaiah 34: 11, describing God's judgement on Zion: 'he shall stretch out upon it the line of confusion, and the stones of emptiness'.

redemption, and a particularly significant one in view of the fact that Elizabeth Barrett had used it previously to describe her desire to be in Wimpole Street with her father.[5] Such associations occur even in passages where Elizabeth Barrett denies them. At one point, where she has just alluded to St. Paul's account of being 'caught up into paradise' and hearing 'unspeakable words, which it is not lawful for a man to utter' (2 Corinthians 12: 1–4), she writes:

> I would not speak profanely or extravagantly [. . .] But to say only that I was in the desert & that I am among the palm-trees is to say nothing . . because it is easy to *understand how*, after walking straight on . . on . . furlong after furlong . . dreary day after dreary day, . . one may come to the end of the sand & within sight of the fountain:—there is nothing miraculous in *that*, you know!—
>
> (15 Dec. 1845, pp. 322–3.)

Even here, in the half-fearful eschewing of blasphemy, the biblical allusions crowd in: to the palm-tree as a symbol of apocalyptic rejoicing (Revelation 7: 9), or of erotic beauty and fertility (Song of Solomon 7: 7), or of the reward of the righteous (Psalms 92: 12); above all, to water in the desert as a symbol of salvation (Numbers 20: 8–11, Psalms 114: 8, among many others).

Elizabeth Barrett is joking in her assurance to Browning that there is 'nothing miraculous' about her image of coming 'to the end of the sand & within sight of the fountain'. Letter after letter reiterates precisely the opposite: the 'miraculous dispensation' (24 Mar. 1846, p. 553) under which she and Browning lived. In writing to Miss Mitford, she was able to give a rational (if disingenuous) explanation of why she agreed to see Browning in the first place: 'He said in his courtesy more, in the way of request, than the thing was worth,—and so I received him here one morning' (*EBB to MRM*, 242).[6] But to Browning himself she wrote:

> It seems to me (as I say over & over . . I say it to my own thoughts oftenest) it seems to me still a dream how you came here at all, . . the very machinery of it seems miraculous. Why did I receive you & only you? Can I tell?—no, not a word.
>
> (4 Dec. 1845, p. 305.)

---

[5] See Part One, p. 34.

[6] This letter is dated 26 May 1845—three days after Elizabeth Barrett had returned the 'intemperate' letter which Browning sent to her after their first meeting! See Part One, pp. 78–84.

In a later letter she makes clear who was in charge of the 'machinery': 'I think again how He of the heavens and earth brought us together so wonderfully, holding two souls in His hand' (29 Mar. 1846, p. 570). And this image of God as 'He of the heavens and earth' implies that Browning represents the former and she the latter; a 'peculiar combination' which never ceased to exercise Elizabeth Barrett's astonishment: 'The isolation on one side, & the best in the whole world, coming in for company! [. . .] It is my special miracle' (25 Mar. 1846, p. 560).

At times, as we have seen already, Elizabeth Barrett comes close to identifying Browning with God himself; in the following image, for example, drawn from the Calvinist doctrine of salvation of the elect by grace, not merit:

It is with me as with the theologians. I believe in you & can be happy and safe *so*: but when my 'personal merits' come into question in any way, even the least, . . why then the position grows untenable:—it is no more 'of grace.'

(21 Dec. 1845, p. 338.)

Jesus says, 'What shall it profit a man, if he shall gain the whole world, and lose his own soul?' (Mark 8: 36); and Elizabeth Barrett echoes: 'Dearest beloved, to turn away from the whole world to you . . *when* I do, do I lose anything . . or not rather gain all?' (16 Aug. 1846, p. 971.) Browning is surrounded by imagery specifically associated with Christ, particularly the imagery of light—for example, 'You have lifted my very soul up into the light of your soul' (15 Aug. 1846, p. 967); and Elizabeth Barrett remembers that the redeemed soul belongs to Christ: on the day after her wedding, she wrote:

What could be better than lifting me from the ground and carrying me into life & sunshine? I was yours rather by right than by gift, (yet by gift also, my beloved!—) for what you have saved & renewed is surely yours.

(13 Sept. 1846, p. 1064.)

Elizabeth Barrett knew perfectly well what she was doing in using such language. Her imagery is neither haphazard nor (in her own terms) hyperbolic. It represents, and celebrates, the effort which her 'return to life' cost her, and also her intelligent appreciation of the new terms on which she was to live. By transposing her transcendent future from Heaven to earth, from the spiritual to the material world, she could no longer see her experience as representative (in the way suggested by such works as 'A Drama of Exile' or 'The Lost Bower'); but she could see it as a *special* providence, a mark of *exceptional* favour, which she did not, of course, deserve, but which was within God's power to grant. The notion of a singular or miraculous dispensation is as valid a part of the Nonconformist side of Protestantism (to which both Elizabeth Barrett and Browning subscribed) as the notion of the general guilt of the Fall being exemplified in each individual. Nor is it only in her letters that she remade her identity according to this new principle. Just as 'A Drama of Exile' symbolized her commitment to her 'old philosophy of life, made of the necessities of sorrow', so in the course of the courtship a new work came into being, which articulated and reflected upon her new identity: *Sonnets from the Portuguese*.

3

Of the forty-four poems in *Sonnets from the Portuguese*, forty-three refer directly to Browning, and all but two of these are addressed to him. The exception is Sonnet I. The poet represents herself as lost in the sad thought of her own past, which 'had flung / A shadow across me':

> Straightway I was 'ware,
> So weeping, how a mystic Shape did move
> Behind me and draw me backward by the hair;
> And a voice cried in mastery, while I strove,
> 'Guess now who holds thee!'—'*Death*,' I said!: but, there,
> The silver answer rang . . 'Not Death, but Love.'[7]

This stands comparison with George Herbert: the measure manages to be both ceremonial and colloquial; the extra syllable in the third line is especially impressive in its suggestion of the dragging power of the gesture it describes. But it is to the 'mystic Shape', abstract and impersonal, that I want to draw attention here. This monitory figure is not Browning, but *what Browning represents*: standing at

---

[7] The text is that of William S. Peterson's facsimile edition of the British Library manuscript of *Sonnets from the Portuguese* (see Bibliography); this manuscript is the one which Elizabeth Barrett gave to Browning in 1849 at Bagni di Lucca (see *RB & JW*, 114–15).

the head of the whole sequence of sonnets, it directs our reading, like a Shakespearean Prologue, to the symbolic nature of the coming drama, a drama which repeats, in the more systematic and condensed mode of poetic art, the experience which Elizabeth Barrett records in her letters. In stylistic terms, the letters have worn better; but that is no reason to consider the *Sonnets* as a collection of random effusions. The sequence, despite its uneven language, has an imaginative authority and coherence, which are new in Elizabeth Barrett's work, and which inform her later poetry, particularly in *Casa Guidi Windows* and *Aurora Leigh*.

The *Sonnets* are like a show place for the images which I have been documenting in the letters. In Sonnet III, to take just one example, Elizabeth Barrett dramatizes her self-image at the time she first knew Browning, and the difference she saw between them: he the 'princely Heart', 'A guest for queens to social pageantries' (some of literary London's hostesses, like Mrs Procter, 'Our Lady of Bitterness', must have blinked when they read this); she the 'poor, tired, wandering singer', who was 'leaning up a cypress-tree' (again that favourite image of mourning). She repeats the image in Sonnet IV:

> Thou hast thy calling to some palace floor,
> Most gracious singer of high poems, . . where
> The dancers will break footing from the care
> Of watching up thy pregnant lips for more.

She, on the other hand, lives in a house with 'the casement broken in— / The bats & owlets builders in the roof'. Once again, this image of desolation has a biblical source: 'the screech owl also shall rest there, and find for herself a place of rest. There shall the great owl make her nest, and lay, and hatch, and gather under her shadow' (Isaiah 34: 14–15).

More important than these parallels in imagery, there is a parallel in the shift of perspective by which Elizabeth Barrett invested in earthly passion the values which she had formerly attributed to the transcendent after-life: 'my soul, instead / Of dreams of death, resumes life's lower range!' she writes in Sonnet XXIV: 'I yield the grave for thy sake, and exchange / My near sweet view of Heaven . . for earth with *thee*!' It is earth, now, which appropriates the values of bliss, harmony, and salvation. Sonnet VII encapsulates this shift:

The face of all the world is changed I think
Since first I heard the footsteps of thy soul
Move still . . oh still . . beside me: as they stole
Betwixt me & the dreadful outer brink
Of obvious death, . . where I who thought to sink
Was caught up into love & taught the whole
Of life in a new rhythm. The cup of dole
God gave for baptism, I am fain to drink,
And praise the sweetness, sweet, with thee anear!
The names of country, Heaven, are changed away
For where thou art or shalt be, there or here:
And this . . this lute & song . . loved yesterday, . .
(The singing angels know!) . . are only dear,
Because thy name moves right in what they say.

In Sonnet XXI, the identification of Browning with God himself is as explicit as in some of the letters: after wondering how she failed to foresee his coming and what it would mean to her, Elizabeth Barrett concludes: 'Atheists are as dull / Who cannot guess God's presence out of sight'. And again in Sonnet XXVIII, where the image of Browning as saviour is most strongly marked (she speaks of his 'lifebreath' and his 'saving kiss'), she repeats an image from the letters, of looking backward over the grave:

> My own, my own . .
> Who camest to me when the world was gone,
> And I, who looked for only God, found *thee*!
> I find thee! I am safe, & strong, & glad!
> As one who stands in dewless asphodel
> Looks backward on the tedious time he had
> In the upper life . .

The 'dewless asphodel' is an allusion to paradise; but this is paradise on earth: 'A Drama of Exile' has come full circle. And in fact it is by literally rewriting one of the sonnets from the 1844 *Poems* that Elizabeth Barrett most convincingly, in terms of her own past way of thinking, signalled her 'return to life'. Browning told her that the sonnet 'Past and Future' 'affects me more than any poem I ever read' (16 Nov. 1845, p. 272). It begins, 'My future will not copy fair my past / On any leaf but Heaven's', and the poet, whose 'wine has run / Indeed out of [her] cup', is left with the 'new vintage' of the Christian heaven to look forward to. But Sonnet XVII (numbered XLII in the published order) tells a different story:

> '*My future will not copy fair my past* . .'
> I wrote that once; and thinking at my side
> My ministering life-angel justified
> The words by his appealing looks upcast
> To the white throne of God, I turned at last,
> And saw thee here instead o thou allied
> To angels in thy soul! Then I long tried
> By natural ills, received the comfort fast;
> While budding, at thy sight, my pilgrim's staff
> Gave out green leaves with morning-dew impearled!
> I seek no copy now of life's first half . .
> Leave here, the pages with long musing curled!
> And write me new my future's epigraph,
> New angel mine, unhoped for in the world!

The sufferings which Elizabeth Barrett had formerly interpreted in terms of God's dispensation, she now sees as 'natural ills'; and, in one of the most intense and striking images of the whole sequence, her 'pilgrim's staff', the rigid religious symbol of her acceptance and endurance of the travail of earthly life, and her hope of an ultimate transcendent goal, flowers into the promise of natural human fertility. Appropriately, since Browning so admired 'Past and Future', Elizabeth Barrett alluded gracefully to her own favourite among *his* works, *Pippa Passes*, seeing herself, 'with morning-dew impearled', as its fresh and hopeful heroine:

> The year's at the spring
> And day's at the morn:
> Morning's at seven;
> The hill-side's dew-pearled;
> The lark's on the wing;
> The snail's on the thorn:
> God's in his heaven—

But everyone knows how it ends.

Bibliography

(Books are listed alphabetically by name of author or editor; the place of publication in London unless otherwise indicated. Short titles follow where appropriate, in square brackets.)

Works

Barrett Browning, E., *Poetical Works*, ed. F. G. Kenyon (1897) [*Works of EBB*].
    Sonnets from the Portuguese, ed. W. S. Peterson (Barre, Mass. 1977). Facsimile of British Library Add. MS 43487.
Browning, R., *The Poems*, ed. J. Pettigrew and T. J. Collins (2 vols., 1981) [*Poems*].
    The Ring and the Book, ed. R. D. Altick (1971).
    Poetical Works, ed. A. Birrell (1897).

Autobiography and Letters

(a)   Browning and Elizabeth Barrett

Benét, W. R., *Twenty-two Unpublished Letters of Elizabeth Barrett Browning and Robert Browning Addressed to Henrietta and Arabella Moulton-Barrett* (New York, 1935).
Browning, R. W. B., *The Letters of Robert Browning and Elizabeth Barrett Barrett 1845–1846* (2 vols., 1899).
Hudson, G. R., *Browning to His American Friends*: *Letters between the Brownings, the Storys and James Russell Lowell 1841–1890* (1965).
Hudson, R. and Kelley, P., *The Brownings' Correspondence* (vols.i and ii of a projected series, Winfield, Kansas, 1984).
Kintner, E., *The Letters of Robert Browning and Elizabeth Barrett Barrett 1845–1846* (2 vols., Cambridge, Mass. 1969) [see 'Note on the Text'].
Landis, P., *Letters of the Brownings to George Barrett* (Urbana, Ill., 1958) [*Letters to George Barrett*].

(b)   Elizabeth Barrett

Heydon, P. N. and Kelley, P., *Elizabeth Barrett Browning's Letters to Mrs. David Ogilvy 1849–1861* (New York, 1973).

273

Hudson, R. and Kelley, P., *Diary by E. B. B.: The Unpublished Diary of Elizabeth Barrett Barrett, 1831–1832* (Athens, Ohio, 1969).

Huxley, L., *Elizabeth Barrett Browning: Letters to her Sister, 1846–1859* (1929).

Kenyon, F. G., *The Letters of Elizabeth Barrett Browning* (2 vols., 1897) [*Letters of EBB*].

McCarthy, B. P., *Elizabeth Barrett to Mr Boyd* (1955).

Miller, B., *Elizabeth Barrett to Miss Mitford* (1954) [*EBB to MRM*].

Pope, W. B., *Invisible Friends*: *The Correspondence of Elizabeth Barrett Barrett and Benjamin Robert Haydon 1842–1845* (Cambridge, Mass., 1972).

Townshend Mayer, S. R., *Letters of Elizabeth Barrett Browning Addressed to Richard Hengist Horne* (2 vols., 1877)

(c)   Robert Browning

Curle, R., *Robert Browning and Julia Wedgwood* (1937) [*RB & JW*].

DeVane, W. C. and Knickerbocker, K. L., *New Letters of Robert Browning* (1951).

Hood, T. L., *Letters of Robert Browning* (1933).

Kenyon, F. G., *Robert Browning and Alfred Domett* (1906) [*RB & AD*].

McAleer, E. C., *Dearest Isa*: *Robert Browning's Letters to Isabella Blagden* (Austin, Texas, 1951).

McAleer, E. C., *Learned Lady*: *Letters from Robert Browning to Mrs Thomas Fitzgerald 1876–1889* (Cambridge, Mass., 1966).

Peterson, W. S., *Browning's Trumpeter*: *The Correspondence of Robert Browning and Frederick J. Furnivall 1872–1889* (Washington DC, 1979).

Biography and Criticism

Chesterton, G. K., *Robert Browning* (1903) [Chesterton].

Creston, D., *Andromeda in Wimpole Street* (1929).

DeVane, W. C., *A Browning Handbook* (2nd edn., New York, 1955) [*Handbook*].

Dowden, E., *The Life of Robert Browning* (1915).

Du Bos, C., *Robert et Elizabeth Browning*, ou *la plénitude de l'amour humain* (Paris 1982).

Griffin, W. H. and Minchin, H. C., *The Life of Robert Browning* (3rd edn., 1938).

Hayter, A., *Mrs Browning*: *A Poet's Work and its Setting* (1962).

Hewlett, D., *Elizabeth Barrett Browning* (1953).

Honan, P. and Irvine, W., *The Book, the Ring, and the Poet: A Biography of Robert Browning* (New York, 1974).

Kaplan, C., Introduction to her edition of *Aurora Leigh* (1978).

Kenmare, D., *The Browning Love-story* (1957).

Lubbock, P., *Elizabeth Barrett Browning In Her Letters* (1906).

Mander, R., *Mrs Browning: The Story of Elizabeth Barrett* (1980).

Maynard, J., *Browning's Youth* (Cambridge, Mass., 1977) [Maynard].

Miller, B., *Robert Browning: A Portrait* (1952) [Miller].

Orr, A., *Life and Letters of Robert Browning* (1891) [Orr, *Life*].

Ricks, C., Introduction to his selection, *The Brownings: Letters and Poetry* (New York, 1970).

Sharp, W., *Life of Robert Browning* (1897).

Sim, F. M., *Robert Browning and Elizabeth Barrett* (1930).

Taplin, G., *The Life of Elizabeth Barrett Browning* (1957) [Taplin].

Tucker, H. F., *Browning's Beginnings: The Art of Disclosure* (Minneapolis, Minn., 1980).

Winwar, F., *The Immortal Lovers* (New York, 1950).

Woolf, V., *Flush: A Biography* (1933).

Index

OXFORD

MORE OXFORD PAPERBACKS

Details of a selection of other books follow. A complete list of Oxford Paperbacks, including The World's Classics, Twentieth-Century Classics, OPUS, Past Masters, Oxford Authors, Oxford Shakespeare, and Oxford Paperback Reference, is available in the UK from the General Publicity Department, Oxford University Press (JH), Walton Street, Oxford OX2 6DP.

In the USA, complete lists are available from the Paperbacks Marketing Manager, Oxford University Press, 200 Madison Avenue, New York, NY 10016.

Oxford Paperbacks are available from all good bookshops. In case of difficulty, customers in the UK can order direct from Oxford University Press Bookshop, 116 High Street, Oxford, Freepost, OX1 4BR, enclosing full payment. Please add 10 per cent of published price for postage and packing.

THE LIFE OF KATHERINE MANSFIELD

Antony Alpers

Until recently it has not been possible to deal freely and frankly with all the events of Katherine Mansfield's life. Conventional mores, respect for the privacy of her lovers, family, and friends, and the lack of some crucial material, have all prevented it. Little was known, for example, of her disastrous one-day marriage, her elopement with her childhood friend, Garnett Trowell, and her subsequent affair with Ida Baker. Now, drawing on newly opened manuscript collections, private papers, and personal contacts to which he has had exclusive access, Antony Alpers has been able to expand his 1953 biography in a new, award-winning interpretation of this volatile and vulnerable genius.

'This is in the way of being a definitive biography, and as such utterly engrossing, simply because Katherine Mansfield herself is always engrossing.' Kay Dick, *The Times*.

LETTERS TO VENETIA STANLEY

H. H. Asquith

This paperback edition of the letters of H. H. Asquith, Prime Minister, to the young Venetia Stanley, whom he adored, includes letters discovered in 1984. Almost all written between January 1912 and May 1915, the letters are loving, informative, and amusing. Whenever he could not meet her, Asquith wrote to Venetia; sometimes three times a day, sometimes during a debate in the House of Commons, sometimes even in a Cabinet meeting. Early in 1914 he began to write to her about politics, divulging military secrets and freely discussing such colleagues as Lloyd George, Churchill, and Kitchener.

Equally arresting is the personal story of Venetia Stanley who was also loved by and eventually married to Edwin Montague, a junior Cabinet Minister in his thirties. The letter in which she told Asquith of her engagement reached him at a time of crisis in his and his country's wartime fortunes.

BURNS

Poems and Songs

Edited by James Kinsley

This edition offers to the student and general reader a complete text of all Burns's acknowledged work, and of poems reasonably attributed to him, based on a critical review of all the accessible manuscripts and early printings. There is a glossary, a chronology, and a bibliography.

COLERIDGE

Poetical Works

Edited by Ernest Hartley Coleridge

This edition by Ernest Hartley Coleridge, grandson of the poet, contains a complete and authoritative text of Coleridge's poems. Here are his earliest extant teenage poems, his masterly meditative pieces, and the extraordinary supernatural poems— 'The Rime of the Ancient Mariner', 'Kubla Khan', and 'Christabel'.

The text follows that of the 1834 edition, the last published in the author's lifetime. The poems are printed, so far as is possible, in chronological order, with Coleridge's own notes as well as textual and bibliographical notes by the editor.

SELECTED POEMS AND PROSE OF JOHN CLARE

Chosen and edited by

Eric Robinson and Geoffrey Summerfield

Illustrated by David Gentleman

This selection by Eric Robinson and Geoffrey Summerfield is based upon their study of Clare's original manuscripts and is an authentic reconstruction of what Clare actually wrote, in some cases going behind printed versions of his work to the primary sources, and in others presenting work never before published. It reveals the variety of Clare's writing, his poetic strengths and sensitivities, and defies the labelling of him as a 'peasant poet' or simple lyricist. Here is to be found also the best of Clare's prose—descriptive and political—which combines the traditions both of Cobbett and White of Selborne.

JOHN CLARE'S AUTOBIOGRAPHICAL WRITINGS

Edited by Eric Robinson

John Clare wrote *Sketches* for his publisher which trace the gradual recognition of his literary talent. It is these sketches and prose fragments he intended as an autobiography—never completed—which are brought together in this collection. They tell of his various jobs as ploughboy, gardener's boy, and militiaman; of his early loves, and loyalty to Patty, his wife; and of his impressions of London, where he mixed in the society of authors such as Hazlitt, Lamb, and Coleridge. Clare spent the final twenty-three years of his life in an asylum, and the volume concludes with *Journey out of Essex,* a nightmare description of his flight from confinement.

'this is the best text yet of Clare's autobiographical prose fragments . . . They add up to one of the best accounts by any writer of the growth of the creative imagination, and one of the most valuable records we have of the mental, emotional and physical world of the English rural poor in the early nineteenth century.' *British Book News*

SELECTED POEMS

W. H. Davies

Edited by Jonathan Barker

This is the first selection from W. H. Davies's poems to appear for over forty years. It contains nearly 300 (more than a third of his total output), selected from the entire range of his poetry, and constitutes a long-overdue critical re-evaluation of his work.

ALEXANDER POPE

Poetical Works

Edited by Herbert Davies

Introduction by Pat Rogers

This edition contains all of Pope's poems, except for his translations from Homer, scraps of verse originally included in letters, and poems of doubtful attribution. It also includes Pope's own notes, the 1728 version of *The Dunciad,* and the 1712 version of *The Rape of the Lock.* The editor has provided a text which attempts to follow Pope's latest wishes both in substance and punctuation: the result is an authoritative text suited to both student and general reader.

THE OXFORD BOOK OF CONTEMPORARY VERSE, 1945–1980

Compiled by D. J. Enright

This anthology offers substantial selections from the work of forty British, American, and Commonwealth poets who have emerged and confirmed their talents since 1945.

'There is more pithy and Johnsonian good sense in his short introduction than in all the many books that have been written about modern poetry . . . one of the best personal anthologies I have come across.' John Bayley *Listener*

FAIR OF SPEECH

Edited by D. J. Enright

The poet and critic D. J. Enright has invited sixteen distinguished contributors to explore the history of euphemisms, and how they are used in various fields of endeavour. Euphemisms are so intimate and integral to our thinking that any study of them is bound to throw light on the human condition, past and present, and the fascinating information and copious entertainment offered by these essays, as the homely alternates with the far-fetched and humour jostles with horror, testify to the richness of the subject.

Contributors include: *Patricia Beer, Robert Burchfield, Richard Cobb, D. J. Enright, John Gross, Simon Hoggart, Derwent May, David Pannick,* and *Catherine Storr.*

'unfailingly entertaining' Dennis Potter in the *Guardian*

DONNE

Poetical Works

Edited by Herbert J. C. Grierson

Sir Herbert Grierson based this edition of Donne's poems on his Oxford English Texts edition (1912), the text of which it reproduces with certain corrections. The volume contains all the poems believed to be genuine, with, in an appendix, those which were attributed to Donne so early and for so long that it did not seem justifiable to omit them altogether. A number of poems tentatively assigned to Donne by modern editors have been omitted. The textual notes record the variants of the old editions with indications of the manuscript evidence.

KEATS

Poetical Works

Edited by H. W. Garrod

This edition by H. W. Garrod includes every poem, verse, drama, and fragment known to have been written by Keats. Based on careful study of the manuscript sources, it offers the student and general reader an authoritative plain text. It also contains a commentary by Buxton Forman on the early printed editions, a chronology of Keats's life, and a note on the wealth of the manuscript material which enables us to see, more clearly than in the case of almost any other English poet, the gropings and agonies through which great poetry comes to truth.

ELIOT'S EARLY YEARS

Lyndall Gordan

Described by Jonathan Raban in the *Sunday Times* as 'the most valuable single book yet published about Eliot', this unusual biographical study of T. S. Eliot's formative years opens a new perspective upon the career of one of our century's most influential poets and critics. Drawing on unpublished manuscripts (his Notebooks and early poems, his mother's poems, his wife's diaries), Lyndall Gordon traces Eliot's journey across the 'waste land' to his conversion to Anglo-Catholicism at the age of 38. Eliot's poetry has a strong autobiographical basis, and the author here shows us its essential

coherence within the context of his life.

'essential for all serious students of Eliot' *T.L.S.*

THE POEMS OF GERARD MANLEY HOPKINS

Edited by W. H. Gardner and N. H. MacKenzie

This Fourth Edition of Hopkins's poems brings together all the known poems and fragments, including the early verse first published in the poet's *Journals and Papers* (1959), and the remainder of his Latin verse, with translations into English of all the Latin poems which are fully original compositions. The edition retains the most important features of the First Edition of 1918, as edited by Robert Bridges, but a number of more authentic readings have been established by checking the poems against the MS sources, and the poems have been arranged in a more strictly chronological order. The Notes include a selection, from the MSS, of the marks used by the poet as guides to rhythm and expression.

'The indispensable Fourth Edition of Hopkins's poems is not only the one complete and accurate text, but for the first time it puts him in his true chronological order of development.' *Guardian*

THE OXFORD BOOK OF SATIRICAL VERSE

Chosen by Geoffrey Grigson

'one of the best anthologies by the best modern anthologist.' *New York Review of Books*

'an immense treasury of wit, exuberance, controlled malice and uncontrolled rage.' *Times Literary Supplement*.

COLERIDGE

Richard Holmes

Coleridge was not only a great poet, he was also a philosopher and explorer of the whole human condition. Richard Holmes describes Coleridge's work as a writer, explains his often difficult and fragmentary ideas, and shows that his concept of the creative imagination still shapes our notions of growth and culture.

'most attractive' *Listener*

'stylish, intelligent and readable' *Irish Times*

SHELLEY

Poetical Works

Edited by Thomas Hutchinson

Revised by G. M. Matthews

This edition by Thomas Hutchinson (1905), corrected and updated by G. M. Matthews (1970), contains every poem and fragment of Shelley's verse that had hitherto appeared in print. The text, based on Mary Shelley's own editions of 1839 has been freshly collated by Thomas Hutchinson, who has indicated in footnotes every material departure from the originals. Shelley's antiquated or eccentric spellings have been modernized except where required by rhyme or metre. The original pointing has been retained except where it tends to obscure or distort the poet's meaning.

There are also headnotes to each poem, detailing its composition and publication, and a list of the principal editions of Shelley's works.

BLAKE

Complete Writings

Edited by Geoffrey Keynes

This definitive edition of Blake's writings—a volume which, the *Times Literary Supplement* observed, 'might serve as a model of how a great editor is able to efface himself from his work'—was first published by the Nonesuch Press in 1957, and reissued in 1966, with substantive corrections and additions, in the Oxford Standard Authors series.

The writings are printed in chronological sequence, with a section of Blake's letters at the end, followed by Notes, and a supplement containing a small amount of new material. Peculiarities of spelling, frequent use of capitals, and abbreviations in Blake's original manuscripts and etched texts are preserved, but certain eccentricities of his punctuation have been regularized. Lines are numbered, and Blake's designs reproduced where they are essential to an understanding of the text.